Authorizations in SAP® HR

 PRESS

SAP PRESS is a joint initiative of SAP and Galileo Press. The know-how offered by SAP specialists combined with the expertise of the publishing house Galileo Press offers the reader expert books in the field. SAP PRESS features first-hand information and expert advice, and provides useful skills for professional decision-making.

SAP PRESS offers a variety of books on technical and business related topics for the SAP user. For further information, please visit our website: *www.sap-press.com.*

Hans-Jürgen Figaj, Richard Haßmann, and Anja Junold
HR Reporting with SAP
2007, 431 pages
978-1-59229-172-4

Jeremy Masters and Christos Kotsakis
SAP ERP HCM Performance Management
2007, 302 pages
978-1-59229-124-3

Jeremy Masters and Christos Kotsakis
Implementing Employee and Manager Self Service
August 2008, approx. 300 pages
978-1-59229-188-5

Satish Badgi
Configuring SAP US Benefits
2007, 85 pages
978-1-59229-164-9

Martin Esch, Anja Junold

Authorizations in SAP® HR

Galileo Press

Bonn • Boston

ISBN 978-1-59229-165-6

© 2009 by Galileo Press Inc., Boston (MA)
1st Edition 2009

German Edition first published 2008 by Galileo Press, Bonn, Germany.

Galileo Press is named after the Italian physicist, mathematician and philosopher Galileo Galilei (1564–1642). He is known as one of the founders of modern science and an advocate of our contemporary, heliocentric worldview. His words *Eppur si muove* (And yet it moves) have become legendary. The Galileo Press logo depicts Jupiter orbited by the four Galilean moons, which were discovered by Galileo in 1610.

Editor Frank Paschen
English Edition Editor Jenifer Niles
Translation Lemoine International, Inc., Salt Lake City UT
Copy Editor Lori Newhouse
Cover Design Tyler Creative
Layout Design Vera Brauner
Production Iris Warkus
Typesetting Publishers' Design and Production Services, Inc.
Printed and bound in Canada

Contents at a Glance

Contents

6 Implementing an Authorization Concept 225

7 Reports for the Authorization System 245

8 Authorizations in Programming 259

Acknowledgments

This book is a very broad cross-section of subjects. It affects all SAP ERP HCM components and the closely related system authorizations. Within the SAP ERP HCM system, it provides very detailed information on particular aspects. To cover all of these areas of expertise, very detailed knowledge was required, which could not have been gathered without the help of many colleagues. Our thanks are due to a large number of people who wrote separate sections, proofread the text, or provided useful tips.

The following customers were of great help: Martina Klapproth-Bienert, Sabine Schwarz, and Roswitha Rogalla at ThyssenKrupp Steel AG, Michael Engl at Schaeffler KG, and Thomas Gaszczak of B. Braun.

The AdManus network, which the enterprises of both authors are part of, has once again proven its value for the creation of this book. Many of the represented consultants made a significant contribution to the book. These include in particular: Viktoria Papadopoulou, Hans-Jürgen Figaj, Joost Klüßendorf, and Klaus Tretter at Projektkultur GmbH; Jörg Edinger, Christian Krämer, Christian Lübke, Jens Richter, Sven-Olaf Möller, and Sven Ringling at iProCon GmbH; Christian Krüger at Knauer & Krüger; and Lars Möller at LM Consulting.

Colleagues at SAP Deutschland helped us to fill the last gaps in our knowledge. These were Katharina Villwock, Stefan Ehrler, Jan Herrmann, and Alexander Woelke. And we would like to thank Satish Badgi, who assisted with Chapter 5 to ensure that it met the standards for the U.S. market.

We would also like to thank the support employees at PIKON International Consulting Group (*www.pikon.com*). They ensured that the access to the IDES system and SAP NetWeaver Portal always worked and provided numerous simulated examples.

Not least, our thanks are due to the SAP PRESS team. We must mention in particular Eva Tripp, who supported us in designing the concept of the book, and Frank Paschen, who encouraged the progress of the book with patience and determination.

All these people deserve a big thank you. We feel associated with them in trying to spread the knowledge of such an essential topic and make it easy to understand.

Martin Esch and **Anja Junold**

In this chapter, you'll find answers to the questions: What is the objective of this book? For whom has it been written? and How is the book structured and how can readers get the optimum benefit from it?

Introduction

This book is about an orphan called *authorizations.* Just like Cinderella in the fairy tale, this topic tends to live in the shadow of most SAP implementation and development projects. *SAP ERP Human Capital Management* (HCM) is not (yet) an exception either. With this book we want to help fill the gaps in information that make this topic so difficult.

The area of personnel management is well suited for dealing with authorizations, because the Human Resources (HR) department has a highly distinct perception of authorizations. From the data protection point of view, the data saved here is particularly critical, because it concerns the employee's privacy, which must be protected at all costs. This is an area to which individual employees and their representatives pay special attention to.

Required Knowledge for Understanding This Book   **[+]**

For this book, we assume that readers have knowledge about the basic SAP authorization concepts and tools and SAP ERP HCM in general. You can find additional reference recommendations in Appendix F.

In this book, we will focus on the use of the general authorization concept in the HCM system and on the three authorization tools that are only available in SAP ERP HCM:

- The structural authorization check (Chapter 3)
- The context-dependent authorization check (Chapter 4)
- The test procedures (see Section 2.7, Test Procedures (Infotype 0130))

SAP ERP 6.0

> The descriptions contained in this book and all screenshots are based on Release SAP ERP 6.0. In order to always keep you up to date, we tried to include all new developments that were provided in OSS Notes up to the publication of this book.

Target Groups of this Book

The following target groups will find useful information in this book:

- **Authorization administrators**
  In this chapter, we address the people who set up authorization roles. They are provided with detailed tools and skills to optimally use the existing tools for their enterprise.
  Those who only assign the roles to the users will benefit from the background knowledge that is provided in this book.

- **Project managers and members of the project team**
  It's vital for this group to keep track of the authorizations topic during the entire runtime of the project. For example, if you're not familiar with structural authorizations within the SAP ERP HCM environment, you'll run the risk of making serious mistakes when setting up applications.
  The process-oriented approach of this book is particularly interesting for this target group, because by approaching authorizations in this way, you will gain knowledge that will also be beneficial for other project tasks.

- **Programmers in the HCM area**
  We dedicated Chapter 8 particularly to programmers, because we believe that a sound basic knowledge about authorizations is indispensable for this target group.

- **Decision makers in HR or IT departments**
  Although some parts of this book provide in-depth information, the initial chapters and Chapter 6, Implementing An Authorization Concept, give a very good overview. Here, decision makers find numerous recommendations for the benefits that are provided by the described authorization tools (see also our recommendations for swift readers in the section, Working with this Book, at the end of this introduction).

► **Data protection officers/Data protection experts**
Because many enterprises store their data in SAP systems and personal data is to be protected specifically in this context, it is useful for all data protection professionals to know the tools and the pitfalls of authorizations in SAP ERP HCM.

Structure of the Book

The first six chapters of this book address the topic of *authorizations in SAP ERP HCM* in great detail: from the requirements of the authorization concept, to the technical tools for implementing these requirements, to Chapter 6 that focuses on the implementation and redesign. Chapters 7 to 10 additionally address the various problems that often occur when working with authorizations and they provide appropriate solutions.

The chapters in detail:

► **Chapter 1: Process-Oriented Authorization Concept**
The process-oriented approach continuously gains in the importance that it deserves. Particularly for the authorization concept, this approach offers clear advantages. This chapter examines the requirements of the authorization concept, and describes a process-oriented procedure for creating such a concept.

► **Chapter 2: General Authorization Check**
After a brief introduction into the general authorization concept, we'll detail the most critical authorization objects of the HCM system, including various special cases and some extension options for the standard. This chapter explains all central elements of the general authorization check.

► **Chapter 3: Structural Authorization Check**
The structural authorization check is based on the organizational management and has become an integral part of most HCM installations. We'll present the standard version and its extension options in great detail.

► **Chapter 4: Context-Dependent Authorization Check**
This chapter is intended for advanced users. Here, the structural and general authorization checks are combined to provide a tool for the con-

text-dependent authorization check, which is indispensable in particular for enterprises that maintain their data in a decentralized manner.

▶ **Chapter 5: Authorization Roles in SAP HCM Components**
After covering the central components of the HCM system, including the master data and organizational management in particular, in Chapters 2 to 4, we'll move on in this chapter to describe the various subcomponents of the HCM system — from A, as in appraisal system, to T, as in travel management. This chapter has a technical orientation and describes each subcomponent and the required authorization objects, along with all aspects of customizing that deal with authorizations.

▶ **Chapter 6: Implementing an Authorization Concept**
In this chapter we'll explain how you need to prepare your HCM system for implementing an authorization concept, how to proceed in this implementation, and which aspects you should consider when redesigning an authorization concept.

▶ **Chapter 7: Reports for the Authorization System**
Once you've established the authorizations, it's interesting and essential for you to know the reports of the authorization management and to understand how to handle them so that you can manage the multitude of authorization roles. In this chapter, we'll present a selection of the most common reports.

▶ **Chapter 8: Authorizations in Programming**
This chapter primarily aims to provide programmers with a tool to implement correct authorization checks in customer-specific reports or applications. And, we'll explain the authorizations available for programmers.

▶ **Chapter 9: Troubleshooting**
Even the best concept and the most careful implementation does not protect you against errors. In this chapter, we'll describe how you can detect them and which supporting tools are available.

▶ **Chapter 10: Selected Problem Areas and Their Solutions**
Here, we'll describe some special problems that occurred in real customer projects and the solutions used to fix them.

The Appendices of this book contain additional information:

▶ Appendix A shows all transactions in the authorization administration environment.

▶ Appendix B comprises all authorization objects of the HCM system, including references to the respective sections.

▶ Appendix C lists all authorization switches, including references to the respective sections.

▶ Appendix D contains all Business Add-Ins (BAdIs) of the HCM system, including references to the respective sections.

▶ Appendix E provides a glossary with the most essential terms used in the authorization system of SAP ERP HCM.

▶ Appendix F includes additional reference recommendations.

Free HR Newsletter

Readers of this book can subscribe to a free HR newsletter by the authors of this book. Among other things, the newsletter is comprised of the latest tips for authorizations in SAP ERP HCM. Just send an email to *newsletter@ admanus.de*, subject *Subscription/book*.

Working with This Book

For those who initially only want to know the most essential things and, if required, read the other parts at a later stage, we recommend the following path in this book:

▶ Chapter 1, Process-Oriented Authorization Concept

▶ Chapter 2, General Authorization Check

  ▶ Section 2.1, Elements

  ▶ Section 2.2, Role Maintenance

  ▶ Section 2.3, Authorization Objects

▶ Chapter 3, Structural Authorization Check

  ▶ Section 3.1, Structural Authorization Check in the Organizational Management

- Section 3.2, Maintenance of the Structural Profiles
- Section 3.3, Function Modules
- Section 3.4, Transfer to other Structures in SAP ERP HCM
- Section 3.5, Use in Personnel Administration
- Section 3.6, Assigning Structural Profiles to the Users
- Chapter 4, Context-Dependent Authorization Check; Section 4.1, Functionality
- Chapter 6, Implementing an Authorization Concept

Of course, you can read the chapters in any arbitrary sequence. Numerous references will help you to refer to the respective chapters or sections to fill knowledge gaps.

Special icons

To make it easier for you to work with this book, we use icons to highlight certain sections. These icons have the following meanings:

[!] Warning

We use this icon to warn you about frequent errors or problems that you may encounter in your work.

[+] Tip

We use this icon to highlight tips that may make your work easier and to help you to find further information on the current topic.

[Ex] Example

We use examples that are based on real life consultation cases to explain and give more information on the current topic.

Once you have missed the first buttonhole you'll never manage to button up. (Johann Wolfgang von Goethe)

1 Process-Oriented Authorization Concept

To set up a successful authorization system, you should not only be familiar with SAP ERP HCM, but also have a complete overview of all of your personnel processes. This chapter introduces a process-oriented authorization concept, which will support you in initially implementing and redesigning already existing authorization concepts.

Implementation and redesigning

If you're about to implement an HCM system, you may not be familiar with all of the authorization requirements. Nevertheless, it is useful to create an authorization concept at an early stage where you include and systematize known requirements.

If you've already implemented an HCM system, you won't be surprised to hear that the requirements increase when you extend the system or integrate new users. The more roles you add, the more complex your authorization system becomes. And, when the maintenance work exceeds the resources of the authorization administrators, you'll know it's time to redesign the concept.

The following sections introduce you to the process-oriented creation of an authorization concept. The approach described is based on the personnel processes in your enterprise. This is quite useful because the running processes already give you a general idea of your work, and often answer the question of which authorizations are needed for which users. You can also more easily identify which tasks should be combined into roles and which shouldn't. And, in addition to forming the basis for the concept, this approach provides documentation about the authorizations in your HCM system.

Basis of the concept and documentation

1.1 Requirements for Authorization Concepts

The first questions you'll need to address are:

▶ What requirements do the interest groups affected by the authorization concept have?

▶ Which content requirements can you derive from these requirements in order to create or redesign such a concept?

1.1.1 Interest Groups

Authorization administrators

First, the authorization administrator himself requires access to the system in order to create roles and user masters for other users. Both functions are generally allocated to two administrators: one is responsible for maintaining the roles, and the other for maintaining the user master records and assigning the roles to users. The authorization administrator basically needs an authorization system that requires less maintenance work and contains a restricted number of roles. The system should cover all requirements, so that each user can do the things he is authorized to.

Human Resources (HR) administrator

The second group is the group of HR administrators. These employees need to access the system for their daily work. They enter personnel data and so, among other things, can provide a correct payroll each month. The authorization concept can support the HR administrators by assuring the quality of the data input. There is generally a conflict of interest between the HR administrator's requirements and the regulations of the data protection officer. Some applications, such as the display of the database tables, would make the HR administrator's work much easier. However, the authorization for these applications is rarely granted, because the system does not check the HCM authorization objects when the database tables are called (see Chapter 2, General Authorization Check). That means that an HR administrator who is only authorized to view some of the employees (e.g., for a specific personnel area) can now view all of them.

Managers

Managers want to report current data, such as leave overviews or time statements, for their area of responsibility and, if required, approve requests for business trips or leaves in the system.

The substitution rule is another problematic issue for this group, because superiors often demand that their substitutes perform all tasks regarding analyses and approvals, but at the same time don't want them to see the manager's salary.

Employees of HR controlling and enterprise management (for strategic tasks) require completely different reports of personnel data across the entire enterprise. This group places its demand on data currency and high report performance. Particularly when many people are employed by the enterprise, this demand can be in stark contrast to complex authorization checks.

HR controlling/ enterprise management

All employees that are authorized to maintain their own data, such as their address or bank details, or call their salary statement online must also be considered. For this interest group, it's important that no other people can access the salary statement. In addition to secure access, you'll also need easy login to the self-service application, because you can't expect users to have yet another user name and password.

Self-service users

IT employees, the HR Competence Center, and external consultants require access to SAP ERP HCM, also. In contrast to the user groups just mentioned, these people usually don't require access to real data. They basically work in the development system to implement new or customer-specific requirements in Customizing or as custom developments. Consequently, it's essential that these employees have as comprehensive a range of authorizations as possible in order to access all data structures and environments without restrictions. In addition, some users must be authorized to access the transport system in order to transport the changes made in the development system into other systems (quality assurance system, production system).

IT employees and consultants

> **Tip**
>
> This means that the authorization concept must be integrated into the overall context of the system architecture and procedures of the system configuration instead of being regarded as an isolated concept.

[+]

Most companies have a person responsible for data security and privacy. This person is responsible for ensuring transparent and documented IT, data protection in the context of IT security, and retraceability of access

Auditor and staff representation

and changes, among other things. His main interest is retraceability. And, it's not sufficient that everyone has the "right" authorizations; this must also be documented. Employees in the area of data security and data protection, the Auditing department, and staff representatives require the respective authorizations to perform the relevant control tasks.

Let's again summarize the requirements of the individual interest groups before looking at the content requirements for the authorization concept:

- ▶ Everyone is able to do the things he is authorized to.
- ▶ There are only a few roles that require less maintenance work.
- ▶ The data is secure.
- ▶ High data quality is ensured.
- ▶ The system performance is acceptable.

1.1.2   Content Requirements

Everyone is able to do the things he is authorized to

To enable everyone to do the things he needs to do in the SAP system, you must first determine all of the tasks that each individual person or the HR department performs and how the SAP system supports them. It's not the goal to assign a minimum authorization and then expand it gradually "upon request." This would lead to a muddle of authorizations without any structure. The more detailed the required authorizations are described at the beginning of the concept, the better a future-oriented authorization concept can be prepared. (We'll look at how you can analyze the required authorizations shortly.)

Fewer roles, require less maintenance work

It's also useful to clearly define the requirements in order to minimize the number of roles. If you've created an overview of the requirements, you can combine individual tasks into roles. Then, you can recognize if you should apply methods to minimize the number of roles. Keep in mind, the fewer the roles, the less maintenance work. But there are also methods in the role definition that simplify maintenance work, and we'll look at these in a moment.

Data security

In addition, authorizations and roles are critical because they ensure that users can only maintain or view data for which they have authorization. Not only does this avoid illegal acts, but it also prevents a variety of errors. To ensure that users maintain or view only data for which they have an authorization, you should provide each user with a user-specific role menu that contains only the transactions and reports required. Furthermore, the data reduction principle applies: As early as during the concept planning phase, you should make sure that as little data as possible is collected and entered.

Another task in the planning phase should be to check the maintenance interfaces up to field level, particularly the infotypes that are supposed to be authorized. Field contents that are not required don't need to be entered and should consequently be removed from the user interface. For this purpose, the SAP system provides the screen modification concept at the infotype level.

As a basic principle, you must always adhere to the legal data protection regulations. Therefore, you should involve the enterprise's data protection officer, the Auditing department, and employee representatives at an early stage in any case.

It's essential to have a high level of data quality to ensure that the HR manager and HR controller can draw the right conclusions from the reports and subsequently make the right personnel decisions. Authorizations also contribute to increased data quality. And the double-verification principle serves to check sensitive data again before it is released. Other potentials for ensuring data quality can be found in the design of the user interface, plausibility checks, dynamic measures, workflows, or intelligent test procedures.

Data quality

> **Tip** **[+]**
>
> The July 2005, May 2006, and October 2006 issues of the AdManus Newsletter (*www.admanus.de/english-newsletter* – select Online Archive) include a detailed, three-part article on this topic.

The authorization check always occupies a significant portion of time of the program flows. Long runtimes and high response times of the system quickly lead to frustration and must definitely be avoided. Particularly if you use the structural authorization check and have a large number of employees, performance problems may occur. For more information, you can go to the end of Chapter 3, Structural Authorization Check,

Performance

which deals with performance optimization. And you should also keep the options provided by the P_ABAP authorization object in mind (covered in Chapter 5), because it enables you to accelerate the program execution.

1.2   Process Analysis

Why process analysis?

For effective personnel management in general and the creation of an authorization concept in particular, it's essential that you know the processes. By visualizing the processes you can understand all of the involved functions and relationships quickly. No one can remember all processes that run in the HR department and elsewhere (self services, for example), although most people can remember the general overview of the job-related instructions or job descriptions. But, this overview isn't sufficient for a thorough concept. For any concept, you'll save a lot of work if you consider all processes right from the start and don't have to integrate them at a later stage. Knowing the processes is useful for the initial creation of the concept, but it's also helpful when you extend the concept. Of course, the processes and the framework architecture must remain up to date so that the initial work for the process definition pays off. To model all HR processes in detail requires a lot of effort but it's not necessary in most cases. It's more important that you know the processes and gear the scope of the process analysis toward the goals of your project. So let's look at the process.

Step 1: Acquiring a process overview

First, you need to acquire a complete overview of the processes in your HR department, for example, using your process documentation if one exists. When you collect information on the processes, it's sufficient to name and structure the processes as individual service units, because detailed process steps are not relevant at this stage. For example, you shouldn't describe all of the steps involved in the process of selecting an applicant, from entering the application to the appointment of the new employee. However, just having the applicant administration service, is not detailed enough. In this case, the individual activities of the service should be specified, such as the correspondence with applicants, organization of job interviews, filing, and so on. Figure 1.1 illustrates one good and one bad example of a process analysis.

Admittedly, to collect information on the processes requires a great deal of effort. But, it will pay off for all subsequent projects in regard to organizational changes or changes to the HR system.

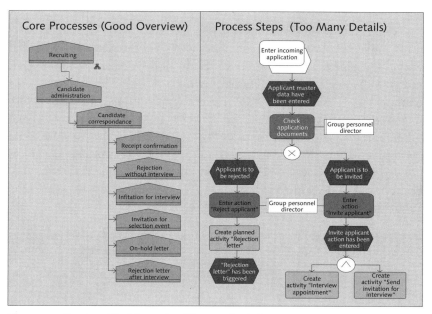

Figure 1.1 Good and Bad Example of Process Analysis

In the second step, you limit the scope of the process analysis in correspondence with your goal, namely, the creation of the authorization concept. Reduce your service catalog to the services that are supposed to be supported by the SAP ERP HCM system. With regard to the excerpt in Table 1.1, you would remove Filing and Advising the Applicants from the overview, because these services don't require system support.

Step 2: Defining the scope of the analysis

To derive roles, you need further information. For example, you need to know:

Step 3: Information on relevant services

► the person that performs the task (e.g., the job or department).

► which transaction, which report, or which infotype supports the service in SAP ERP HCM (if required, in conjunction with a program, such as the Manager's Desktop (MDT) or Employee Self-Services (ESS)).

▶ whether a more detailed description or process modeling is required, (e.g., because it runs through multiple stages).

You can enter this information into an Excel table for all relevant services. Table 1.1 illustrates an example where team leaders are provided with three analyses of their areas of responsibility. You can call the analyses via the MDT. The master data is then recorded by branch office administrators (ADMIN/BRANCH) using Transaction Code (TAC) PA30. In ESS, the employee can enter the (locked) bank details, and the branch office administrator then unlocks the details. The X in the Modeling column indicates that, when maintaining the organizational assignment, you must describe in detail how the information on the position is supposed to be transferred from the Organization department to the administrator.

Service	User Group	Application	TAC	Infotype	Report	Modeling	Action
Manager Info About Employees							
Employee list	Team leader	MDT			RPLMIT00		
Birthday list	Team leader	MDT			ZHR_BIRTH-DAY_LIST		
Recurring payments and deductions	Team leader	MDT			ZHR_RECUR_DEDUC		
Maintain Master Data							
Maintain employee's personal data	ADMIN/BRANCH		PA30	IT 0002			Maintain
Maintain challenge data	ADMIN/BRANCH		PA30	IT 0004			Maintain

Table 1.1 Sample Excerpt from a Service Overview with Reference to the System and Permitted Action for Each User Group

Service	User Group	Application	TAC	Infotype	Report	Modeling	Action
Maintain bank data	ADMIN/ BRANCH		PA30	IT 0009			Maintain and unlock
Maintain bank data	ESS user	ESS		IT 0009			Maintain locked record
Maintain organizational assignment	ADMIN/ BRANCH		PA30	IT 0001		x	Maintain

Table 1.1 Sample Excerpt from a Service Overview with Reference to the System and Permitted Action for Each User Group (Cont.)

As a result of such a service overview, you can obtain an overview of

▶ all *activities* for which an authorization must be created in SAP ERP HCM.

▶ all *positions/people* that require an authorization in SAP ERP HCM.

Step 4: Who is authorized to perform which actions?

At this stage you know which actions the positions/user groups are authorized to perform in the system. In the next step, you determine how the users are authorized to access the data, for example, via write access or read access (see Table 1.1, Action column). Some services may be performed by several users, for example, one user can enter sensitive data of a locked record and another may only release it (double-verification principle).

Finally, you must answer the question as to which people or areas of responsibility the users are authorized to edit or view. There are two different concepts here: Is the general authorization check sufficient? In this check, the access depends on the data provided in Infotype 0001 (Organizational Assignment), such as personnel area, employee subgroup, or responsible administrator. Or do you determine the area of responsibility considering the organizational structure? The prerequisite s for using the structural authorization check are a clear organizational management

Step 5: For which area of responsibility?

that is always kept up-to-date, and the implementation of the structural authorization (and of the context-dependent authorization, if required).

[+]

> **Tip**
>
> The greater the number of users in SAP ERP HCM, for example, due to increased decentralized usage, an increased range of functions, or the integration of additional locations, the greater the need for the structural authorization check.

As the number of users increases, so does the number of roles. This is particularly true when the SAP ERP HCM system is used in a decentralized manner, because many users have the same authorizations but for different person subgroups (e.g., time administrators for their respective departments). Instead of creating a specific role for each of these users, it's sufficient to create one role and structural profile with a dynamic start object (see Chapter 3, Structural Authorization Check). The maintenance work can be considerably reduced if the number of different roles/profiles for time administrators can be reduced from 100 to 2 for an enterprise with 10,000 employees, for example.

Consequently, you should enter the area of responsibility in the Excel table. In the general authorization check, you can create a column for each field (Personnel Area, Employee Subgroup, and so on) and enter the value for each user, for example, Personnel Area 1000 (Hamburg) or Employee Subgroup 10 (salaried employee). If you perform the structural authorization check, you must maintain the evaluation path and the start object you use to determine the area of responsibility from the organizational structure (see Table 1.2). In our example, the Manager's Desktop is used. Here, you always determine the area of responsibility via the organizational structure, and the start object corresponds to the logged-on user (applies also to Manager Self-Services, MSS). You also determine the area of responsibility for the branch office administrators via an evaluation path with a dynamic start object (logged-on user), as shown in the Start Object column in Table 1.2. If you determined the area of responsibility of a branch office administrator using the fields of Infotype 0001 (Organizational Assignment), or via a defined start object (e.g., Organizational Unit 57600000), you would need a new column in the Excel table for each administrator.

This example illustrates that you can already reduce the effort of the authorization administration by intelligently using the given options.

Service	User Group	...	Evaluation Path	Start Object
Manager Info About Employees				
Employee list	Team lead	...	MDTSBES	Dynamic
Birthday list	Team lead	...	MDTSBES	Dynamic
Recurring payments and deductions	Team lead	...	MDTSBES	Dynamic
Maintain Master Data				
Maintain employee's personal data	ADMIN/ BRANCH	...	Z_BRANCHADMIN	Dynamic
Maintain challenge data	ADMIN/ BRANCH	...	Z_BRANCHADMIN	Dynamic
Maintain bank data	ADMIN/ BRANCH	...	Z_BRANCHADMIN	Dynamic
Maintain bank data	ESS user	...		
Maintain organizational assignment	ADMIN/ BRANCH	...	Z_BRANCHADMIN	Dynamic

Table 1.2 Area of Responsibility Determined via Structural Authorization

You have now created a qualitative analysis of the required authorizations. The table with the relevant services and user data, system reference, action, and area of responsibility forms the basis for deriving the roles (see Section 1.3, Role Definition). You have also created a clear and complete documentation of the authorizations that are supposed to be assigned, which derives from your HR processes.

You can use the HR service catalog to accelerate the collection of information on the processes. This HR service catalog is comprised of more than 800 services that are provided by HR departments. Figure 1.2 shows an extract of the catalog. It has proved its worth in numerous process man-

HR service catalog as accelerators

agement projects and is increasingly used and extended on an ongoing basis by the authors of this book (for further information see *www.ipro-con.de/referencemodel*).

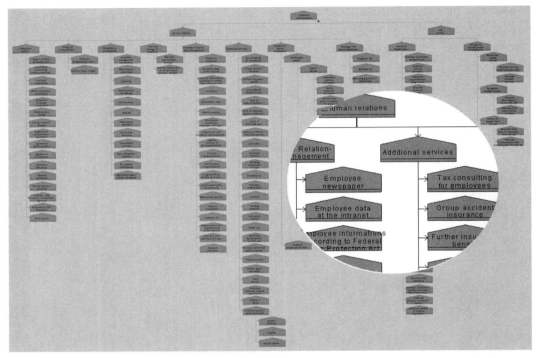

Figure 1.2 Extract from the HR Service Catalog, Personnel Administration Subtree

Using such a reference model saves you from spending many workshop days to create the enterprise-specific service catalog. In addition, the reference model supports you visually in acquiring information on the services and increases the quality because fewer details are forgotten.

The services are divided into HR main processes and subprocesses. At the highest level, the services are divided into company pension scheme, payroll, personnel administration, HR controlling, personnel develop-ment, workforce planning, recruiting, travel management, organizational structure, and time management.

If you use the reference service catalog, you must first adapt it to the specific requirements of your enterprise. For this purpose, the employees that provide these services get together and add missing services, remove services that haven't been provided, and customize terminology if required. In this way, an enterprise-specific HR service catalog is created, and you can determine which tasks your HR department actually covers.

This HR service catalog has been created in ARIS, which is a database-based modeling tool offered by IDS Scheer AG. The catalog's advantage is that you can directly enter and analyze the information described back in Steps 2 and 3 in the attributes of the service. You can also download Excel tables from the ARIS database, and can customize them according to your requirements and, as described earlier in Steps 4 and 5. Figure 1.3 shows an example of this process. In the figure, the Maintain organizational Assignment service is marked by an X, and it's indicated that this service is the interface between two departments/areas of responsibility.

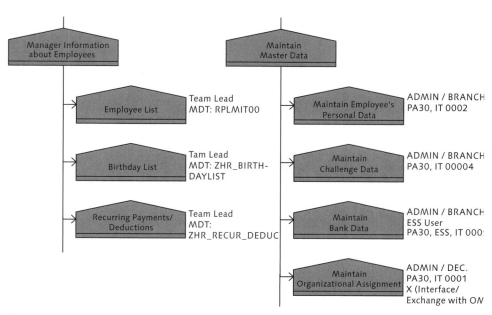

Figure 1.3   Extract from the Service Catalog with Attributes

1.3   Role Definition

Based on the qualitative process analysis created in Section 1.2, you can now derive roles. For this purpose, you should sort the tables by user groups. You can then identify which tasks can be combined into roles. If you determine the area of responsibility statically from the organizational assignment or from a static start object (when using the structural authorization), the number of roles or profiles will quickly increase. Therefore, examine the usage of the concepts introduced in this book in sections 2.8., Extensions, and Chapter 3, section 3.3, Function Modules, in order to reduce the number of roles.

Don't forget cross-process authorizations

When designing the roles, always keep in mind the cross-process authorizations that are combined into one or a few roles. This includes the following:

- ▸ Troubleshooting
- ▸ Printing
- ▸ Variant maintenance
- ▸ SAPoffice
- ▸ Download
- ▸ Table display

Consider exceptional cases

During the role definition process, it's also essential to discuss exceptional cases, such as substitution rules, temporary assignments, trainee programs, concurrent employment relationships, and transition periods. Decide how the cases are supposed to be resolved in detail — on a technical or organizational basis. We recommend finding a general solution for exceptional cases instead of resolving each individual case. Substitutes, for example, should permanently have the necessary authorizations. Otherwise, in the case of absence or illness, manual interaction is required repeatedly, which doesn't just involve unnecessary effort, it also constitutes a source of error (for example, due to the analysis of the change documents).

> **Tip**   **[+]**
>
> Please refer to Chapter 2, General Authorization Check, Chapter 5, Authorization Roles in SAP HCM Components, and Chapter 7, Reports for the Authorization System, for more information on the setup and maintenance of roles.

Before maintaining the roles in the system, you should think about the naming conventions. The next section provides essential information on this topic.

1.4   Naming Conventions

If you use a clear naming convention structure right from the start, you'll have a better overview of the roles at a later stage. Please note that you cannot rename the roles afterward! You can only copy a role and delete the old one. However, in this case, you'll lose the change history as well as the user assignment in the case of a central user administration.

> **Warning**   **[!]**
>
> You must use the central user administration if identical user records are needed in several systems with multiple clients. Then, you can maintain and distribute user records from a central system.

It's not advisable to customize and use the default roles provided by SAP because they may be modified for release changes or updates. However, you can copy default roles and use them as a template or create completely new roles.

Use a clear and logical naming convention structure in order to simplify the role administration work. For all objects in the SAP system, you can distinguish between SAP namespaces and customer namespaces. The latter usually start with Y and Z. For role names, only the SAP prefix is set. All other descriptions can be freely chosen. The role name may consist of up to 30 characters and may include the following information:

▶ **First letter**
You can select, for example, Y or Z, in order to ensure a clear differentiation from the SAP namespace. This is not mandatory; however, it is critical that the role doesn't start with *SAP*.

▶ **Application**
Here, you can choose H for HCM, S for System (or basic authorization), F for Financials, and so on.

▶ **Role category**
Here, you should distinguish between single, composite, and reference role, for example, S or :, C or &, R or -. To reduce the complexity of the role name, you should use a sign instead of a letter.

▶ **System**
This information is required if you don't use the central user administration. For example, use P12 for the production system with System Number 12, and so on.

▶ **Component**
To which SAP ERP HCM component does the authorization refer? Personnel administration (PA), personnel development (PD), and so on.

▶ **Organizational area**
To which organizational area, such as personnel area, employee subgroup, or assistant assignment, is the access granted? For example, use PA1000 for Personnel Area 1000, and so on.

▶ **Short name**
Enter an appropriate short name for the activity that the role covers, for example, MASTER DATA.

▶ **Function**
Which function does the user of the role have? Is he a leader (L), an administrator (AD), or an assistant (A)?

▶ **Action**
Which actions, such as reading or writing, can be used with the role? Use, for example, ALL (for All), DIS (for Display), CHA (for Change), and so on.

[+]

> **Tip**
>
> For reference roles, the name should contain the field that has been defined for the organizational level (see Chapter 2, General Authorization Check). Let's assume the personnel area was an organizational level. Then, instead of the organizational area, the field name (ADMIN) could be included in the role name.

For example, a single role could be named as follows:

Example of a single role

    P:PA_PA1000_LEADER_MASTERD_DIS

To improve readability, the name contains separators; however, these are not necessarily required. This role is structured as shown in Table 1.3.

Position	Example (ID)	Information	Example (Long Text)
1	P	Application	Personnel
2	:	Role category	Single role
3 – 4	PA	Component	Personnel administration
5	_	Separator	
6 – 11	PA1000	Organizational area	Personnel Area 1000
12	_	Separator	
13 – 18	LEADER	Function	Lead
19	_	Separator	
20 – 26	MASTERD	Short name	Processing master data
27	_	Separator	
28 – 30	DIS	Action	Display

Table 1.3 Sample Structure of a Single Role

In addition to defining the naming convention, with regard to organizational aspects, you should also specify that the description of a role is always maintained when a role is created (Figure 1.4). This is required in order to enable auditors as well as role and user administrators to determine which authorizations are included in a role without having to study the authorization objects in detail.

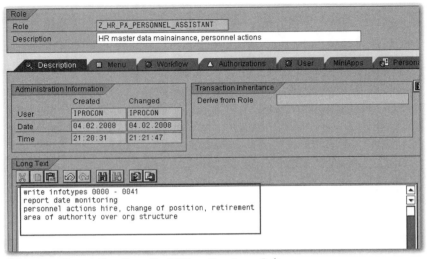

Figure 1.4 Description (Long Text) When Creating a Role

1.5 Critical Success Factors

This section lists some critical success factors from this chapter that you must take into account when creating a new authorization concept or redesigning an existing one.

▸ Involve the data protection officer, Auditing department, and employee representatives at an early stage in order to be able to meet the requirements of these interest groups right from the start.

▸ Define processes and responsibilities before beginning the detailed work on the authorization concept. This is the only way you can create a qualitative basis for the concept work.

▸ Select a person who is familiar with the data and processes of the HCM system to design the roles. This is not the task of the system administrator. Instead, you should select someone who has a profound knowledge of the HCM authorization objects and the SAP role and authorization concept. This is the only way you can set up an authorization concept that exploits the full functionality of the HCM system.

▶ Choose a concept that supports you in keeping the number of roles and structural profiles as few as possible. This reduces the later maintenance work.

▶ Schedule sufficient time to test the roles. In a large project, you should perform all integration tests and trainings for the roles that are later used in the production environment. In this way, you can avoid frustration among users.

▶ Consider dependencies on the system architecture, such as transport routes, connected data warehouse systems, or e-recruiting, and structures in the HCM systems, for example, personnel areas and the organizational management. There are often specific requirements for the authorization concept that depend on the architecture.

▶ Challenge complex regulations from time to time and don't be afraid to abandon antiquated customs. Often, regulations are complex because they couldn't be implemented in another way in a legacy system. This frequently enables you to optimize the authorization system.

The general authorization check is the central tool in the authorization system on which all other authorization concepts are based. In this chapter, we'll describe the most critical functions of the role maintenanc, and the use of the authorization objects utilized in the HCM System.

2 General Authorization Check

Out of the three authorization concepts available in SAP ERP HCM, the general authorization check is always implemented first, because it forms the basis for all subsequent authorization concepts.

In the following sections, we'll initially give you an overview of the components of the general authorization check. Then, we'll detail the different role types and their maintenance (Transaction PFCG), and the most critical authorization objects. In Section 2.5, Customizing of the Profile Generator, you learn more about how you can customize the Profile Generator for proposing authorization objects in the role maintenance. Another section is about time logic that plays a critical role for establishing the periods of responsibility (see Section 2.6, Period of Responsibility and Time Logic). Test procedures are an essential instrument of the general authorization check. We'll describe their functionality in Section 2.7, Test Procedures (Infotype 0130). To conclude this chapter, we'll present various options for extending the standard.

2.1 Elements

The goal of this section is to provide you with a sound basic knowledge based on which we'll outline the general authorization check. For this purpose, we'll briefly discuss the most critical terminology of the SAP authorization system and their interrelations, but we won't detail the SAP authorization concept.

Components of an
authorization role

Like all other SAP components, an authorization role in SAP ERP HCM comprises authorization objects, authorizations, and authorization profiles. The authorization profiles are only technical values that build the connection between role and authorization.

Figure 2.1 shows the relationships between the individual elements.

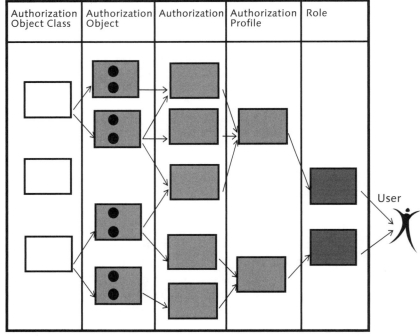

• Authorization Field

Figure 2.1 Elements of the General Authorization Check

Authorization
object and object
class

Authorization objects protect the access to a functional area or data area in the SAP system. The check can be implemented both when starting a transaction and at any other point in the program. Authorization objects comprise one to ten fields that give a detailed description of the concrete authorizations. Therefore, an authorization object is a kind of variable, including fields that can be filled with different values. Authorization objects are grouped into classes for the sake of clarity; the *authorization object class* for SAP ERP HCM is called *Human Resources*.

An authorization object, whose fields are filled, result in an *authorization.* Sometimes, this must be very detailed, for example, the read authorization for a specific infotype in a certain employee subgroup; however, it can also be very general, for instance, executing all functions available in the Manager's Desktop (MDT).

Authorization

The combination of different authorizations, which consist of authorization objects, results in an *authorization profile.* Each *role* comprises exactly one authorization profile. A *role* (for example, HR administrator) is created when setting up a user menu, and comprises a combination of various transactions, for instance, PA30 (Maintain HR Master Data), PA40 (Personnel Actions), and so on.

Authorization profile and role

| **Tip** | [+] |

In older releases, there was only one profile that was directly assigned to the user. Today, the profile is created based on the role, and you only assign the role to the user. As of Release 4.6B the profile is generated when creating a role.

In the next section, we'll detail how you can create a role and assign it to a user.

2.2   Role Maintenance

You can access the role maintenance from the SAP Easy Access menu TOOLS • ADMINISTRATION • USER MAINTENANCE • ROLE ADMINISTRATION • ROLES or through Transaction PFCG. Figure 2.2 shows the initial screen of the role maintenance.

| **Customizing the Profile Generator** |

If you enter transactions in the menu of the role maintenance and you change to the Authorizations tab, the Profile Generator is used. We'll describe the customizing of the Profile Generator in Section 2.5, *Customizing of the Profile Generator*. Prior to that, in Section 2.3, *Authorization Objects*, and Section 2.4, *Required System Authorizations*, we'll present the authorization objects that can be used as default values in the Profile Generator.

Use the F4 help option of the ROLE field to view the standard roles delivered by SAP. Most of the roles relevant for the HCM system start with SAP_HR*. We'll present the most common HCM roles in Chapter 5, Authorizations in SAP HCM Components.

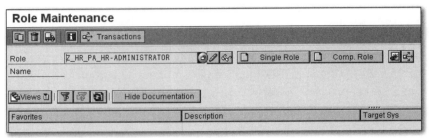

Figure 2.2 Initial Screen of the Role Maintenance

Creating a role To create a new role, you can either use a standard role as a template or select the SINGLE ROLE button (the composite roles will be explained shortly). If your enterprise has no naming conventions for role names, refer back to Chapter 1, *Process-Oriented Authorization Concept*.

To create a new role, proceed as follows:

1. Enter a name in the ROLE field, and click on the SINGLE ROLE button.

2. Enter a brief description, and change to the Menu tab (Figure 2.3). Here, you can compile the user menu using the following buttons:

   ▶ TRANSACTION
   To enter individual transactions (you need to know the transaction code)

   ▶ REPORT
   To enter ABAP reports, queries, reports from the Business Warehouse, and transaction codes with variant (we'll explain the creation of a transaction with variant in Chapter 10, Selected Problem Areas and Their Solutions)

   ▶ OTHER
   To enter Internet addresses, and so on

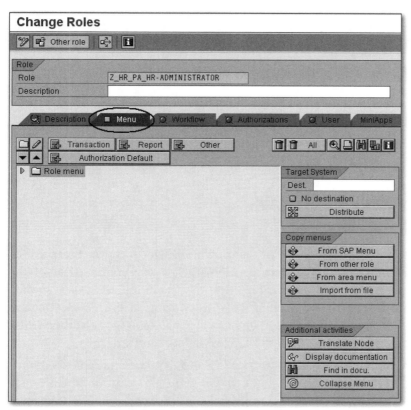

Figure 2.3 Setting Up a Role Menu

▶ AUTHORIZATION DEFAULT

The transactions entered here are not visible in the user's menu. This makes sense if, for example, the user uses a web browser that requires access to the back-end system. The user, however, is not supposed to execute these transactions. In addition to transactions, you can also enter RFC functions and web services here. You can then maintain the authorization defaults on the AUTHORIZATIONS tab.

▶ COPY MENUS

To import complete menu parts from the SAP Easy Access menu, from other roles, from an area menu, or from a file (see SAP PRESS book, *HR Reporting with SAP*, Chapter 16 for more details if necessary)

[+] Double-click on an entered transaction to change the name of the transaction.

[+] The traffic light colors on the tabs indicate the maintenance status (Figure 2.4):
  ▶ Green: Menu entries, authorizations, and users are maintained.
  ▶ Yellow: Authorizations and users are assigned, but not yet generated/synchronized.
  ▶ Red: Menu entries, authorizations, or users are not maintained.

Figure 2.4 Maintenance Statuses of the Tabs

3. After you have compiled the menu, change to the **Authorizations** tab and click on the **Change authorization** DATA button. Based on the menu entries, proposals for the authorization objects to be checked are compiled (see Section 2.5, Customizing of the Profile Generator). This brings you to the screen for maintaining the authorization objects (Figure 2.5). Here are a few helpful hints:

  ▶ Depending on the settings of the Profile Generator, not all authorization objects to be checked will be proposed. You can customize the proposals of the Profile Generator (see Section 2.5, Customizing of the Profile Generator).

  ▶ Use the Selection criteria and Manually buttons to insert additional authorization objects.

  ▶ For more information about the Organizational levels... button, refer to Section 2.2.3, Reference Roles.

  ▶ Note the ▦ button. In the legend, you can find an explanation for all colors and icons of this screen.

  ▶ Use the menu path, Utilities • Technical Names on, to show the technical names of the authorization objects and fields.

  ▶ If you click on the yellow traffic light (Figure 2.5), you can directly assign the full authorization (in each field *) for an object or all objects below the highest traffic light.

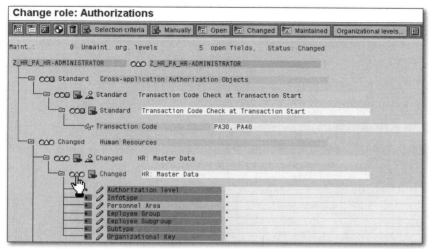

Figure 2.5 Maintaining Authorizations

▶ Use the 🖉 button on the left of the authorization field to maintain the authorization values. For some fields, you can only obtain reliable input values through the F1 help (Figure 2.6).

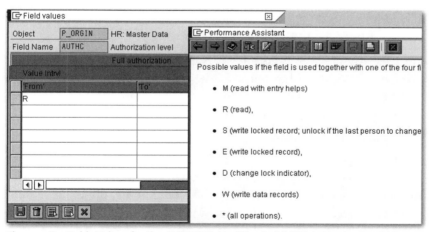

Figure 2.6 Fields Values for the AUTHC Field of the P_ORGIN Authorization Object

▶ To delete an authorization object from the role, you first have to deactivate it using the 🖳 button. Only then will you receive the delete symbol for the authorization object.

▶ When all authorization objects have been maintained (green traffic light), click on the Generate button. You are proposed a technical name for the authorization profile. We recommend not changing this name because you usually don't work with profiles, but with roles. Give the roles a meaningful or systematic name.

▶ Assign the full authorization as described in the following paragraph.

Creating the SAP_
ALL role

In a development system, the users often require authorizations to all transactions and authorization objects. The fastest way to create a role with full authorization is as follows: In the screen, CHANGE ROLE: AUTHORIZATIONS (see Figure 2.5) select the menu path, EDIT • INSERT AUTHORIZATION • FULL AUTHORIZATION. Because these users generally are not supposed to be assigned with the user maintenance authorization, deactivate all authorization objects that start with the user master maintenance in the basis administration object class.

After you have created the role, you need to assign it to the users. This can be done in many different ways that will be described in the following section.

2.2.1 Role Assignment

You can assign roles to users directly or indirectly. For direct assignment, you create a relationship between the role and the user. For indirect assignment, you connect the role and an organizational object. Via the organizational structure, you can inherit the role to a person or user.

Both options have advantages and disadvantages. For direct assignment, it often happens that users regularly changing departments (e.g., trainees) accumulate several roles, because only new roles are added, but not invalid roles are removed. At the end of the training, the trainee might have more rights than the mentor. Moreover, the employee doesn't automatically have the appropriate rights when he changes to another department. Generally, he must request new required rights each time. However, you can flexibly control when and for how long a user may have specific rights. For example, an employee might have to complete remaining work for old tasks after a task change. For direct assignment, the old role would then be delimited to a later point.

This exactly is the disadvantage of assignment through the organizational structure. In case of a change, the old authorizations are automatically removed and new ones assigned. The optimal way depends on whether the authorizations in your enterprise are primarily derived from the organizational structure or from the persons.

Direct User Assignment

Due to data protection requirements it is often necessary to separate the role maintenance from the user assignment. The system offers two options for user assignment:

- Assignment in the role maintenance (Transaction PFCG)
- Assignment in the user master record (Transaction SU01)

If the role administrator simultaneously has the authorization for role assignment, he can use Transaction PFCG to implement the assignment on the USER tab. On this tab, you can enter the user names, including an assignment time period. Subsequently, click on the USER COMPARISON button to add the profile and role to the user master record. Alternatively, you can implement the user comparison automatically when saving the role. Select the menu path UTILITIES • SETTINGS and then the option for automatic comparison when saving the role.

User assignment via Transaction PFCG

Tip	[+]
Changes to the role, the authorization profile, or the assigned users always require a user comparison.	

If you assign the users separately to the role maintenance, for example, by the user administrator, this is done using Transaction SU01. Here, you enter the single roles or composite roles on the ROLES tab. The profiles belonging to these roles are automatically displayed on the PROFILES tab. A manual assignment of profiles that were generated in the role maintenance (Transaction PFCG) on the PROFILES tab, should no longer be possible because the role concept is available. Moreover, the user is automatically entered for the role on the USER tab.

User assignment via Transaction SU01

[+]

Tip

For more information on the subject, user maintenance and user master record, refer to *SAP Authorization System* published by SAP PRESS.

Scheduling daily
user master
comparisons

If you delimit the assignment time period right from the start, you must
perform a regular user master comparison. Use Transaction PFUD or the
TOOLS • ADMINISTRATION • USER MAINTENANCE • ROLE ADMINISTRATION •
USER MASTER DATA RECONCILIATION path in the SAP Easy Access menu to
go to the selection screen of the RHAUTUPD_NEW report (Figure 2.7).
Schedule this as a job that runs every night. The report performs a complete user master comparison for all roles and updates the user master
records with regard to authorizations. The roles are deleted from the user
master record according to the assignment end or entered in the user
master recording according to the assignment start.

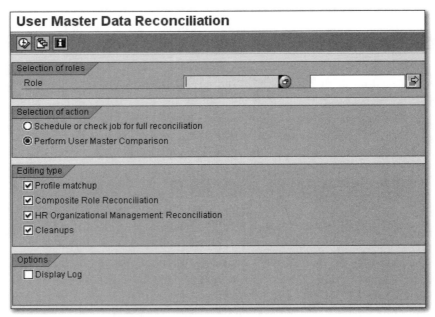

Figure 2.7 Selection Screen of the RHAUTUPD_NEW Report

In the next setion, we'll present another option for assigning users
through objects of Organizational Management.

Indirect User Assignment

Active plan versions and a clearly maintained organizational management are prerequisites for indirect assignment of roles to users by means
of the organizational structure. Moreover, Infotype 0105 (Communication) must be maintained together with the user name to establish the
connection between the person and the user. You can assign roles to the
object types shown in Figure 2.8. The RHAUTUPD_NEW report performs the user master comparison for the selected roles. Therefore, you
should schedule this report for indirect assignment periodically just like
described above. In the selection screen, you must check the HR ORGANI-
ZATIONAL MANAGEMENT: COMPARISON flag. For individual roles, you can
also start the user master comparison by means of Transaction PFCG.

Prerequisites for
assignments via
OM

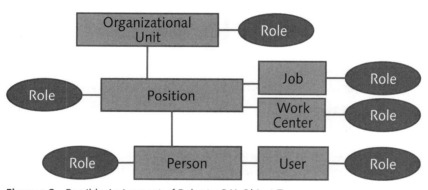

Figure 2.8 Possible Assignment of Roles to OM Object Types

Tip	[+]

If you want to assign roles to additional object types, you must adapt the
US_ACTGR evaluation path, because it determines the user based on the
contained object types to subsequently assign the roles to the user.

For indirect role assignment, you should proceed as follows.

Procedure for
assignments via
OM

1. To assign roles, click on the ORGANIZATIONAL MANAGEMENT button on
   the USER tab. If this button is not visible, select the COMPLETE VIEW
   option in the menu path GOTO • SETTINGS ON THE INITIAL SCREEN OF
   THE ROLE MAINTENANCE.

2. In the ROLE: Choose Agent Type, select the  button to create the assignment. A list with possible agent types is opened that you can connect with the role (Figure 2.9).

Figure 2.9 Selecting Agent Types

3. Select the corresponding object type from the list of possible agent types, and enter the appropriate object ID. Figure 2.10 shows the assignment of a role to positions.

4. Now select the ⊞ button to compare the user master records. The traffic light changes to green.

Our example in Figure 2.10 has the following result: Because only Mr. Kaufman is connected to a user (US) via Infotype 0105, Subtype 0001, will the Z_HR_PA_HR-ADMINISTRATOR role be inherited to him. Mr. Beckenbauer receives no authorizations.

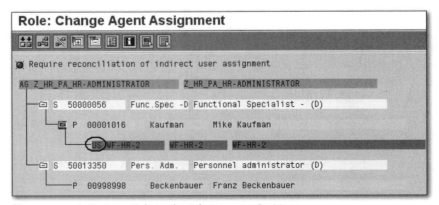

Figure 2.10 Assigning a Role to the Administrator Positions

> **Warning** [!]
>
> If you have a missing authorization for assigning roles to OM object types, refer to SAP Note 312682. A customizing setting in the PRGN_CUST table might be required.

> **Tip** [+]
>
> You can also implement the role assignment in Organizational Management (Transaction PPOME). In the standard version, however, the Object Type AG (Role) is not available. SAP Note 578271 comprehensively describes the required steps to integrate the Object Type AG in Transaction PPOME.

The effort for role maintenance and user administration can be particularly extensive if the HCM system used is decentralized. There are two concepts for reducing the effort: composite roles and reference roles. Composite roles can facilitate the user administration if multiple users require the same roles. We'll present this concept in Section 2.2.2, Composite Roles. Reference roles, however, reduce the effort in the role maintenance. In Section 2.2.3, Reference Roles, you will learn more about when it makes sense to derive roles, how you must proceed when inheriting role menus and authorizations of a reference role, and what aspects you must take into consideration here.

2.2.2 Composite Roles

The more users you connect to your SAP ERP HCM system, the higher the number of roles. If multiple employees have the same functions that contain multiple roles (Figure 2.11), you can facilitate the user administration by means of the composite role concept. Instead of assigning the roles separately to each user, you can combine them in a composite role and assign them to only one composite role. Composite roles may comprise any arbitrary number of single roles, and you can add or remove single roles at a later stage. All users with a composite role automatically receive the new single role after a comparison.

> **Warning** [!]
>
> Composite roles don't contain authorizations and can't be combined to form another composite role.

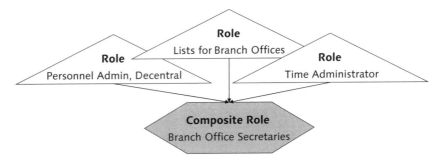

Figure 2.11 Example for the Use of Composite Roles

[+] **Deviating Naming Convention for Composite Roles**

Before introducing the composite role, you should establish a naming convention that deviates from the single role. This facilitates your work, because otherwise you can't distinguish single roles from composite roles at first glance in the role maintenance. For tips on the naming convention, refer to Chapter 1, Process-Oriented Authorization Concept.

But how do you have to proceed if you want to combine roles into a composite role?

1. Call the role maintenance using Transaction PFCG.

2. Enter a name for the new composite role in the ROLE field.

3. Click on the Create Composite Role button.

4. Enter a description of the composite role in the following screen, and save your entries.

5. Go to the Roles tab, and enter all the single roles that you want to combine for the composite role (Figure 2.12).

6. On the Menu tab you can display the individual roles and restructure them using the Import menu button. For this purpose, note the information about importing composite role menus and transferring them to the user menu. You can obtain it using the 🔳 button.

7. Assign the composite role to the users as described in Section 2.2.1, Role Assignment, and finally click on the USER COMPARISON BUTTON.

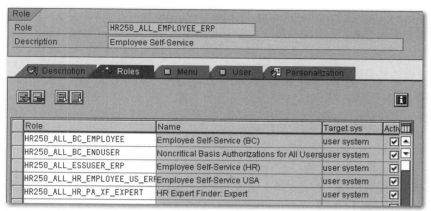

Figure 2.12 Combining Single Roles to Composite Roles

When you complete these steps, the users of your user master record are assigned both to the composite role 🌐 and the single roles ⊕. Additionally, the users are entered on the user tabs of the single roles; however, they cannot be maintained there.

> **Tip**
>
> You can obtain an overview of the composite roles and their assigned single roles on the initial screen of the role maintenance using the VIEWS • ROLES IN COMPOSITE ROLES button.

[+]

Based on our experience, we highly recommend the use of composite roles. Composite roles enable you to modularize role concepts, and therefore, increase the overview over the multitude of roles. In addition, they facilitate the user maintenance work of the authorization administrator.

In the next section, you'll be presented with another concept for reducing the maintenance effort in the authorization management, namely the reference roles.

2.2.3 Reference Roles

While some years ago, there were only a few SAP users at the headquarters, more and more decentralized users have been added for some time now. For example, when implementing Self Services or outsourcing HCM tasks in decentralized Competence Centers, the number of users frequently increases by leaps and bounds. The result is that the number of roles also increases and the administration becomes more extensive. Deriving roles enables you to reduce the maintenance work, and provides an efficient authorization management.

Using reference roles

Deriving roles makes sense if multiple users are supposed to obtain the same user menu with different authorizations, or if multiple users are supposed to have the same user menu with the same authorizations for different areas of responsibility (organizational levels) (Figure 2.13).

> **What is an Organizational Level?**
>
> The organizational level is the employee's area of responsibility. For whom does the user have authorizations to implement certain functions? The area of responsibility can be the personnel area or a administrator key, for example.

[Ex]
> **Example**
>
> You have multiple time administrators with identical tasks, but each time administrator has a different area of responsibility. Without deriving roles, you would have to maintain a separate role for each time administrator. Thanks to the deriving option you only have to maintain one role.

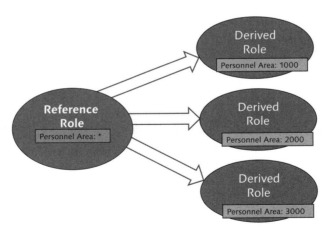

Figure 2.13 Reference Role at the" Personnel Area" Organizational Level

Using this concept does not reduce the number of roles, but instead of maintaining multiple roles after you've changed the menu or the authorizations, you only need to adapt the reference role. The changes are then automatically transferred to the derived roles. A prerequisite for deriving a role is that the new role contains no menu entries or authorizations.

We generally differentiate between two forms of derivation:

▶ You accept the entire menu for the derived role, but you change the authorizations of the derived role.

▶ You accept the menu and the authorizations, and only maintain the organizational level of the derived role (see Figure 2.13).

You can obtain an overview of the inheritance relationships between roles on the initial screen of the role maintenance using the VIEWS • INHERITANCE HIERARCHY button. To view the inheritance relationship of an individual role proceed as follows:

Viewing or deleting inheritance relationships

1. Execute Transaction PFCG, and select the appropriate role.

2. Select the DISPLAY ROLE or CHANGE ROLE buttons to go to the next screen.

3. In the menu, open the path ROLE • WHERE-USED LIST. From this inheritance overview, you can directly navigate to other roles. To resolve an inheritance relationship, select the RESOLVE INHERITANCE RELATIONSHIP button on the DESCRIPTION tab in the role maintenance of the derived role.

In the following sections, you'll learn how you can derive roles, what you have to take into consideration, and why you initially must define new organizational levels.

Inheriting a Menu

For this form of derivation, the menu and all of its transactions are inherited by the reference role. The authorizations are separately maintained in the derived role. To derive the menu, you must proceed as follows:

1. Select Transaction PFCG, role maintenance.

2. Create a new role.

3. In Figure 2.14, you can see the TRANSACTION INHERITANCE section on the DESCRIPTION tab. As long as no transactions are directly assigned

to this role, you can select the reference role in the Derive from Role field. (A role becomes a reference role, when roles have been derived from it.)

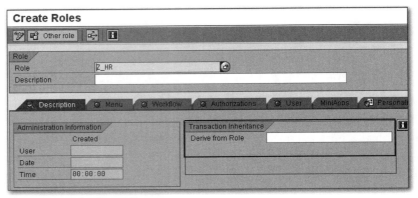

Figure 2.14 Inheriting a Menu

4. Save your entries, and maintain the AUTHORIZATIONS tab as described in Section 2.2, Role Maintenance.

5. You can't maintain menu entries in the derived role any longer.

By means of these settings you achieved that the menu of the reference role is inherited to the derived role. Future changes to the menu of the reference role are automatically transferred to the derived role. In the derived role you can't add or delete menu entries.

Inheriting the Menu and Authorizations

By means of the following steps you transfer the authorizations to the derived role:

1. For the derived role, select the AUTHORIZATION DATA button on the AUTHORIZATIONS tab.

2. The COPY DATA button is only available for derived roles. Use this button to copy all authorizations of the reference role to the derived role except for the organizational levels (Figure 2.15).

3. Now maintain the organizational level(s) of each derived role using the ORGANIZATIONAL LEVELS button. In this context, note the explanations provided in the following section.

Figure 2.15 Copying Authorization Data to the Derived Role

Alternatively, you can copy the authorizations to multiple derived roles based on the reference role:

Alternative

1. Select the AUTHORIZATIONS tab in the role maintenance of the reference role, and click on CHANGE AUTHORIZATION DATA.

2. The 🔡 button (generate derived roles) is only available for reference roles. Use this button to copy all authorizations of the reference role to all derived roles except for the organizational levels. You must also use this button if you change the reference role.

Defining Organizational Levels

In SAP ERP HCM, the plan version is the only organizational level in the authorization concept (Figure 2.16). However, the plan version is not a commonly used field to differentiate areas of responsibility. In other components, for example, the company code, business area or the plant are defined as organizational levels. Consequently, the concept of the reference role in the HCM system would be virtually useless.

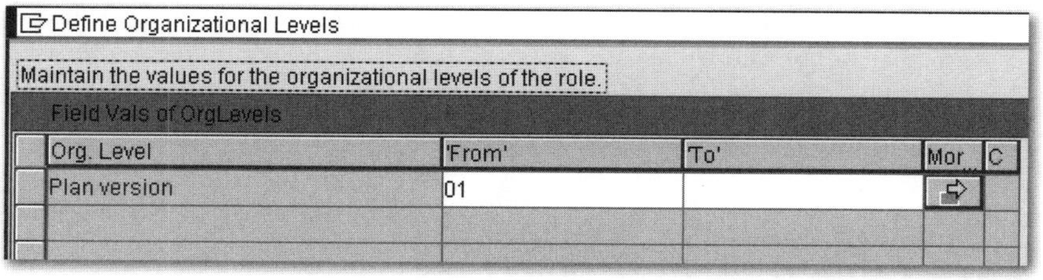

Org. Level	'From'	'To'	Mor	C
Plan version	01		⇨	

Figure 2.16 In the Standard Version, the Plan Version is the Only Organizational Level

However, it is possible to create new organizational level fields using the PFCG_ORGFIELD_CREATE report. The report creates an organizational level field for an individual authorization field to be selected, for example, PERSA (personnel area). Theoretically, you can define each autho-

**PFCG_ORGFIELD_
CREATE**

rization field for the organizational level field. The report also deletes the default values for this field in the Profile Generator (see Section 2.5, Customizing of the Profile Generators).

Initially, start the report in the test mode. Subsequently, you receive a comprehensive list that indicates how extensive the customizing requirements would be. The list is comprised of all affected roles, including the maintained values of the authorization object to be changed. If the traffic light is yellow, this means that you must manually customize the role. After you have created an organizational level field, this is included in the list of organizational level and can now be maintained in the derived roles (Figure 2.17).

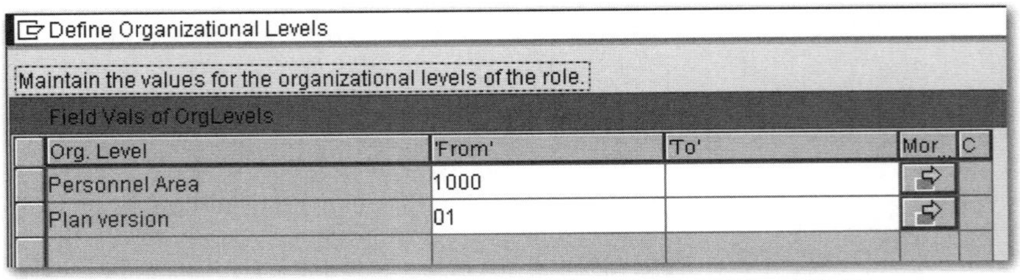

Figure 2.17 Defining the Personnel Areas as an Organizational Level Field

[+]   **Defining Organizational Levels**

You must implement the report for creating an organizational level field separately for all clients and all systems (development system, production system). You can obtain more information in the program documentation of the PFCG_ORGFIELD_CREATE report. For deleting an organizational level field that you created yourself, use the PFCG_ORGFIELD_DELETE report. After an upgrade, start the PFCG_ORGFIELD_UPGRADE report to provide the new organizational level field to the newly delivered authorization data.

2.3   Authorization Objects

No superordinate system

Authorization objects are the central elements of authorizations. Unfortunately, there are no superordinate systems of authorization objects or locations in the SAP transactions where the objects are checked. Depending on the application, the subjects to be protected may vary and must, therefore, be checked specifically.

It becomes all the more important to precisely know the authorization objects of a subject. We will now examine this task, and limit our detailed description to the seven most critical objects of the HCM. The remaining objects in the context of the respective HCM subarea will be explained in Chapter 5, Authorization Roles in SAP HCM Components.

In Transaction SU21 (Maintenance of Authorization Objects) you can find an overview of the detailed documentation about the authorization objects and their fields. Figure 2.18 shows the results of this transaction: In the CLASS/OBJECT column, you see the HCM authorization objects with their technical names and the descriptions.

Overview and documentation using Transaction SU21

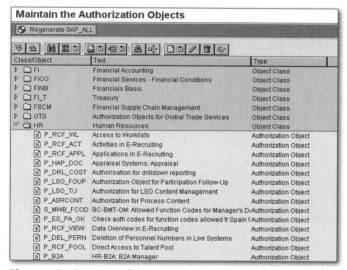

Figure 2.18 Overview of the Authorization Objects Using Transaction SU21

2.3.1 Transaction Authorizations

Transaction authorizations is the most simple and most effective tool for authorization checks. For example, if you don't permit transactions of Organizational Management for a user, the user can't access this data at all. In the following section, we'll describe how the transaction authorizations work in combination with system and HCM authorization.

Generally, you maintain the transaction authorizations on the MENU tab of the role maintenance (Transaction PFCG). An example is provided in Figure 2.19.

Each entry of a transaction at this point is translated into an authorization of the S_TCODE system authorization object (Transaction Code Check at Transaction Start). Figure 2.20 shows the entries in S_TCODE for the transactions of Figure 2.19. You can also see that the created entries on the AUTHORIZATIONS tab can't be changed.

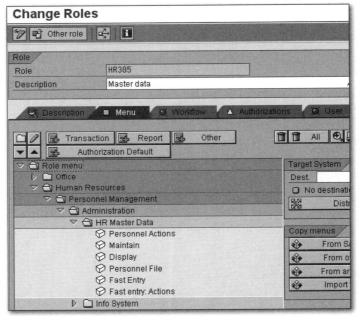

Figure 2.19 Maintaining the Transaction Authorizations via the Role Menu

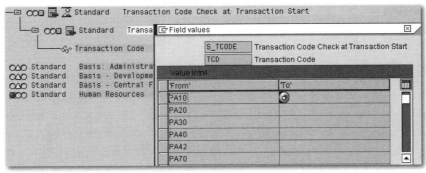

Figure 2.20 Entries in the S_TCODE System Authorization Object

To avoid a situation where every transaction is processed using the role maintenance function, the S_TCODE authorization object can also be transferred manually to the profiles using the MANUALLY button and maintained without the need to go through the menu. You can also use the placeholder "*" here — for example, "ZPT*" would allow all transactions that start with ZPT. This can facilitate the maintenance of transaction authorizations; however, the advantages of a clear menu for the roles are withdrawn.

Direct maintenance of S_TCODE

In addition to the already described transaction authorization, the P_TCODE object is also checked in many HCM transactions at transaction start (HR: transaction code) and proposed by the Profile Generator (Figure 2.21). This may appear to be unnecessary, but it enables the double-verification principle for the maintenance of authorizations: S_TCODE is only maintained by the person responsible for the system authorizations, P_TCODE is maintained by the person responsible for HCM authorization.

HCM with additional transaction check Using P_TCODE

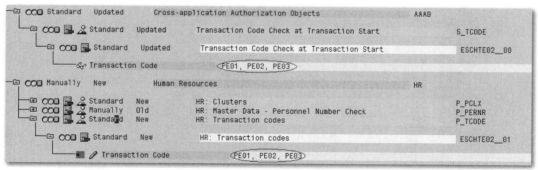

Figure 2.21 Some transactions in HCM additionally require the P_TCODE authorization object.

Most transactions in HCM require authorizations for both objects. This generally applies to system transactions, for example, Delete Personnel Numbers (PU00) or Maintenance of Payroll Schemas and Calculation Rules (PE01/02). Moreover, transactions, like Single Data Entry in Statements (PM11) or Shift Planning (PP61), additionally check whether a HCM transaction authorization exists. In practice, this lets you simply accept the HCM transaction object, instead of checking for every single case to see whether it is really necessary.

P_TCODE comprises — just like S_TCODE — only one single field, namely the transaction code. Here, you can use the placeholder "*" as well.

[+]

> **Tip**
>
> To obtain a list of all transactions that check the HCM transaction authorizations, proceed as follows: Call the Repository Information System using the transaction code maintenance (Transaction SE93) via **Utilities • Find**. Enter "P*" under Transaction code and "P_TCODE" under Authorization Object.

2.3.2 Infotype Authorization in Personnel Administration

P_ORGIN (HR: Master Data) presumably is the most popular authorization object in SAP ERP HCM. This object checks all accesses to infotypes of the administration and time management, technically speaking, the access to tables with the prefix PA.

In Figure 2.22 you can see the fields of the P_ORGIN authorization object.

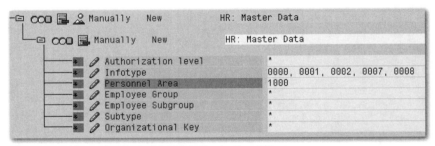

Figure 2.22 Example of a P_ORGIN Authorization Object

Authorization level   The authorization level can have the following characteristics:

- ▶ M (read with entry helps)
- ▶ R (read)
- ▶ S (write locked record; unlock if the last person to change the record is not the current user)
- ▶ E (write locked record)

- ▶ D (change lock indicator)
- ▶ W (write)

You can enter the permitted actions individually in the fields, or authorize all possible actions by entering "*".

Double Verification Principle	**[Ex]**

Using the options of the Authorization level field, you can implement the following double-verification principle for maintaining arbitrary infotypes:

- ▶ User A has Authorization Level E. The infotype records that he created must be unlocked by another user.
- ▶ User B has the Authorization Level S. He as well, can only write locked records, but can unlock locked records if they were not created by him.

Note that only unlocked records are considered for time evaluation and payroll.

For more information about the double-verification principle, refer to the role maintenance (PFCG) on the tab, **Authorizations • Change Authorization Data button • Expand Authorization Object**. If you place the cursor on the Authorization Level field and then press the [F1] key, you receive the field documentation. There, you must click on the marked link, double verification principle.

In the fields, INFOTYPE and SUBTYPE, you can enter all infotypes and subtypes of personnel administration and time management for which you want to permit the actions specified under authorization level. In our example, the Infotypes 0000, 0001, 0002, 0007, and 0008, and all subtypes are permitted.

Infotype/subtype

Warning	**[!]**

If you assign individual explicit authorization in the SUBTYPE field instead of using "*", you must ensure that you also authorize the " " entry (blank). Otherwise it may be possible that no authorization exists for infotypes without subtype.

The PERSONNEL AREA, EMPLOYEE GROUP, EMPLOYEE SUBGROUP, and ORGANIZATIONAL Key fields relate to Infotype 0001 (Organizational assignment) of the personnel number that is accessed. In Figure 2.22, all persons belonging to Personnel Area 1000 are accessible without any restrictions for the listed infotypes.

Fields from Infotype 0001

Extension of the example
Imagine that an employee did not have Infotype 0008 (Basic pay) as given here in our example, but he had read authorization and access to non–pay-scale employees. What would you have to do? In this case, you would have to divide the authorization into two authorizations for the same object. This is shown in Figure 2.23.

What would you have to do? In this case, you would have to divide the authorization into two authorizations for the same object. This is shown in Figure 2.23.

Infotype 0008 was removed from the first authorization, and a second authorization was established with a pure read authorization level that has an additional restriction of the permitted employee subgroups.

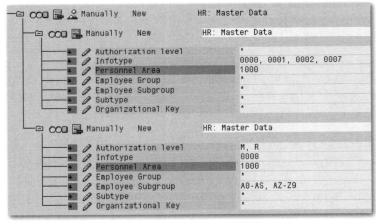

Figure 2.23 Special Authorization for Infotype 0008

Additional extension of the example
Now imagine that the employee for which these authorizations are valid, also had read access to another personnel area. Figure 2.24 shows that a third characteristic of the P_ORGIN object must be created.

OR link between the authorizations
If a user, with the authorizations specified in our example, tries to access the system, for example, for creating a record in Infotype 0007 for Personnel Area 1000, Employee Group AS, the system will search for an authorization that allows this access. This access must be permitted in at least one of the characteristic of P_ORGIN. Because the first authorization permits all maintenance actions for Infotype 0007 in Personnel Area 1000, this access is granted.

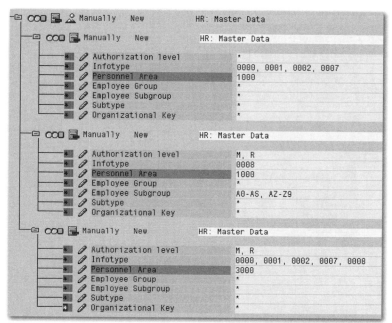

Figure 2.24 Read Authorization for Personnel Area 3000

Clarity in Case of Multiple Authorization [+]

It is possible that authorizations overlap, so that multiple authorizations may permit the access. This does not impair the system behavior, but can lead to complexity and consequently result in difficult authorization maintenance. Generally, we recommend assigning an authorization only once within a role.

Another problem in structuring the authorization of an object is the subtype field. In principle, it is possible to combine infotypes with and without subtype within an authorization as you can see in our example in Figure 2.25. However, you must always enter a Subtype " " (blank) so that infotypes without subtype are also authorized. It might be a bit clearer if you separate authorizations for infotypes with subtypes and infotypes without subtypes (Figure 2.26). For the authorization check it is not relevant which form you select.

These considerations are also valid for authorization objects with subtypes, whereas you can omit the entry " " (blank) for PLOG — see Section 2.3.5, Personnel Planning (PLOG).

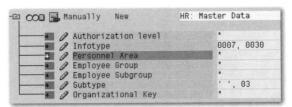

Figure 2.25 Working with Subtypes: Variant 1

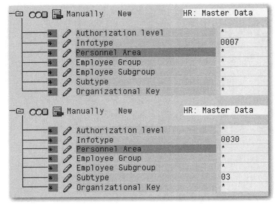

Figure 2.26 Working with Subtypes: Variant 2

"Special feature" — organizational key

The special feature of the organizational key field of Infotype 0001 is that you can use all fields of Infotype 0001 for authorizations. Via Customizing you can fill the 14-place organizational key with any content, for example, with the personnel subarea, the cost center, or a combination of both fields. The IMG path is: PERSONNEL MANAGEMENT • PERSONNEL ADMINISTRATION • ORGANIZATIONAL DATA • ORGANIZATIONAL ASSIGNMENT • SET UP ORGANIZATIONAL KEY. In the authorizations of the P_ORGIN object, you can permit, for example, the cost centers 20000 to 29999, in the ORGANIZATIONAL KEY field.

[+] **Tip**

The Organizational Key field is the only option available in the standard version to use the cost center within the authorizations. The structural authorization does not process the cost center.

Another option would be to accept the cost center of Infotype 0001 in the Authorization Object P_NNNNN (see Section 2.8.1).

SAP provides the P_ORGIN authorization object in active mode. To replace it with another authorization object (for example, P_ORGXX, see Section 2.3.3, Additional Authorization Objects for Master and Time Data), you must deactivate it in the maintenance of the authorization main switches of IMG: PERSONNEL MANAGEMENT • PERSONNEL ADMINISTRATION • TOOLS • AUTHORIZATION MANAGEMENT • EDIT AUTHORIZATION MAIN SWITCH • MAINTAIN AUTHORIZATION MAIN SWITCH. There, you need to switch the AUTSW ORGIN switch from "1" to "0".

Activation/
Deactivation

2.3.3 Additional Authorization Objects for Master and Time Data

As a supplement or alternative to P_ORGIN, there are two additional authorization objects that authorize the access to infotypes.

HR: Master Data - Extended Check (P_ORGXX)

This object can be used as an alternative or supplement to the authorization object, HR: Master Data. It extends the Infotype 0001 fields (Organizational assignment), that can be used for authorizations to the administrator fields (Figure 2.27).

Figure 2.27 Administrator Fields of Infotype 0001

This object is very useful for the decentralized data maintenance in time management and administration. Sometimes it is a good alternative to the structural authorizations, but is less flexible, because the organizational changes only impact the authorizations if you additionally maintain the corresponding fields of Infotype 0001.

You must activate this authorization object in Customizing by entering "1" in AUTSW ORGXX (HR: Master Data – Extended Check) of the authorization main switches of Table T77S0.

The following fields are checked:

▶ **Infotype/Subtype**
   analog to P_ORGIN authorization object (HR: Master Data) (see Section 2.3.2, Infotype Authorizations in Personnel Administration)

▶ **Authorization Level**
   analog to P_ORGIN authorization object

▶ **Administrator for Payroll/Personnel Master Data/Time Recording, Administrator Group**
   checks Infotype 0001 (Organizational assignment)

[+]   **Interaction of P_ORGIN and P_ORGXX**

Generally, the authorization objects, P_ORGIN and P_ORGXX, are alternatives to each other. If you've activated both of them, you must ensure that the authorization check is carried out as an AND link: The authorization must be issued in both objects.

As you can see in Figure 2.28, the employee has authorizations for the Infotypes 0000, 0001, 0002, 0007, and 2001 but only for persons that have maintained the ADMINISTRATOR GROUP and ADMINISTRATOR FOR TIME RECORDING FIELDS in Infotype 0001.

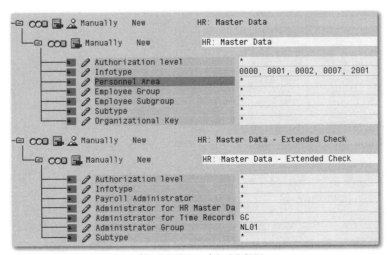

Figure 2.28 Interaction of P_ORGIN and P_ORGXX

HR: Master Data – Personnel Number Check (P_PERNR)

The P_PERNR object enables you to additionally authorize infotypes for administration and time management based on the personnel number of the individual user. It is used for Employee Self Service scenarios, and in some instances when the personnel administrator is to be assigned fewer rights with regard to his own data than he would be granted usually (for example, he is not permitted to change his salary).

In addition to the already known fields, authorization level and infotype/subtype, the authorization object only contains the Interpretation of assigned personnel number field that can have the following content:

▶ E (excluded authorizations for assigned personnel number)

▶ I (additional authorizations for assigned personnel number)

If you enter both the characteristic I and E, the characteristic E will always be preferred. The characteristic "*" is not supported in this context.

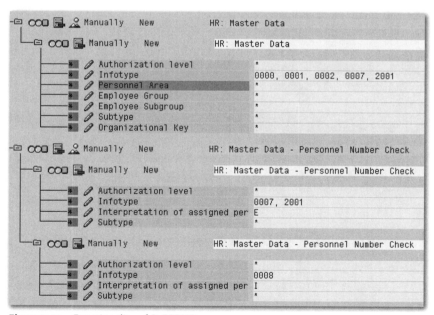

Figure 2.29 Functionality of P_PERNR

Figure 2.29 shows the two different functionalities of the object, *HR: Master Data – Personnel Number Check.*

Parameter E ensures that the infotype authorizations issued in the P_ORGIN object are reset for the own personnel number (and only for this number). The result is that you can only process the Infotypes 0000, 0001, and 0002 without any restrictions, and Infotypes 0007 and 2001 for all personnel numbers except for your own.

Additional
authorizations for
your own per-
sonnel number (I)

Parameter I ensures that you can issue further accesses for your own personnel number in addition to rights issued in other authorization objects. The example shown in Figure 2.29 enables you to maintain Infotype 0008 for your own personnel number without any limitations beyond the infotypes permitted in P_ORGIN — an example that you shouldn't take too seriously.

In order to use the P_PERNR authorization object, you must activate it in Customizing by entering "1" in AUTSW PERNR (HR: Master Data – Personnel Number Check) of the authorization main switches of Table T77S0.

The connection between the user according to the SAP logon and the personnel number is determined via Infotype 0105 (Communication), Subtype 0001 (SAP System user name).

[+] | **Tip**

You can find the customizing of Infotype 0105 (Communication) under PERSONNEL MANAGEMENT • PERSONNEL ADMINISTRATION • COMMUNICATION. If you have any problems, refer to this section to find information about how the labeling of Subtype 0001 as the SAP system user name must be like.

2.3.4 HR: Cluster – Cluster Authorization Object (P_PCLX)

Clusters are a form of complex data storage that is widespread within SAP ERP HCM. In the "classic" HCM components clusters are indispensable. A critical example is the storage of payroll and time management results. More recent components of the HCM system increasingly omit the cluster storage and use transparent tables instead.

The P_PCLX authorization object always checks in the locations where the clusters are read or written, but you can't activate or deactivate it.

The following two fields are checked:

▶ **Area identifier for Cluster in tables PCLx**
Here, you can enter a two-digit cluster ID or "*".

▶ **Authorization Level**
R (Read), U (Write to the database), S (Export data to a buffer without changing the database for simulations)

We will detail the names of the most critical clusters for each area of application in Chapter 5, Authorization Roles in SAP HCM Components. The input help for the Area Identifier for Cluster in Tables PCLx field in the authorization maintenance function provides a full list of all of the clusters.

We'll explain the three most frequently used clusters or cluster groups in the following sections:

Cluster PC comprises one-place abbreviations for attendances and absences that are displayed in the monthly calendar of the time management and in numerous evaluations. You can't maintain the Infotypes 2001 and 2002 (Attendances and absences) if you don't have the write authorization for this cluster.

The user-defined texts, which you can create and maintain for each individual infotype record, are not stored in the infotypes, but in Cluster TX (TY for applicant infotypes). If you want to read or maintain these texts, you need the corresponding access for Cluster TX or TY.

If you activated the logging of infotype changes in the master data, each change to the selected infotype is written in Cluster LA for long-term documents or SA for short-term documents (for applicant master data in Clusters LB or SB). The user who implements the data changes does not requires rights for these clusters, however, the user who evaluates the change documents, does require authorizations.

[+] **Simplification for Issuing Cluster Authorizations**

Each HCM user who works with clusters, that means virtually all users, requires an authorization in the P_PCLX object. A technically feasible option to simplify the authorization maintenance would be to enter "*" in both fields of this object and to assign the authorization to each user.

Generally, the clusters are read together with the infotypes. So if the infotype access is protected by other authorization objects, you don't have to repeat it in P_PCLX. Clusters are usually written in special reports (for example, time evaluation) that typically can only be executed by selected users.

If you use this option, you must ensure that the protection via the infotypes is consistent, in particular for reporting. Some reports that read clusters don't include infotype checks. These must not be provided to the users. For more information refer to Chapter 5, section 1.16, SAP Reports Without Logical Databases.

2.3.5   Personnel Planning (PLOG)

Where is PLOG necessary? The name *personnel planning* is confusing for this authorization object, because it not only plays a significant role here, but also in many other subcomponents of the HCM system. From the technical point of view, these are database tables that start with HRP. In terms of content, the following HCM components are involved:

▸ Organizational Management

▸ Personnel Development; that means all areas in which qualifications and development plans are significant

▸ Training and Event Management including the SAP Learning Solution components

▸ Performance Management

▸ Shift Planning

▸ E-Recruiting

▸ Compensation Management

▸ HR Funds and Position Management/position budgeting and control in the public sector

▸ Management of global employees

You can find more details on the individual SAP HCM components in Chapter 5, Authorization Roles in SAP HCM Components.

The fields of the PLOG object are similar to the fields of the P_ORGIN object from personnel administration. These are also infotypes and subtypes. The following fields are checked:

▶ **Plan Version**
This is the central key component of all datasets of the HRP* tables; usually "01" or "*" is entered here.

▶ **Object Type**
In contrast to personnel administration (Object Type P) the object type is explicitly checked in this authorization object. This enables you, for example, to only read the organizational units (Object Type O) and to write the positions (Object Type S). The *external object types* (for instance, the cost center) are not checked here. The only exception: P (Person) is the checked as the only external object type.

▶ **Infotype/Subtype**
These are permitted infotypes/subtypes complying with the object type. The Subtype field is highly significant for relationships (subtypes of Infotype 1001); however, you must also observe the direction (A or B) of the relationship.

▶ **Planning Status**
Planning statuses are the permitted statuses. If you don't differentiate here, like so many others, the "*" entry is the means of choice.

▶ **Function Code**
Here, you are provided with the function codes available for processing. This field corresponds to the AUTHORIZATION LEVEL field in P_ORGIN, but has a higher differentiation, because you must permit each function code explicitly.

Figure 2.30 shows the special meaning of the subtypes of Infotype 1001 in the PLOG authorization object. The figure shows the authorization that all positions (S) including all infotypes must be fully maintained and all organizational units are only displayed. Because the maintenance of a position (S) also includes the relationship to an organizational unit, you must permit the maintenance of Subtype B003 of Infotype 1001 for Object Type O (Organizational unit).

Like for all other authorization objects the following rule applies: The authorization for a specific action must only be stored in an authorization of the respective object and not in all objects.

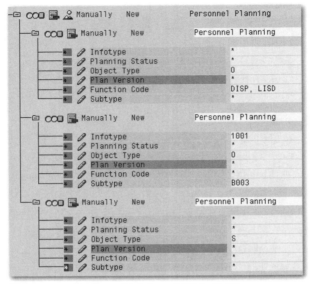

Figure 2.30 Subtype of Infotype 1001 in PLOG

[+]

What you must look for in the display and delete options in the function code field

In many maintenance transactions of Organizational Management, the call of overview screens is allocated with its own function codes. Consequently, a display authorization only makes sense if you use the DISP (for individual display) and LISD (for overview screen) function codes.

In some of these transactions, for deletion options you must also differentiate between deleting an individual infotype (Function Code DEL) and deleting a complete object (Function Code DELO).

PLOG only in combination with structural authorization

In the PLOG authorization object, you can easily determine that the authorizations stored here are of formal nature. They don't describe which part of the organizational structure or of the event catalog may be processed by the user. Therefore, this authorization object is incomplete without the structural authorization check, which we'll detail in the next chapter.

2.4   Required System Authorizations

In this section, we'll present the basic authorization objects that are essential for HCM. We'll exclude all authorizations that are part of the basic version for each user, for instance, the use of SAPoffice.

Initially, we'll explain the authorization objects that are required for reporting and for query evaluations. Then, we'll describe authorization objects that are primarily assigned to component supervisors (responsible for the customizing of the HCM system) and system administrators (responsible for the system basis).

2.4.1   Checks when Calling Reports

As a basic rule, you should protect the call of reports through transactions, as we already described in Section 2.3.1, Transaction Authorizations. If you permit — probably only for individual user groups — the call of reports using Transaction SA38 (SYSTEM • SERVICES • REPORTING), you require the S_PROGRAM object (ABAP: Program Flow Checks).

In this object you permit the following user actions: IMPLEMENT, SCHEDULE FOR BACKGROUND PROCESSING, and VARIANT MAINTENANCE. These permitted user actions relate to specific authorization groups, the second field of the authorization object.

S_PROGRAM fields

Warning
Programs, for which the authorization group is not maintained, can be called by each user who has Transaction SA38 and any authorization in S_PROGRAM.

[!]

The authorization group is part of the program attributes that you can maintain when creating a report. Because the authorization group is not maintained in several standard SAP programs (or not maintained in the way you require), you will have to implement these reports, which you authorize by means of Transaction SA38, retroactively. You can use the RSCSAUTH (Maintain/Restore Authorization Groups) report to maintain the authorization group (Figure 2.31).

Maintaining authorization groups

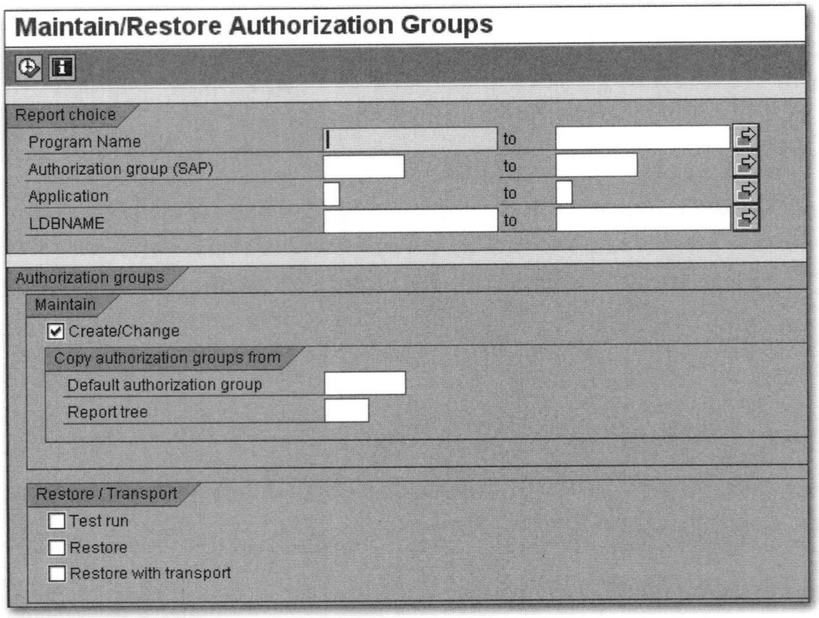

Figure 2.31 Maintenance of the Authorization Groups

In the upper part of the screen, REPORT CHOICE, use specific criteria to select the standard reports to which you want to assign the authorization groups entered under DEFAULT AUTHORIZATION GROUP. If you have also created authorization groups in report trees, include these using the REPORT TREE option provided in the screen section, AUTHORIZATION GROUPS.

The RESTORE/TRANSPORT options are needed after upgrades and other new releases of standard programs.

[+]

Checking S_PROGRAM also after Transaction Start

In some reports, which are usually not implemented by the end user (for example, posting runs in FI), the S_PROGRAM authorization object is also checked if you call the report using a transaction code.

To determine the transactions used here, call Transaction SU24, which we'll describe in Section 2.5, Customizing of the Profile Generator, select the Authorization Object tab on the initial screen (Figure 2.38), and enter "S_PROGRAM". You are provided with a list of all transactions in which this object is checked.

The option of maintaining variants is protected by the authorization object just described. If you call a report using a transaction, in which S_PROGRAM is not checked, the variant maintenance is available for every user. There are two possible ways to carry out a protection:

▶ The user creating the variant, protects the variant himself by setting the checkmark for PROTECT VARIANT (Figure 2.32).

▶ The variant name starts with *CUS&* or *SAP*. These variant names are automatically protected against changes by other users.

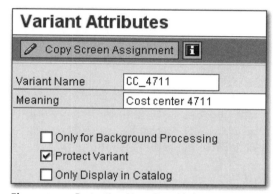

Figure 2.32 Protecting Your Own Variant

Warning
Variants that have been protected can only be changed or deleted by the user who created it. This can quickly result in data accumulation. For this purpose, use the RSVARENT report to undo the variant protection.

[!]

You should generally assign other authorizations in the reporting environment only to system administrators, component supervisors, or other selected users. These include the following:

▶ **Scheduling of jobs**
You require Transactions SM36 (Define Background Job) and SM37 (Simple Job Selection). You should treat Transaction SM36 with special caution, because it enables you to enter external commands and consequently implement unauthorized activities in the SAP system.

The relevant authorization objects are

▶ S_BTCH_ADM (Background Processing: Background Administrator)

▶ S_BTCH_JOB (BackgroundProcessing: Operations on Background Jobs)

▶ S_BTCH_NAM (Background Processing: Background User Name)
You should treat S_BTCH_NAM with special caution, because this object authorizes you to start a job using the name of another user (and consequently his authorizations) and to bypass the authorization concept.

▶ **Execution of programs in the background**
The authorization is assigned through the S_BTCH_JOB object (Background processing: Operations on Background Jobs) using the RELE entry in the OPERATIONS ON A JOB field.
In Section 10.2, Starting Reports via Customer Programs (ThyssenKrupp Steel AG), we'll describe how you can solve the problem of authorization assignment for job scheduling and starting programs in the background by providing a customer-specific solution.

▶ **Access to spool**
By default, you can access own spool requests without any authorization check. You can use the authorization object S_SPO_ACT (Spool: Actions) to view spool request of other users.

▶ **Printout**
S_SPO_DEV (Spool: Device Authorizations) comprises the printer names on which users may print out lists. Due to data protection requirements, you must carefully check where you are permitted to print out protected data.

▶ **Maintenance of user-independent variants in ALV grids**
The S_ALV_LAYO authorization object (ALV Standard Layout) enables you to save the layout variant of the *employee list* report shown in Figure 2.33 user-independently. This authorization should only be assigned to component supervisors or system administrators.

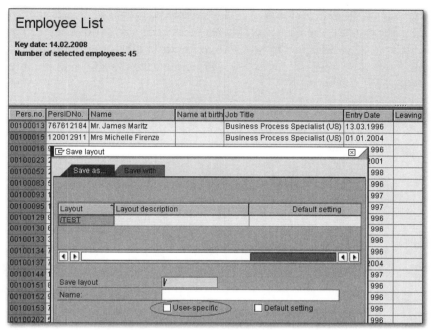

Figure 2.33 Maintaining User-Independent Layouts in the ALV Grid

2.4.2 Access to InfoSets and Queries

Special authorization is required in the queries context in order to access InfoSets. This must be configured in addition to role maintenance. You can use various user groups to determine which users can access which InfoSets. You can determine whether a user can create and change queries in this InfoSet or can only execute queries. You can access the (query) user maintenance section via the following path in the SAP Easy Access menu: HUMAN RESOURCES • INFORMATION SYSTEM • REPORTING TOOLS • SAP QUERY• ENVIRONMENT • USER GROUPS. When you have defined a user group and assigned users to this group, you must then assign the InfoSet (see Section 4.1.4 of the book, *HR-Reporting using SAP*, published by SAP PRESS).

As soon as a user has been assigned to a query user group and has been granted the transaction authorization for SAP Query (SQ01) or Ad-hoc Query (S_PH0_48000513), for example, via his user menu, he can already execute the queries. This user has access to all queries of the InfoSet that are assigned to his user group. Also, this user can run queries that you add directly to his or her user menu using the role maintenance function.

However, this user cannot save changes to the queries. Thus, for more advanced work in the query area, you need the S_QUERY authorization object (SAP Query Authorization) displayed in Figure 2.34.

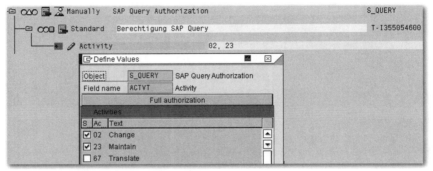

Figure 2.34 S_QUERY Authorization Object

S_QUERY field   This object only has one field, Activity. You have the following options here:

► **02 (Change)**
The user can create new queries based on the InfoSets of his user group(s) and save the changes of existing queries. You can reserve permission to change queries for individual users by means of the user group assignments.

► **23 (Maintain)**
The user can execute Transactions SQ02 (InfoSet Maintenance) and SQ03 (User Group Maintenance) and transports. Ideally, end-users should not have this authorization.
To extend InfoSets using ABAP code, the additional S_DEVELOP authorization object is also required with the characteristics AQ* for the object name field and PROG for the object type.

▶ *67 (Translate)*

Here you can set a language comparison for SAP query objects.

Tip	[+]
The InfoSet maintenance (S_QUERY with Activity 23 (Maintain)) should only be implemented in the development system and then transported to the production system. Otherwise, if you process the InfoSet in the production system this results in errors for the query implementation.	

If a user has authorization to create and change queries and to maintain InfoSets and user groups (S_QUERY and Activities 02 and 23, see Figure 2.34), he then can access all queries without being explicitly assigned to each (query) user group. Without this comprehensive authorization, the user must always be assigned to a (query) user group to implement specific queries. If a query accesses tables outside the logical database, the S_TABU_DIS authorization object is also checked.

Access to the HR data to be evaluated is administrated by the usual HCM authorization objects and the structural or context-sensitive authorization check.

No Authorization Check on Additional Fields in the InfoSet	[+]
If a field is included in the InfoSet as an additional field by means of directly reading the database table rather than by means of the logical database, no authorization check is carried out.	
This would enable you to fulfill the following requirement: A user wants to report on the internal address of Infotype 0032 (Internal data), but is not authorized to view company car data and so cannot have full authorization for this infotype.	

2.4.3 Table Maintenance

You require the *Table Maintenance* authorization object (via standard tools, for example, SM30) (S_TABU_DIS) for maintaining SAP and customer-specific Customizing tables, if it is implemented using standard means like SM30 (SYSTEM • SERVICES • TABLE MAINTENANCE).

Here, you can check the activity (change, display, maintenance beyond system boundaries) for each authorization group. The authorization

S_TABU_DIS fields

group of a table corresponds to their authorization class according to Table TDDAT.

Whereas S_TABU_DIS provides protection only for complete tables, you can use the S_TABU_LIN object (Authorization for organizational unit) to protect parts of the table or to release them for display or maintenance. Figure 2.35 shows an example. Here, the maintenance permission (Activity 02) is issued for grouping of work schedules (MOSID) 01.

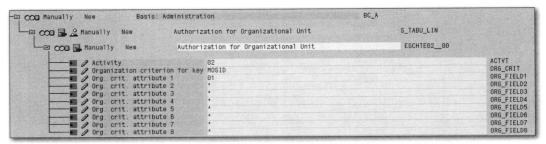

Figure 2.35 Maintenance Right: Grouping for Working Schedules 01

S_TABU_LIN
Customizing

S_TABU_LIN works with *organizational criteria*. You can define and activate them in Customizing under SAP NetWeaver • Application Server • System Administration • Users and Authorizations • Line-oriented Authorizations • Define or Activate organizational criteria. Figure 2.36 displays the organizational criteria provided by SAP. You can also define your own organization criteria.

If you assign the rights by means of S_TABU_LIN, you must additionally authorize the table via S_TABU_DIS.

The other way around, S_TABU_LIN is only checked if you've defined organization criteria for the key fields of the selected table.

[+] **Tip**

Instead of working with the authorization objects described here, for the maintenance of tables implemented by the end user it often makes sense to create own maintenance transactions and protect them by means of transaction codes or a customer-specific authorization object.

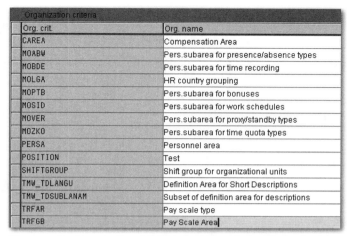

Figure 2.36 Organizational Criteria for Line-oriented Authorization

2.4.4 Customizing Authorizations in the Implementation Guide (IMG)

In principle, Customizing is carried out in the development system and is then transferred to the production system by means of transport requests.

In HR it is possible that a larger number of users requires Customizing Authorizations, for example, for decentralized maintenance of work schedules. Here, you usually create a project IMG for the specific activities, for instance, for customizing tables in the work schedule environment. When you generate the IMG you can simultaneously generate the required authorizations.

The S_PROJECT authorization object (Project Management: Project Authorization) is used to protect activities in IMG. Here, only the Activity and PROJECT NAME fields are relevant for Customizing rights.

S_PROJECT authorization object

Everyone working in Customizing needs authorizations for maintaining the respective tables (see Section 2.4.3, Table Maintenance) in addition to this object (and the transaction authorization for IMG – SPRO). Moreover, specific maintenance transactions are often called from IMG (for example, OOOT for object types of Organizational Management), for which you also require a transaction authorization.

2.4.5 Batch Input Authorizations

For processing batch input sessions and for any other action involving the sessions, you require the S_BDC_MONI authorization object (Batch Input Authorizations) (Figure 2.37).

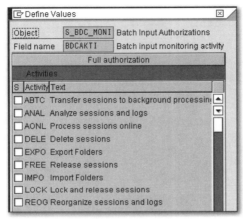

Figure 2.37 Permitted Activities Involving Batch Input Sessions

S_BDC_MONI fields

The BATCH INPUT MONITORING ACTIVITIES field enables you to implement different actions with regard to batch input sessions. Using the SESSION NAME field you can generically specify which sessions may be processed and to which extent. This means that you must observe the naming conventions when creating a batch input session so that the persons responsible can process them.

[+] **Tip**

If you distribute the responsibilities for processing the sessions decentralized, you need to provide systematics for the session names in advance in order to generically allocate the rights.

2.4.6 Authorization for Download and Upload

These two rights, which are very critical with regard to data protection, must be assigned explicitly by means of the S_GUI authorization object (Authorization for GUI Activities).

S_GUI fields

S_GUI only comprises the Activity field that includes the export and import authorization. Using S_GUI enables you to not only protect the explicit download, for example, to Microsoft® Excel®, but also to copy data from the SAP system to the clipboard by means of the key combination, CTRL+Y.

The download from statements (see Chapter 5, Authorization Roles in SAP HCM Components) must also be authorized through this object.

Analog to the export authorization, you must also pay special attention to the assignment of import authorizations. Each non-authorized or inexpertly implemented data import to the SAP system may risk the consistency of the already existing data.

2.4.7   Number Range Maintenance

The number ranges are maintained using the following transactions:

▶ PA04 (Personnel Administration)

▶ PB04 (Former Recruitment)

▶ OONR (Organizational Management and Corresponding Object Types)

For all of these transactions, you require the S_NUMBER system authorization object (Number Range Maintenance).

2.4.8   HCM-Specific Authorizations for System Administrators

In this section, we'll present the HCM authorization objects that are specifically intended for system administrators and component supervisors: P_PE01, P_PE02 and P_DEL_PERN.

It would be ideal if you could authorize specific component supervisors only for the display of personnel calculation schemas and rules. Unfortunately, according to SAP Note 709949 the two objects intended for this purpose, P_PE01 and P_PE02, currently don't work. Refer to Chapter 10, Selected Problem Areas and Their Solutions, to obtain information how you can solve this problem using transaction variants of Transactions PE01 and PE02 (Maintenance of Personnel Calculation Schemas and Rules).

Display in PE01 and PE02

Deleting personnel numbers

Only in exceptional cases you may perform the final deletion of personnel numbers in the production system. For this purpose the P_DEL_PERN authorization object (Deleting of Personnel Numbers in Live Systems) exists. You can delete according to the double-verification principle by assigning one role with the deletion application and another role with the deletion itself. The authorization is checked in the RPUDELPP report. The following field is checked: ROLE DEFINITION FOR DELETING PERSONNEL NUMBER IN LIVE SYSTEMS (application, deletion).

Evaluation of change documents

For evaluating the change documents, that is the logging of infotype changes, you need read access to the Clusters LA and LB (Long-term documents master data or applicants) and Clusters SA and SB (short-term documents master data or applicants).

The requirements of the authorization check in customer-specific reports are covered in Chapter 8, Authorizations in Programming, along with the problem of authorizations available for programmers.

After we've presented the most critical authorization objects of HCM and system basis, in the next section you'll learn more about how you can maintain default values for these authorization objects.

2.5   Customizing the Profile Generator

The Profile Generator is used if you've entered transactions in the menu of the role maintenance and you can change to the AUTHORIZATIONS tab from there. During this step, the Profile Generator generates default values for the authorization objects, including specific entries that are based on the transactions entered in the menu.

Transaction SU24

You can access the Profile Generator by means of Transaction SU24 or in IMG under PERSONNEL MANAGEMENT • PERSONNEL ADMINISTRATION • TOOLS • AUTHORIZATION MANAGEMENT • MAINTAIN AUTHORIZATION MAIN SWITCHES • MODIFY PROFILE GENERATOR STANDARD VALUES. The initial screen is displayed in Figure 2.38.

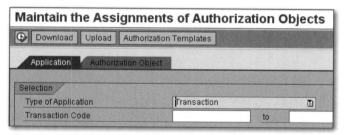

Figure 2.38 Initial Screen of the Profile Generator

You have the following two options to continue: you either have all transactions listed in which a specific authorization object is checked (Authorization Object tab), or you require a list of all authorization objects that are checked in a specific transaction (Application tab). Figure 2.39 shows the first part of the list after you have entered "PA20" on the Application tab.

Status	Object	Object Description	Check Ind.	Proposal
☐	P_ABAP	HR: Reporting	Check	NO
☐	P_APPL	HR: Applicants	Check	NO
☐	P_ORGIN	HR: Master Data	Check	YS
☐	P_ORGINCON	HR: Master Data with Context	Check	NO
☐	P_ORGXX	HR: Master Data - Extended Check	Check	NO
☐	P_PCLX	HR: Clusters	Check	YS
☐	P_PERNR	HR: Master Data - Personnel Number Check	Check	YS
☐	P_PYEVRUN	HR: Posting Run	Check	NO
☐	P_TCODE	HR: Transaction codes	Check	NO
☐	PLOG	Personnel Planning	Check	YS
☐	S_ADMI_FCD	System Authorizations	Check	NO

Transaction Code PA20 — Saved — Authorization Objects — Field Values

Figure 2.39 Excerpt of the Authorization Objects checked in PA20

If an authorization object is checked in a transaction depends on whether the objects is allocated to the transaction and whether the Check Indicator is set. If you're not sure whether a specific object is checked at a specific location, you can look this up in Transaction SU24.

The maintenance of the check indicator is usually unnecessary, especially because you can't remove HCM objects from this list in the system. However, you can add objects, which may be necessary if SAP has forgotten

HCM objects can't be deactivated

an entry, for more recent (context-dependent) authorization objects, for example.

While you shouldn't touch the check indicator, it's worth taking a look at the indicator of the default value .

Use the button to switch to the change mode. There, you can set the Proposal field to YES or NO. Wherever you indicated YES, the entries of these authorization objects are proposed in the role maintenance if you enter the respective transaction, in this case "PA20", in the Menu. If you don't want any proposal for this authorization object, you simply enter NO.

Select the Field Values button in the change mode, if you want to know the content of the proposals. Figure 2.40 shows you the authorizations proposed for transaction PA20.

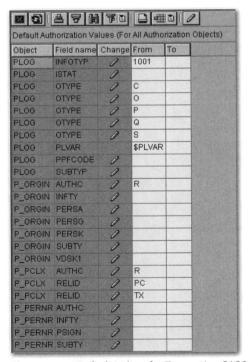

Figure 2.40   Default Values for Transaction PA20

Figure 2.40 indicates that for each authorization object for which you entered YES in the PROPOSAL column, each field of this object is proposed at least once. The proposal may have content or not. Multiple entries can be proposed per field, for example in the OTYPE field in PLOG.

Figure 2.41 shows how the field values, which are displayed in Figure 2.40, are implemented in role maintenance.

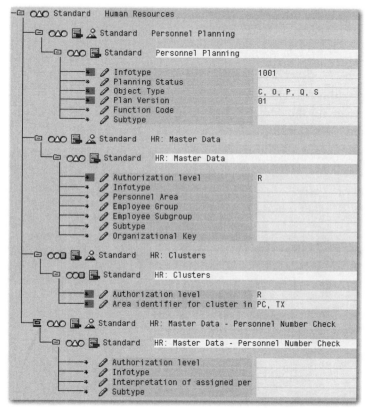

Figure 2.41 Default Values of the Profile Generator for PA20

In terms of content, the proposal offers a useful entry point for the maintenance of authorizations of Transaction PA20:

The proposal is the entry point in the authorization maintenance

▶ PLOG authorizations are necessary to be able to read Organizational Management information from Infotype 0001, and to maintain the *person-position relationship*. We'll detail this in Chapter 5, section 5.12, Personnel Administration and Time Management.

▸ You also require authorizations for the infotypes that can be viewed by means of PA20. However, only two of the four possible master data objects are proposed here. In this context you must make adjustments, if necessary.

▸ Usually, cluster authorizations (P_PCLX) for the listed Clusters PC (Abbreviation attendances and absences) and TX (Text for employee infotypes) are also indispensable.

▸ For P_TCODE, there is no default value. This makes sense because no entry is required for PA20.

Keeping the default values

You can leave the default values of the Profile Generator as they are. Then, you maintain the deviations and supplementations for each individual case in the role maintenance.

Customizing the Profile Generator

Additionally, you can customize the default values in Transaction SU24 according to your requirements. For example, you can refine the default values for PLOG for the subtype of Infotype 1001. This saves at least one part of the customizing in the role maintenance.

[!] | **The Profile Generator Works Independently of the Authorization Main Switches**

Unfortunately, the Profile Generator does not react to the settings of the authorization main switch at all. Regardless of whether you use the P_PERNR authorization object or not, you always receive a proposal in the role maintenance (see Figure 2.41) due to the customizing in the Profile Generator (see Figure 2.40).

Therefore, you should customize the Profile Generator to the objects that you utilize if you use other authorization objects than P_ORGIN and P_PERNR for the master data check.

To process the default values, proceed as follows:

Add another authorization value by placing the cursor on the corresponding field and clicking on the ✎ button. If you selected the P_PCLX RELID field, for example, a maintenance popup opens for these values (Figure 2.42). You've already seen this in the role maintenance Transaction PFCG (see Figure 2.6). If you enter a new value, it is displayed in the proposal list.

Carry out the same process to remove the authorization defaults. If you want to remove the authorization default completely, switch the PRO-POSAL indicator from YES to NO.

Fields containing the organizational level (see Section 2.2.3, Reference Roles), automatically obtain the entry, $<Fieldname>. You can't change anything here, but you can only maintain the value directly in the role.

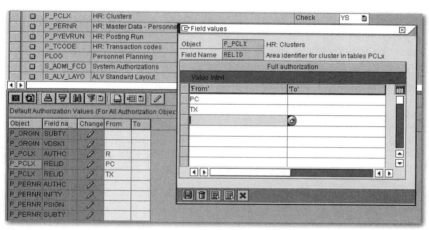

Figure 2.42 Adding Default Values in the Profile Generator

If you use customer-specific authorization objects, you can add them to the transactions using the Profile Generator. This doesn't automatically impact the authorization check, but the default values in the role maintenance. So if you check a customer-specific authorization object in the user exits of the personnel master data, you can add them in the Profile Generator for Transactions PA20 and PA30 to have the object proposed in the role maintenance.

Depending on your personal working method, it might be a good solution to simply omit the default values, because they often impede your work.

Deactivating default values

93

Example

If you add Transaction PA20 to a role that already contains Transaction PA30, all default values belonging to PA20 will be rebuilt, even if these authorizations already exist in the role. In this case, it can be easier to have no proposals at all.

You can delete the default values either for each transaction or for each authorization object. If necessary, select all entries of the list via `CTRL`+`A`, and implement the proposal indicator by clicking on the Proposal button.

If you decide to deactivate the default values after you've already worked with the Profile Generator for a longer period of time, you should proceed step by step, because the withdrawal of the Profile Generator considerably changes the authorization maintenance work.

[+] **Tip**

If you decide to deactivate the default values, you should make an exception for P_TCODE. Experience has shown that the Profile Generator works with high precision here and avoids tedious extra work, for instance, for the entry in the menu or in S_TCODE.

In case you've changed the settings of the Profile Generator, you must perform steps 2a and 2d of Transaction SU25 (Profile Generator: Upgrade and First Installation) during release changes. This is necessary to compare the new Profile Generator settings delivered by SAP and your customer settings.

2.6 Period of Responsibility and Time Logic

The access to an area of responsibility is never unlimited from 01/01/1800 to 12/31/9999. Instead, a period of responsibility is established for each individual person to which a user has access. In this section, we'll detail how this period is derived and which (time) logic is used in the SAP ERP HCM system to determine the periods of responsibility.

The most critical authorizations objects, P_ORGIN and P_ORGXX (see Sections 2.3.2, Infotype Authorizations in Personnel Administration, and 2.3.3, Additional Authorization Objects for Master and Time Data), are filled with data of Infotype 0001. The area of responsibility, for example, the personnel area, is derived from these authorization fields. Each employee assigned to the authorized personnel area in Infotype 0001 can be processed by the user. If the employee changes to another personnel area, the period of responsibility terminates for one user and a new period of responsibility starts for another.

However, it is not practical to terminate the responsibility on the change date, because the employee still has to do some work after the change that must be implemented by the "old" administrator. For this purpose, SAP ERP HCM provides the AUTSW ADAYS authorization main switch. It is available via the following IMG path: Personnel Management • Personnel Administration • Tools • Authorization Management • Maintain Authorization Main Switches • Maintain Authorization Main Switches. Here, you can set the tolerance time that extends the period of responsibility beyond the date of the change. The default value is 15 days.

Tolerance period after changing the responsibility

Additionally, the date-dependent check is not carried out for each infotype by default. An administrator can always access uncritical infotypes, for example, IT0002 (Personal data), if the responsibility has been available or will be available at any point in time. For most infotypes, however, the date-dependent check is set. You can change the setting in the Table View V_T582A by checking the Access authorization indicator (Figure 2.43).

In the following example, we want to explain how you can determine the period of responsibility:

Determining the period of responsibility

Let's assume that the P_ORGIN authorization object is set. One administrator is responsible for all employees of a specific personnel area. Therefore, the P_ORGIN authorization object of his role has been filled with Personnel Area 1000.

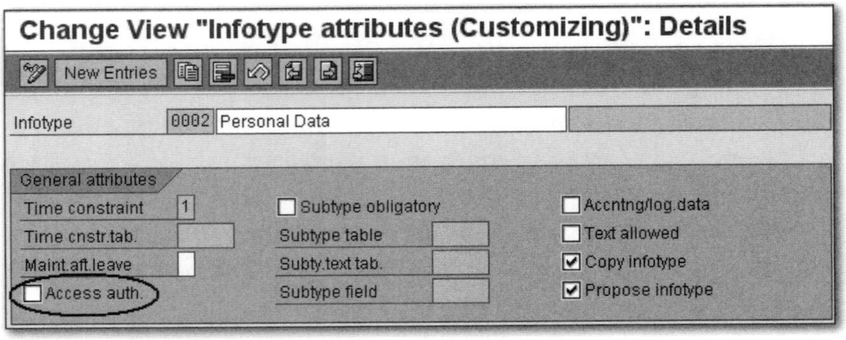

Figure 2.43 For IT0002 the date-dependent check is deactivated by default.

When the user logs on to the system, all organizational assignments with Personnel Area 1000 will be determined initially. These assignments have validity periods according to the start and end date of IT0001. The validity periods initially determine the responsibility intervals. If the tolerance period is > 0, the respective responsibility interval is extended by this tolerance period.

In case responsibility intervals generally exist, they are migrated to the time logic to determine the period of responsibility.

Here, it is first checked whether a date-dependent check (according to T582A as previously described) is to be performed. If no date-dependent check is to be performed, the user has read or write access from 01/01/1800 to 12/31/9999.

Time logic for read and write access

Read and write access follow a different logic. It is a prerequisite that the period of responsibility has existed or existed:

If the user is authorized to *read* the data of the employee and

▸ a responsibility currently exists, he may view the data from 01/01/1800 to 12/31/9999.

▸ no responsibility currently exists, he may view the data with the valid-from date 01/01/1800 to the responsibility end date.

If the user is authorized to *maintain* the data of the employee and

▸ a responsibility currently exists, he may maintain the data with the valid-from date 01/01/1800 to the responsibility end date.

▶ no responsibility exists any longer (the tolerance period has expired), he may no longer maintain the data.

[+]

> **Tip**
>
> The start of the period of responsibility is only set to 01/01/1800 if the administrator is responsible for the employee from the very start (as of the hiring date); otherwise, the start of the period of responsibility is used.

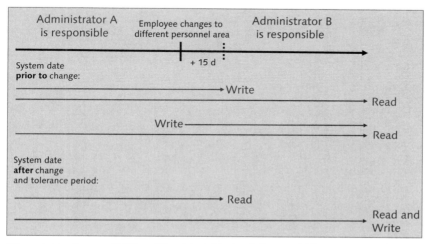

Figure 2.44 Responsibilities of the Administrator Before and After a Personnel Area Change

In summary, the periods of responsibility listed in Table 2.1 are determined if responsibility intervals exist.

Prerequisite	Period of responsibility
No date-dependent check, read or write	01/01/1800 to 12/31/9999
Date-dependent, read authorization, current date is within a responsibility interval	01/01/1800 to 12/31/9999
Date-dependent, read authorization, current date is outside all responsibility intervals	01/01/1800 to responsibility end date

Table 2.1 Summary of the Periods of Responsibility

Prerequisite	Period of responsibility
Date-dependent, write authorization, current date is within a responsibility interval; first day of assignment = start of responsibility	01/01/1800 to 12/31/9999
Date-dependent, write authorization, current date is within a responsibility interval; first day of assignment ≠ start of responsibility	01/01/1800 to 12/31/9999
Date-dependent, write authorization, current date is outside a responsibility interval	No responsibility

Table 2.1 Summary of the Periods of Responsibility (Cont.)

Extension in the Time Logic

For implementing a customer-specific time logic in the general authorization check you are provided with a special Business Add-In (BAdI) as of R/3 Release 4.6c.

BAdIs enable you to implement requirements for the authorization check that exceed the SAP standard without having to modify it. They also enable you to change the standard code at places predefined by SAP and implement customer-specific checks.

[+] **Tip**

SAP Note 570161 provides a comprehensive description and sample implementation of BAdI HRPAD00CHECK_TIME.

The BAdI can be used for the following requirement: Contrary to the standard logic, when accessing Infotype 0008 (Basic pay) the period of responsibility is always supposed to be assigned for the entire period, that is, from 01/01/1800 to 12/31/9999, in case of write access with SY-DATUM within a responsibility interval, and in case of SY-DATUM outside a responsibility interval no write or read access is supposed to be possible.

If you want to forbid the change option for individual infotypes in a specific period of time, you can use Infotype 0130 (Test Procedures). We'll describe this concept in Section 2.7, Test Procedures (Infotype 0130).

2.7   Test Procedures (Infotype 0130)

Infotype 0130 (*Test Procedures*) is another instrument of the authorization check that is only used in HCM. Within HCM, it is exclusively supported for infotypes of personnel administration and time management (database tables PA*).

2.7.1   Necessity and Functionality

The test procedures fill a gap in the standard authorizations. If the access to an infotype is permitted, for example, for a specific employee group, this is valid for all dataset of this infotype, independent of the validity date of the infotype record. If the user has the organizational responsibility for the respective employee, he may edit all data from the past to the future.

Period-based protection through test procedures

Example	[Ex]

In time management, it is often necessary that the decentralized time administrators can process the time data (for example, Infotypes 2001 and 2002) only for as long as it is still relevant for payroll. Changes to already processed time data can usually only be implemented by the central HR department, because its employees generally have a better overview of the effects on the payroll facts.

For these cases, you can use Infotype 0130 (Test Procedures). This test procedure is a data record of Infotype 0130 with a specific subtype, for example, Subtype T1 (Time data 1st level). The infotype record contains a data that indicates up to which date the time data related to this test procedure has already been checked. This date indicates for the affected infotypes that a special authorization protection exists here.

The Subtype T1 is delivered by SAP. You can create additional subtypes in Customizing.

As soon as a record of Infotype 0130 exists for the personnel number, and if time data, which is connected to this record via Customizing, is changed, the system tests whether its validity is after the date of the test procedure. If not, the changes are rejected. This only applies to the time administrator, of course. Employees of the HR department require an additional authorization to make changes (see Section 2.7.3, Authorization Assignment).

The data record shown in Figure 2.45 was created manually. This is indicated by the MP013000 program that is entered in the TESTED USING field. MP013000 is the dialog program for maintaining Infotype 0130.

You can write the records of Infotype 0130 automatically, which we'll cover shortly.

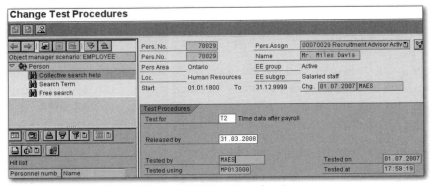

Figure 2.45 Example for Infotype 0130 (Test Procedures)

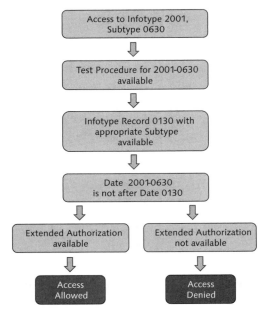

Figure 2.46 Overview of the Test Procedure Process

> **Tip**
>
> Note that Infotype 0001 (Organizational Assignment) and all applicant info-types are excluded from the test procedure.

[+]

2.7.2 Customizing

For setting up the test procedure, you need to implement some Customizing activities:

Test procedure authorization main switch

1. The first prerequisite for customizing the test procedure is to activate the AUTSW APPRO authorization main switch.

2. Now, you determine the test procedure you want to use in the IMG. This is done via **Personnel Management • Personnel Administration • Tools • Authorization Management • Test Procedures • Create Test Procedures** (Figure 2.47).

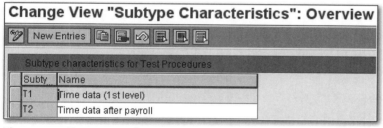

Figure 2.47 Determining the Test Procedure

3. Then, you define the infotypes and subtypes that are to be assigned to the respective test procedure via **Personnel Management • Personnel Administration • Tools • Authorization Management • Test Procedures • Assign Infotypes to Test Procedures** (Figure 2.48). The customizing of the test procedures is now completed.

Multiple test procedures possible

You can assign arbitrary infotypes of administration and time management with and without subtypes to the test procedures. You can use multiple test procedures. In this case, you require a record of Infotype 0130 including the appropriate subtype for each test procedure.

You can assign the same infotype and/or subtype to multiple test procedures. Then the authorization may not be issued if only one of the involved subtypes of Infotype 0130 denies the access due to the date.

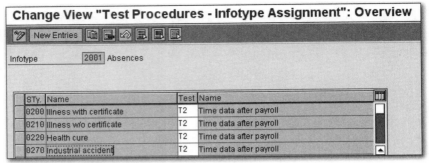

Figure 2.48 Assigning Test Procedures to the Infotypes and Subtypes

2.7.3 Authorization Assignment

The test procedures involve the infotypes of personnel administration and time management. These are contained in the following authorization objects:

- P_ORGIN (HR: Master Data)
- P_ORGINCON (HR: Master Data with Context)
- P_ORGXX (HR: Master Data—Extended Check)
- P_ORGXXCON (HR: Master Data—Extended Check with Context)
- P_PERNR (HR: Master Data—Personnel Number Check)

Additional authorization for changing checked records

In these authorization objects, you explicitly assign the authorizations for accessing infotypes and subtypes. Wherever an infotype/subtype is related to a test procedure, you don't assign an authorization to this infotype/subtype if it overlaps the period of the test procedure by at least one day. To change the infotype/subtype nevertheless, you require the write authorization to Infotype 0130 (as you can see in the P_ORGIN object in Figure 2.49).

If you use multiple test procedures, you can differentiate the write authorization to Infotype 0130 based on the subtypes.

Figure 2.49 Write Authorization for the Test Procedure

2.7.4 Automatic Writing of the Test Procedure Infotype

For a consistent authorization protection by means of Infotype 0130 (Test procedure) it is very important that all involved personnel numbers are provided with an appropriate record of Infotype 0130. If no infotype record exists, the system won't be checked.

No test without the record of Infotype 0130

Consequently, the automatic provision of this infotype is mandatory. For this purpose, SAP provides the RPTAPPU0 report (Report for time leveling) as a sample (Figure 2.50).

The sample report specifically relates to the time data and supports the following process:

SAP sample report

1. Calling of the report for time leveling through the responsible administrator

2. Checking the list of time types that is provided by the report from the time management cluster

3. Releasing the data for each employee in the list and writing the *test procedure* infotype in the background

Best Practice for the Use of Test Procedures   **[+]**

Admittedly, this procedure is only feasible in rare cases. The requirements are usually designed to lock all of the data, for which the payroll has been run, for decentralized maintenance. For this purpose, you must create your own report that sets Infotype 0130 to the to-date of the payroll after the payroll has been implemented for all employees.

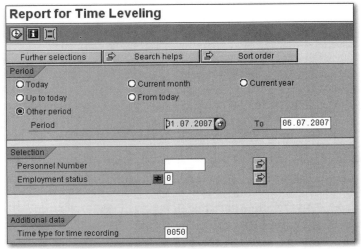

Figure 2.50 Sample Report for Writing the Test Procedure Infotype

2.8 Extensions

Whereas you can use the standard tools only to a certain limit, you can implement virtually any requirement using the extensions, Authorization Object P_NNNNN, customer-specific authorization object, and Business Add-Ins. The only question is whether this is worth the effort. In this section, we'll describe the extension options, and provide various examples.

2.8.1 The Authorization Object P_NNNNN

The P_ORGIN and P_ORGXX authorization objects check the fields, PERSONNEL AREA, Organizational Key, and PERSONNEL ADMINISTRATOR. If you want to check additional fields of Infotype 0001, for example, COST CENTER or PERSONNEL SUBAREA, you can use the P_NNNNN authorization object. You can create this authorization object yourself and equip it with all fields of Infotype 0001 and customer-specific additional fields.

Note that you can only use one customer-specific authorization object based on Infotype 0001. Using a report, the coding for the authorization check of the new authorization object is integrated in the standard authorization check and, so, automatically checked together with the other objects. Formally, this process is a modification; however, it is explicitly supported by SAP. The maintenance effort won't increase here.

To create the customer-specific authorization object, you must proceed as follows:

Creating an authorization object

1. Select the following path in the SAP Easy Access menu: TOOLS • ABAP WORKBENCH • DEVELOPMENT • OTHER TOOLS • AUTHORIZATION OBJECTS • OBJECTS, or start Transaction SU21.

2. You are working in the maintenance of the authorization objects. You won't find the P_NNNNN authorization object in the list of existing authorization objects. It doesn't exist there as such, but is rather a kind of placeholder. On the MAINTAIN THE AUTHORIZATION OBJECTS screen, select the CREATE • AUTHORIZATION OBJECT button.

3. On the Maintain authorization object screen, enter a name starting with Y or Z, and select Class HR.

4. On the same screen, specify the authorization fields. To be able to use the new authorization object in the master data check, it must at least comprise the fields INFTY, SUBTY, and AUTHC (Figure 2.51).

TCD and INFSU Authorization Fields	**[+]**
You can additionally use the fields, TCD and INFSU. The former is used to check transactions, and the latter is an eight-place field comprising an infotype and subtype.	

5. Save the new authorization object and the click the REGENERATE SAP_ ALL button to integrate the new authorization object and the full authorization in the SAP_ALL role.

Noting the program documentation

6. After you have generated the authorization object, call SYSTEM • SERVICES • REPORTING in the menu or start Transaction SA38 and enter the report name, RPUACG00.

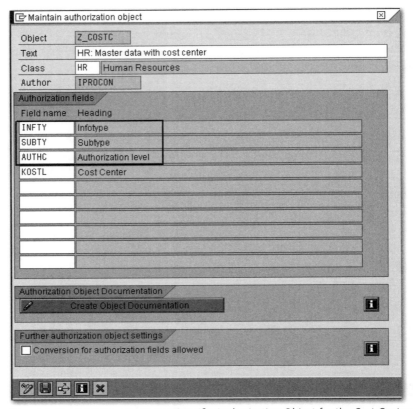

Figure 2.51 Creating a Customer-Specific Authorization Object for the Cost Center Check

7. Enter the name of the new authorization object and your user name as the password. For implementation without the test checkmark, you must enter an access key.

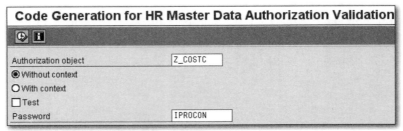

Figure 2.52 Report for Generating a Customer-Specific Authorization Object (Without Context Sensitivity)

8. In the menu, call the Extended table maintenance transaction via SYS-TEM • SERVICES • TABLE MAINTENANCE • EXTENDED TABLE MAINTENANCE or enter transaction code SM31; then activate the new authorization object in Table T77S0 by setting the AUTSW NNNNN switch to "1".

Integrating the object into the standard authorization check

The time logic and periods of responsibilities are valid both for the new authorization object and the standard authorization objects (see Section 2.6, Period of Responsibility and Time Logic).

Warning: Don't Forget the PROFL Field for the Context-Sensitive Authorization Check	**[!]**
If you use the context-sensitive authorization check or switch to context-sensitive authorization, you must add the PROFL field to the customer-specific authorization object. When you start the RPUACG00 generation report, select With Context (see Figure 2.52). Then activate the authorization object by switching the AUTSW NNCON switch in Table V_T77S0 to "1."

2.8.2 Customer-Specific Authorization Object

You can customize the customer-specific authorizations according to your requirements. In contrast to the P_NNNNN authorization object, you can't check them automatically, but you need to call customer-specific programs or BAdIs. In the examples for extending the standard authorization check using BAdIs, which we'll provide in Section 2.8.3, BAdI for General Authorization Checks, customer-specific authorization objects are also used.

As described in Section 2.8.1, The Authorization Object P_NNNNN, you can create a customer-specific authorization object using Transaction SU21. It can contain one to ten fields. There are no requirements with regard to the field selection, which means that you are not delimited to Infotype 0001 (Organizational Assignment) as is the case for P_NNNNN.

Therefore, the authorization object can only serve as an additional security as you can see in the following example. In this case, it is sufficient if the authorization object is contained in the role of the user. For this reason, it is equipped with a dummy field (Figure 2.53).

Use of a Customer-Specific Authorization Object

Some decentralized administrators are supposed to create or maintain a specific infotype from a report result (for example, an employee list). However, they are not to be assigned with authorizations for Transaction PA30 due to data protection reasons. For maintaining the infotype they require an authorization for some master data infotypes, for instance, IT0001, IT0008, and so on. You can deactivate this check when you navigate out of the report by means of BAdI HRPAD00AUTH_CHECK (see Section 2.8.3, »BAdI for General Authorization Check). To be on the safe side, you can additionally set up a customer-specific authorization object containing a dummy field with fixed value "*", assign it to the user by means of a role, and query it in the BAdI.

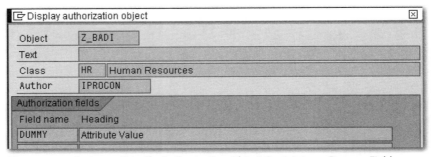

Figure 2.53 Customer-Specific Authorization Object Containing a Dummy Field

2.8.3 BAdI for General Authorization Checks

From Release 4.6C onward, the authorization check provides the BAdI HRPAD00AUTH_CHECK for the general authorization check.

You can find the BAdI in the IMG under PERSONNEL MANAGEMENT Ð PERSONNEL ADMINISTRATION Ð TOOLS Ð AUTHORIZATION MANAGEMENT Ð BADI: SET UP CUSTOMER-SPECIFIC AUTHORIZATION CHECK. Here, you can also find the BAdI documentation.

Methods of the BAdI The BAdI for the general authorization check comprises the following methods:

▶ **CHECK_MAX_LEVEL_AUTHORIZATION: Maximum check for authorization level**
This method is an initial basic test whether you are authorized to access all employees and applicants or infotypes with the specified

authorization level (R, W, S, E, D, M). For write accesses (LEVEL = S, E, D, W) it is additionally checked whether you are permitted to create data records.

▶ **CHECK_MAX_INFTY_AUTHORIZATION: Maximum check for infotype authorization**
This method is an initial basic test whether you are authorized to access all employees or applicants with the given infotype and the given authorization level (for instance, write access).

▶ **CHECK_MAX_SUBTY_AUTHORIZATION: Maximum check for subtype authorization**
This method is an initial basic test whether you are authorized to access all employees or applicants with the given subtype of the infotype and the given authorization level.

▶ **CHECK_MAX_PERNR_AUTHORIZATION: Maximum check for personnel number authorization**
This method is called by applications that want to determine whether a full authorization has been issued, in other words, whether you can access all infotypes/subtypes of a given personnel number.

▶ **CHECK_MIN_LEVEL_AUTHORIZATION: Minimum check for authorization level**
This method is an initial basic test whether you are authorized to access at least one (not necessarily existing) data record of an infotype with the given authorization level. This method is called particularly when you start personnel transactions.

▶ **CHECK_MIN_SUBTY_AUTHORIZATION: Minimum check for subtype authorization**
This method is an initial basic test whether you are authorized to access at least one (not necessarily existing) data record of a personnel number for a given subtype of an infotype and the given authorization level.

▶ **CHECK_MIN_PERNR_AUTHORIZATION: Minimum check for personnel number authorization**
This method is called by applications that want to determine whether a minimum authorization has been issued, in other words, whether you can access at least one infotype record of a given personnel number.

▶ **CHECK_AUTHORIZATION: Authorization check**
This method checks the combination of authorization level, employee/applicant, personnel number, infotype, subtype, start and end date for each infotype record, and also for hiring actions. This method is implemented for every single infotype record (at least) once.

Infotype 0130 (Test Procedures) controls the release check and, therefore, assumes a special function. For write accesses to this infotype, the authorization check is not provided with start and end date. Instead the method is called with start date = end date = release date (P0130-RELDT).

▶ **CHECK_PERNR_AUTHORIZATION: Check for personnel number authorization**
This method checks outside the infotype concept whether the access to the personnel number is permitted (for instance, from Financial Accounting).

▶ **SET_ORG_ASSIGNMENT: Set organizational assignment**
This method fills the buffer with data records of IT0001 (Organizational assignment) to optimize the performance. Possibly, the data must be read from the *Organizational Assignment* infotype. For performance reasons, you should therefore use the method, SET_ORG_ASSIGNMENT, to fill the buffer of the authorization check with organizational data. As a result, you only have to reread the data from the database when the personnel number is changed.

▶ **SET_PARTIAL_ORG_ASSIGNMENT: Set partial organizational assignment**
This method fills the buffer with already known data records of IT0001 (Organizational Assignment) in case of hiring measures, if not all fields of IT0001 have been filled yet. The same performance aspects apply as for the method, SET_ORG_ASSIGNMENT.

▶ **DELAYED_CONSTRUCTOR: Replacement of the CONSTRUCTOR**
This method interface enables you to obtain information about the instance generation environment, and to implement the authorization check context-dependently to a certain extent. SAP recommends using own context dependencies so that you don't have to store any coding here.

In principle, the ...MAX... methods are available for performance reasons. If "no authorization" is returned, you can't expect any performance benefits. If these methods return "is authorized" (IS AUTHORIZED = TRUE switch), you must ensure that no additional check is carried out.

The ...MIN... methods are just additional security mechanisms. They are used to prevent access to transactions or reports in advance, and to achieve performance benefits. If these methods return "no authorization" (IS AUTHORIZED = FALSE switch), no additional authorization checks are performed.

[!]

> ### Warning
>
> You must consider all of these methods during implementation to ensure that the standard authorization check continues to work! Otherwise, you will deactivate the complete authorization check. Listing 2.1 provides you with information about how you can implement the complete standard authorization check in the first step, and then a customer-specific authorization check.
>
> For the implementation, you can revert to the classes, CL_HRPAD00AUTH_ CHECK_STD and CL_HRPAD00AUTH_CHECK_FAST, which are used in the standard version.

```
METHOD if_ex_hrpad00auth_check~check_authorization.
*************************************************************
* Standard authorization check
*************************************************************
  CLEAR is_authorized.
  CALL METHOD me->check_authorization
    EXPORTING
      level                       = level
      tclas                       = tclas
      pernr                       = pernr
      infty                       = infty
      subty                       = subty
      begda                       = begda
      endda                       = endda
      uname                       = uname
      process_only_partial_checks = process_only_partial_
      checks
    IMPORTING
      is_authorized               = is_authorized
```

```
    EXCEPTIONS
      invalid = 1
      internal_error= 2.

  IF NOT sy-subrc IS INITIAL.
    IF sy-subrc = 1.
      RAISE invalid.
    ELSE.
      RAISE internal_error.
    ENDIF.
  ENDIF.

************************************************************
* Extension of the time management authorization check
************************************************************
  IF tclas = 'A'.
    CALL METHOD z_check_auth_xxx_time
      EXPORTING
      level                        = level
      tclas                        = tclas
      pernr                        = pernr
      infty                        = infty
      subty                        = subty
      begda                        = begda
      endda                        = endda
      process_only_partial_checks  = process_only_partial_
      checks
    CHANGING
      is_authorized                = is_authorized
    EXCEPTIONS
      invalid                      = 1
      internal_error               = 2.

  IF NOT sy-subrc IS INITIAL.
    IF sy-subrc = 1.
      RAISE invalid.
    ELSE.
      RAISE internal_error.
```

Listing 2.1 Example for BAdI HRPAD00AUTH_CHECK, CHECK_AUTHORIZATION Method

We'll now describe another two practical examples in which BAdI HRPAD00AUTH_CHECK is used.

Upon request of the employee representatives, the access to the attendances and absences is to be limited for specific time administrators. A customer-specific authorization check determines which infotypes an administrator may access with which authorization level. In BAdI HRPAD00AUTH_CHECK, initially all standard checks are carried out. Upon successful completion, the customer-specific object is checked. This check prevents that attendances and absences are viewed or maintained from the time before the administrator was assigned with the responsibility, and that no attendances or absences of the previous year can be accessed any longer as of a given key date.

Time management

The assistants or their representative are not supposed to view the salary data of their superiors in the report of the Manager's Desktop. In BAdI HRPAD00AUTH_CHECK and the CHECK_MAX_PERNR_AUTHORIZATION method it is checked, whether a user may view a specific employee, and in the CHECK_AUTHORIZATION method it is checked, what information about an authorized person a user may see. The persons involved are recognized by means of customer-specific relationships between the positions of the secretary's office and the superior. The critical infotypes can be found via a customer-specific table.

Decentralized reporting

2.9   Critical Success Factors

The following section deals with critical success factors that you must particularly take into account when using the general authorization check:

▶ Make use of all available options to simplify the maintenance and to reduce the maintenance effort as much as possible: Composite roles, reference roles, and additional organizational levels.

▶ Make future-oriented decisions when selecting the authorization objects for the master data. Here, you should take into account Chapters 3, Structural Authorization Check, and Chapter 4, Context-Dependent Authorization Check.

- You should also consider these two chapters to establish which organizational check parameters you want to use for mapping the responsibilities in your enterprise. Select the authorization objects to be used and the fields to be provided accordingly.

- Define the handling of critical system authorizations, particularly the call of reports, table maintenance and display, queries, and download.

- Decide in good time how you want to use the Profile Generator, and implement your decision in Customizing.

- Think about the time variance for responsibilities, and consider the use of the required procedures (for example, Infotype 0130 (Test Procedures)) for your authorization concept.

In SAP ERP HCM, many things don't work without a structural authorization check — or only if a great deal of maintenance effort is involved. This chapter describes the benefits of structural authorizations and where you can best use them.

3 Structural Authorization Check

The structural authorization check supplements the general authorization check. It uses the arrangement and flexibility of structures in the HCM system to simplify the authorization profiles and increase their dynamics. The structural authorization check is used in three essential areas:

▶ Display and maintenance of objects in Organizational Management (OM)

▶ Display and maintenance of all other HCM objects that are stored in tables of the HRP* structure

▶ Organizational restrictions for the display and maintenance of personnel administration data

A structural authorization check as it is described here exists only in SAP ERP HCM. The following sections first introduce the concept of structural authorizations in Organizational Management. After demonstrating how you can configure a structural authorization, we will describe additional fields of application. The section on the maintenance of structural authorizations ends with the description of how you can assign structural authorizations to users. Then, some specific problems are specified and, finally, we'll again focus on the extension options of the tool.

Only in SAP ERP HCM

3.1 Structural Authorization Check in Organizational Management

PLOG doesn't check the content

When examining the PLOG object, it's apparent that it doesn't provide the option to exclude or permit access to certain objects. For example, if the authorization for Infotype 1000 of object type S is granted, it applies to all positions of the enterprise. The PLOG authorization object doesn't enable you to determine for which areas of the enterprise positions may be displayed or managed. But this can be done using the structural authorization check.

OM tool: evaluation path

Basically, the structural authorization uses the means of the evaluation paths . Based on a root object, which is defined by its eight-digit object ID, the evaluation path determines all objects under the root object in the structure. The authorization is issued for all of these objects.

[+]

> **Tip**
>
> For more information, refer to the SAP PRESS book, *HR Personnel Planning and Development Using SAP.*

Figure 3.1 illustrates the O-O-S evaluation path as an example. This path lets you access all positions located under a hierarchy of organizational units.

Evaluation Path	0-0-S	All positions under an organizational unit in the org. structure			

No.	Obj.Type	A/B	Relat'ship	Relationship name	Priority	Rel.obj.type	Ski
5	0	B	002	Line supervisor of	*	0	☐
10	0	B	003	Incorporates	*	S	☐

Figure 3.1 O-O-S Evaluation Path

Figure 3.2 shows a structure of organizational units (object type O), positions (object type S), and persons (object type P) as an example. The O-O-S evaluation path describes exactly these object types.

If root object 80000815 is linked to the O-O-S evaluation path, all objects illustrated in Figure 3.2 are permitted. If you specify root object 80004711, an authorization is only issued for the white objects.

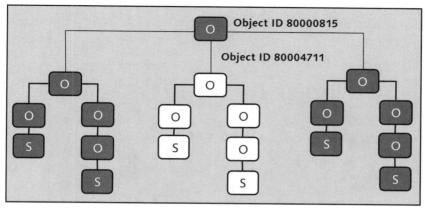

Figure 3.2 Example of a Structural Authorization Check

Such an authorization check is completely flexible regarding changes to the structure. For example, if a new organizational unit is — directly or indirectly — assigned to the root object on April 1, 2008, this organizational unit and all linked positions are permitted objects as of April 1, 2008.

Flexibility of the structural check

Skipping Object Types   **[+]**

What would you have to do if the authorization was supposed to be issued for the positions but not for the organizational units? And what if you must access the structure via the organizational units because the positions are not hierarchically linked? In this case, you could use the Skip indicator for the evaluation path. If you check the Skip flag in the first row of the O-O-S evaluation path (or in a copy), only the positions (object type S) are permitted, but not the organizational units.

Figure 3.3 provides an overview of the interaction of the general and structural authorization check. Every time objects of the HRP* database table are accessed, the structural and general authorization checks are performed. Only if both checks return a positive result will the authorization be issued.

Now that we've explained the concept of the structural authorization, the following section describes how you can configure structural authorizations.

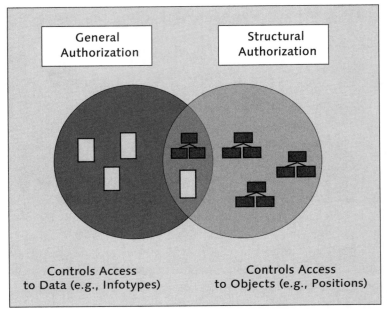

Figure 3.3 Interaction of the General and Structural Authorization Checks

3.2 Maintaining the Structural Profiles

Transaction OOSP

You must maintain the structural profiles outside of the role maintenance (Transaction PFCG) in a specific Transaction called Authorization Profiles (OOSP). Here, the profiles are initially created independently of the users and then, in a second step, assigned to the users (see Section 3.6, Assigning Structural Profiles to Users).

Maintenance parameters in authorization profile maintenance

Figure 3.4 shows the maintenance parameters in the authorization profile maintenance. The fields not shown in the figure are described below:

▸ **Plan Version|**
Can be left empty and if so, applies to all plan versions.

▸ **Object Type**
(Almost) only internal object types of the HCM system including P (Person) and AP (Applicant). For external objects, structural authorization checks are only performed in exceptional cases (for example, LW – Logistics work center)

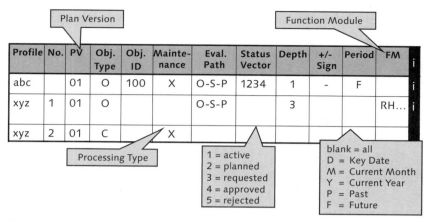

Figure 3.4 Maintenance Parameters in Authorization Profile Maintenance

---

External Object Types in Structural Authorizations [+]

To determine whether a structural authorization check is performed for an external object, you should use the following path in the IMG: PERSONNEL MANAGEMENT • ORGANIZATIONAL MANAGEMENT • BASIC SETTINGS • DATA MODEL ENHANCEMENT• MAINTAIN OBJECT TYPES • EXTERNAL OBJECT TYPES. Only if PKEYS is entered in the Key structure field and if the Inverse Relationship flag is checked can you use this external object type in a structural authorization. If you check this, for example, for the cost center, you will determine that you cannot perform a structural authorization check for the cost center in the standard version.

▶ **Maintenance**
You can display the object and also maintain its respective infotypes. Table T77FC indicates which functions are supposed to be considered as maintenance functions. The check is only relevant if the maintenance process is also permitted in the general authorization.

▶ **Depth**
If the field has the value 0 or is left blank, it indicates that all levels under the root object are permitted; a number refers to the number of the levels permitted under the root object (Figure 3.5).

▶ **Plus/Minus Sign**
Reverses the direction for counting the depth (Figure 3.5).

119

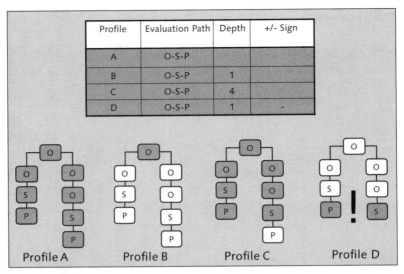

Profile	Evaluation Path	Depth	+/- Sign
A	O-S-P		
B	O-S-P	1	
C	O-S-P	4	
D	O-S-P	1	-

Figure 3.5 Effects of Depth and Plus/Minus Sign

▶ **Period**
Here, you define how the responsibility of the structural authorization is checked; for example, whether the user has to be authorized for exactly this key date or only for the year in which he or she accesses the data. See Section 3.7, Period of Responsibility and Time Logic, for more detailed information.

▶ **Function module**
The function module is maintained instead of the object ID; for more information, see Section 3.3, Function Modules.

Checking permitted objects You can find the 🛈 button next to the profile description. This button calls the RHAUTH01 report. This report lists the objects that are included in the structural profile and indicates the total number. The button provides an excellent check for whether the structural profile contains all expected object types and object IDs. However, note that the personnel number in the development system or test system has to be assigned to a respective person in Organizational Management if the structural profile determines the permitted objects based on the logged-on user.

The next section describes how a structural profile can dynamically determine the start object instead of entering a defined ID in the Object ID field.

3.3   Function Modules

The structural authorization is pretty flexible. However, entering a defined object ID as a root object is a rigid process and, therefore, requires a lot of maintenance work. Changing the responsibilities in the context of organizational restructuring often affects the structural profiles and particularly the object IDs in this case.

Consequently, when designing the structural authorization, you should always ask yourself whether the number of permitted OM objects can be determined in another way than described previously.

Two examples:

In this example, a manager who uses the Manager's Desktop or Manager Self-Service is supposed to access the data of the employees he's responsible for.

Managers

Usually, the manager's responsibility is already mapped in OM. He holds a position that is linked as a chief position with the subordinate organizational unit. Additional positions and perhaps additional organizational units, including the respective positions, are linked to his organizational unit. The employees for which the manager is responsible hold these positions.

This information enables you to dynamically determine the number of permitted persons, as well as the root object from OM. This is done by the default function module, RH_GET_MANAGER_ASSIGNMENT. In the structural profile, this function module is used instead of the object ID (Figure 3.6).

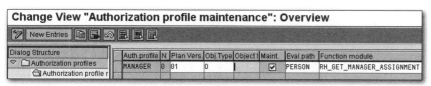

Figure 3.6   Structural Profile with Function Module

Every manager is provided with the same structural profile. The function module determines the root object as follows:

1. It determines the personnel number of the logged-on user via Infotype 0105 (Communication), subtype *SAP User Name* (usually 0001).

2. It reads the position held by the person.

3. It determines the organizational unit with which the position is linked as a manager — this organizational unit is then reported to the structural profile.

4. With the identified object ID, it continues with the stored evaluation path, O-O-S-P in this example, which determines the organizational units, positions, and persons that are linked to the root organizational unit.

Function modules reduce the number of profiles

This tool considerably increases the flexibility of the structural authorization, because it automatically considers all changes that are made under the root object, and the profile can also remain unchanged when the manager changes his position (as long as he is still a manager) or when he or his position is responsible for a different organizational unit. Moreover, you only need one structural profile for all managers.

The second function module supplied by SAP for this purpose is called RH_GET_ORG_ASSIGNMENT. It also determines an organizational unit as a root object, but doesn't use a manager relationship. Instead, the root object is defined by the simple assignment "Position belongs to organizational unit."

Time Administrators

In this second example, time administrators are supposed to be authorized to maintain data of the employees in their own organizational unit.

Customer-specific function modules

If time administrators are also responsible for organizational units to which they are not directly assigned, you must create a specific function module. This is quite simple. First, create a new relationship (e.g., "Is time administrator for") and use it to link the position of the time administrator to another organizational unit. Then, create a new evaluation path by copying the ORGASS default evaluation path and extending it by the customer-specific relationship. Finally, copy the default function module RH_GET_ORG_ASSIGNMENT, and only change the evaluation path in this function module.

Such function modules can use any data from the HCM system or from customer-specific tables to determine the root object.

3.4   Transfer to Other Structures in SAP ERP HCM

Structural authorization checks are critical wherever data is stored in HRP* tables. The use of the fields in the profile maintenance fully corresponds to the one described in Section 3.2, Maintaining the Structural Profiles. You can also use the function modules that were introduced in this section.

The following HCM components outside OM use the structural authorization:

Components of the HCM system with structural check

▸ **Training and Event Management including Learning Solution**
  Here, the business event catalog forms the structure. Figure 3.7 shows a sample restriction of the access to a subcatalog.

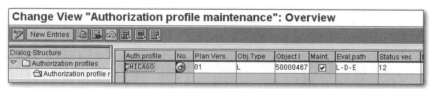

Figure 3.7 Structural Profile with Restriction to Subcatalog

In this case, the root object is a business event group with object ID 50000467; the object types are L (Business event group), D (Business event type), and E (Course).

▶ **Qualifications**
It also includes a catalog that defines the structure: the qualification catalog with object types QK (Qualification group), Q (Qualification), and QB (Qualification block), if required.

▶ **Budget Planning and Position Control (Public Sector)**
Object type BU (Budget Structure Element) has a hierarchical structure and can be structurally authorized via an evaluation path.

The HCM components mentioned so far each have their own hierarchical structure. The authorizations for these structures use the evaluation path or function module. In addition, there are applications in SAP ERP HCM that don't have a specific structure, but nevertheless entries — without an evaluation path — have to be made in the structural profiles (Figure 3.8). These are all subcomponents, which we haven't mentioned yet, for which the PLOG authorization object is responsible, namely:

▶ Development plans with object type B (Development Plan)

▶ Shift planning with object type SR (Planned staff requirement) (Figure 3.8)

▶ Performance management with object type VA (Appraisal template)

▶ VB (Criteria Group), and VC (Criterion)

▶ Management of global employees with object type CP (Central person).

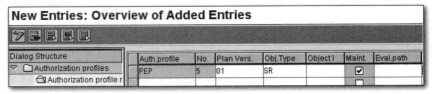

Figure 3.8 Structural Authorization for Object Type SR (Requirement)

The structural check cannot be deactivated here In the HCM components described earlier, the structural authorization is a required supplement to the single OM authorization object, Personnel Planning (PLOG, see Section 2.3.5). All data that is checked with this object is also subject to the structural authorization check. You cannot deactivate this check in the standard version.

However, you can deactivate it for personnel administration, because the structural authorization check is only an option here. We'll describe this option in the next section.

3.5 Use in Personnel Administration

If the integration between OM and personnel administration is activated, you can also use the structural authorizations for personnel administration (object type P). In this case, however, the ORGPD authorization switch in the AUTSW group of Table T77S0 must have a value between "1" and "4" (Transaction OOAC (HR: Authorization main switch)). That means, by assigning a value other than 0, you activate the structural authorization for personnel administration. Section 3.8, How the Structural Authorization Check Handles Nonintegrated Persons, explains the different meaning of the values "1" through "4."

Authorization main switch

The structural authorization check in personnel administration also uses the flexibility of the structural authorization already described also for personnel master data and time data. It represents an alternative for using:

▶ The Organizational Key field in the P_ORGIN (HR: Master Data) authorization object.

▶ The different administrator IDs of Infotype 0001 in the P_ORGXX (HR: Master Data – Extended Check) authorization object.

As long as the organizational assignment of the persons is reliably maintained in OM, you don't have to maintain the mentioned fields in Infotype 0001 if you use the structural authorization.

Example [Ex]

Managers are only authorized to view a specific selection of infotypes for the employees of their organizational units.

For this purpose, the structural profile, MANAGER, described in Section 3.3, Function Modules, is required. In the HR: Master Data object, you only have to list the infotypes under INFTY and the R authorization level. No organizational restrictions are required.

You must consider the following aspects for maintaining the structural profiles in conjunction with the infotypes of personnel administration:

▶ The evaluation path in the profile maintenance must include object type P.

▶ The combination of the structural authorization with the organizational fields of the authorization objects, *HR: Master Data* and *HR: Master Data – Extended Check*, is an AND link. That means the check of the default object and the structural check both have to be successful to assign an authorization.

Disadvantages of the structural authorization check

Although the structural authorization is the preferred method for personnel administration in most cases, you must take the following into account: The fully accurate maintenance of Organizational Management is an essential prerequisite for a consistent structural authorization protection; however, the structural authorization is more complex than the general authorization alone. Consequently, there's a great deal of learning effort involved for the affected administrators, as well as testing effort for configuring and changing the authorizations.

[+] **Tip**

You can also activate the structural authorization check in the (classic) recruitment using a switch. See Chapter 5 for more detailed information.

3.6   Assigning Structural Profiles to Users

Transaction OOSB (User Authorizations), shown in Figure 3.9, is used to assign the profiles to users.

Change View "User Authorizations": Overview

User name	Auth.profile	Start date	End date	Exclusion	Display Objects
CHICAGO	CHICAGO	01.01.1900	31.12.9999	☐	ℹ
COMMCLERK_A	COMMCLERK_A	01.01.1900	31.12.9999	☐	ℹ
HASSMANN	ALL	01.01.1900	31.12.9999	☐	ℹ
MAESTEST	MANAGER	01.01.2007	31.12.9999	☐	ℹ
SAP*	ALL	01.01.1900	31.12.9999	☐	ℹ
SMITH	MANAGER	07.01.2000	31.12.9999	☐	ℹ

Figure 3.9 Assigning Profiles to Users

In this transaction, the structural profiles — together with a validity period — are assigned to the users. A user may have several structural profiles.

If you check the Exclusion field, the profile is negative, that is, it indicates all objects that the user is not authorized to view or edit. The Information button works in the same way as in profile maintenance: It displays the permitted objects.

What happens if the table doesn't contain entries for a specific user? In that case, the authorization check uses the entry of the SAP* user. So, the profile stored for this user is applicable if an entry has been left out. That means you have two possible alternatives:

Fall-back to SAP*

Leave everything as it has been provided by SAP: SAP* provides an ALL profile that contains the full structural authorization for all object types. This is advisable if you use the structural authorization only for a small user community, and if the other users were assigned with an unrestricted structural authorization anyway.

Alternative 1

If you want to avoid a user that isn't assigned to a profile at all, that is, if you don't want a structural authorization to be issued in this case, you must create an "empty profile" and assign it to the SAP* user. The "empty profile" could, for example, contain only an object type that you don't use. Alternatively, you can delete the entry for SAP*. In this case, too, the user to which no structural profile is assigned doesn't have an authorization.

Alternative 2

These two variants are useful if you have to maintain multiple structural authorizations. They prevent you from assigning the SAP* authorization to users by mistake that aren't supposed to have this authorization.

This becomes more important if Transaction OOSB (User Authorizations) does NOT check the user's input.

[!]

Assigning a Profile to the SAP* User

If most of the users are supposed to get the same profile, it may be useful to assign this profile to the SAP* user.

Let's look at an example: All time administrators are authorized to edit data of the employees in their own organizational unit. If an enterprise had 10,000 employees, approximately 100 time administrators would have the same structural profile with the RH_GET_ORG_ASSIGNMENT function module. If you assign the time profile — instead of the 100 entries — to the SAP* user, you can avoid a great deal of maintenance effort. At the same time, it would be a minimum fall-back profile for users who haven't been assigned by mistake.

3.7 Period of Responsibility and Time Logic

In Organizational Management, all relationships have a *validity period*. For example, if an employee changes the organizational unit and is transferred to a new position, a new relationship period for the new position starts (Figure 3.10).

Staff Assignments (Structure)	ID		Assigned as	Assigned until
iProCon GmbH	O	50004104		
Business Development & Consulting	O	50004105	01.05.2000	Unlimited
Chief Executive Manager	S	50008992	01.05.2000	Unlimited
Franz Beckenbauer	P	00090009	01.01.2007	Unlimited
Senior Consultant & Business Developper	S	50008982	01.05.2000	Unlimited
Hochschulkontakt-Manager	S	50008993	01.05.2000	Unlimited
Stefanie Graf	P	00090010	01.01.2007	05.11.2007
SAP HR Consulting	O	50004106	01.05.2000	Unlimited
Geschäftsführer	S	50008983	01.05.2000	Unlimited
Consulting 1	O	50004107	01.05.2000	Unlimited
Senior Consultant	S	50008984	01.05.2000	Unlimited
Senior Consultant	S	50008989	01.05.2000	Unlimited
Consultant	S	50008990	01.05.2000	Unlimited
Junior Consultant	S	50008991	01.05.2000	Unlimited
Stefanie Graf	P	00090010	06.11.2007	Unlimited
Senior Consultant	S	50009050	01.01.2007	Unlimited

Figure 3.10 Stefanie Graf Changes the Organizational Unit as of 11/06/2007

When maintaining the structural profiles (Transaction OOSP), you can restrict the structure's validity period to the current key date (Figure 3.11), current month, current year, past, or future (see Section 3.2, Maintenance of the Structural Profiles).

Auth.profile	No.	Obj.Type	Eval.path	Period	Function module
MANAGER	0	0	PERSON	D	RH_GET_MANAGER_ASSIGNMENT

Figure 3.11 The Analysis of All Persons the Manager is Responsible for is Carried out on the Key Date (D)

Therefore, for this restriction it is always checked whether there is an intersection with the relationship period along the structure. If the check can be carried out down to the lowest level — the person — the period of responsibility is identical with the relationship period (between person and position).

In the following section, the different values are described that the periods of responsibility for the leads of Org Units A1 and A2 can have in the PERIOD column. You can also use Figure 3.12 for orientation. A structural profile as shown in Figure 3.11 and the system date 11/06/2007 are required:

▶ **Period = D (Key Date)**
Only the manager of OrgUnit A2 can view the person (11/06/2007).

▶ **Period = F (Future)**
Only the manager of OrgUnit A2 can view the person (11/06/2007 to 12/31/9999).

▶ **Period = M (Month)**
Both leaders can view the person (11/01/2007 to 11/30/2007).

▶ **Period = Y (Year)**
Both leaders can view the person (01/01/2007 to 12/31/2007).

▶ **Period = P (Past)**
Only the manager of OrgUnit A1 can view the person (01/01/1800 to 11/05/2007).

▶ **Period = Blank (All)**
   Both leaders can view the person (01/01/1800 to 12/31/9999).

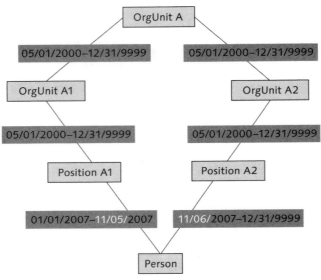

Figure 3.12 Organizational Change as of 11/06/2007 – Diagram

Grace period for structure period
The PLOGI ADAYS authorization switch extends the validity period of the structural profile. By default, the default value of the switch is blank (Figure 3.13).

Group	Sem.abbr.	Value abbr	Description
PLOGI	ADAYS		Waiting Period Personnel Planning

Figure 3.13 Standard Version of PLOGI ADAYS

This setting in combination with the key date validity of the analysis of the persons (see Figure 3.11) would mean that the leader, Franz Beckenbauer (see Figure 3.10), can no longer view his employee, Stefanie Graf, as of 11/06/2007. You can quickly check this by selecting the **i** button in the assignment of the profile to the user (Transaction OOSB) or starting the RHAUTH01 (Show Authorization Views) report. The result is shown in Figure 3.14.

Show Authorization Views

User: IPROCON1
User's authorization profiles: MANAGER

Auth.profile	OT	Object ID	Eval.path	Period	Begda	Endda	Function module
MANAGER	O	50004105	PERSON	D	01.01.1900	31.12.9999	RH_GET_MANAGER_ASSIGNMENT
MANAGER	P	90009	PERSON	D	01.01.2007	31.12.9999	RH_GET_MANAGER_ASSIGNMENT
MANAGER	Q		QALL				

Figure 3.14 The Manager Can No Longer View His Employee as of 11/06/2007

Set the grace period above the PLOGI ADAYS authorization switch to 20 days (Figure 3.15), for example. Then, Franz Beckenbauer can view his employee again (Figure 3.16).

Group	Sem.abbr.	Value abbr	Description
PLOGI	ADAYS	20	Waiting Period Personnel Planning

Figure 3.15 Grace Period of 20 Days

Show Authorization Views

User: IPROCON1
User's authorization profiles: MANAGER

Auth.profile	OT	Object ID	Eval.path	Period	Begda	Endda	Function module
MANAGER	O	50004105	PERSON	D	01.01.1900	31.12.9999	RH_GET_MANAGER_ASSIGNMENT
MANAGER	P	90009	PERSON	D	01.01.2007	31.12.9999	RH_GET_MANAGER_ASSIGNMENT
MANAGER		90010	PERSON	D	01.01.2007	05.11.2007	RH_GET_MANAGER_ASSIGNMENT
MANAGER	Q		QALL				

Figure 3.16 Extension of the Relationship Using PLOGI ADAYS

Maintaining PLOGI ADAYS   [!]

You won't find the PLOGI ADAYS authorization switch in the Maintain Authorization Main Switches IMG activity, where the other switches of the AUTSW group can be found. To maintain the PLOGI ADAYS switch, navigate directly to the table maintenance of T77S0. Don't get confused by the documentation for this switch ((F1) help). It's incorrectly identical to the documentation for the AUTSW ADAYS authorization switch (see Section 2.6, Period of Responsibility and Time Logic). SAP Note 375216 explains the functionality of this switch, which is available from Release 6.20 onward, in more detail.

If you use the general and structural authorization with both authorization switches, the following applies for our example of an organizational change as of 11/06/2007, as well as the key date 11/06/2007:

1. As long as the manager, Franz Beckenbauer, cannot view his employee, Stefanie Graf, via the structural profile, he cannot do anything.

2. If you extend the structural profile by a grace period using PLOGI ADAYS, the manager can view Stefanie Graf and read/analyze her data for the past. However, he cannot maintain infotypes (for which the access authorization in Table T582A is activated) for Stefanie Graf.

3. If the period of responsibility of the general authorization is additionally extended via AUTSW ADAYS, the manager can maintain infotypes for Stefanie Graf for this tolerance period.

Best practice

Usually, a blank in the date field is sufficient for the structural profiles of central areas. For decentralized profiles, use Y for users with read access and D for users with write access for further restrictions.

Summary

Let's summarize the essential aspects for the periods of responsibility and time logic once again:

- The period check of the structural authorization is executed prior to the period check of the general authorization.
- The period of responsibility of the structural authorization arises from the last relationship period if the check has a positive result.
- The period of responsibility is transferred to the general authorization and further restricted, if required.
- The period check can be extended by a tolerance period — in the general authorization using the AUTSW ADAYS authorization switch and in the structural authorization using the PLOGI ADAYS authorization switch.

Of course, the responsibility period and period checks can only be performed for persons that are linked to the organizational structure. However, specific person groups (for example, trainees or retirees) are often not included in the organizational structure. The next section describes how the system handles nonintegrated persons.

3.8 How the Structural Authorization Check Handles Nonintegrated Persons

In personnel administration, the structural authorization only records persons that are integrated in Organizational Management. Persons that are excluded from the integration via the PLOGI characteristic are not considered in the structural check. This also applies to persons for which no position has been entered in Infotype 0001, that is, the infotype still contains the default position (usually 99999999).

Linking the nonintegrated persons with the organizational structure via special evaluation paths such as the temporary assignment relationship doesn't solve the problem. The structural check still ignores nonintegrated persons.

To control how these persons are handled with regard to authorizations, the authorization switches, AUTSW ORGPD and AUTSW DFCON, are provided. Their values 1 to 4 have the same meanings. ORGPD controls the normal authorization check while DFCON controls the context-sensitive check. You can maintain the switches via IMG path Personnel Management • Personnel Administration • Tools • Authorization Management • Maintain Authorization Main Switches • Maintain Authorization Main Switches.

Authorization main switch

Initially, the four switch settings enable you to use the Organizational Unit field of Infotype 0001 for the authorization check. If you want to use the settings, you must enter all authorized organizational units separately into the structural profile (see example in Figure 3.17). Then, you must decide whether the authorization is supposed to be rejected or issued if an organizational unit is missing. This results in the following combinations:

Rules for checking nonintegrated persons

▶ Switch setting 1: The organizational unit is analyzed, no authorization is issued if it is not maintained.

▶ Switch setting 2: The organizational unit is not analyzed, an authorization for persons without an integrated position is generally rejected (makes only sense if all persons are integrated).

▶ Switch setting 3: The organizational unit is analyzed, an authorization is issued if it is not maintained.

▶ Switch setting 4: The organizational unit is not analyzed, an authorization for persons without an integrated position is generally issued.

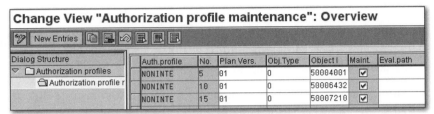

Figure 3.17 Organizational Units for Nonintegrated Persons

[+] | **Exceptions for DFCON**

While switch setting 0 of the ORGPD switch deactivates the structural authorization check for personnel master data, the DFCON authorization switch differentiates between 0 and 1 as follows (see SAP Note 647278):

1: Only users with unrestricted access (that is, "*" in all fields of the context-dependent authorization object including the PROFL field) can access nonintegrated persons whose organizational unit is not maintained.

0: Users with restricted master data access (for example, for personnel areas) but "*" in the PROFL field can also access nonintegrated persons whose organizational unit is not maintained.

3.9   Performance Optimization

The performance of the structural authorization check results from the number of read accesses required to determine whether a specific object is permitted or not. The larger the number of different object types with different evaluation paths contained in the profile and the more objects that exist under the root, the longer the access times.

Use as few evaluation paths as possible

If some object types may be viewed completely, such as the entire qualification catalog, the evaluation path shouldn't contain a root object and evaluation path (Figure 3.18).

Change View "Authorization profile maintenance": Overview

New Entries

Dialog Structure		Auth.profile	No.	Plan Vers.	Obj.Type	Object I	Maint.	Eval.path	Status vec
▽ ☐ Authorization profiles		QALL	1	01	Q		☐		
☐ Authorization profile r		QALL	3	01	QK	I	☐		

Figure 3.18 Profile Without Evaluation Path

An additional potential for optimization is to use as few evaluation paths as possible. For example, combine all object types that you determine via the organizational structure into one evaluation path. Have the structural check read the organizational hierarchy only once in order to determine all permitted organizational units, positions, persons, jobs if required, work centers, and so on.

In addition, make sure that only evaluation paths with a specified target object are used. The evaluation path illustrated in Figure 3.19, lists all objects linked to the position. Depending on the system landscape, this may include, for example, object types US (User) or BP (Business Partner), which then would be unnecessarily included in the structural check.

Evaluation Path			SBESX	Staff assignments along organizational structure			

	No.	Obj.Type	A/B	Relat'ship	Relationship name	Priority	Rel.obj.type
	10	O	B	003	Incorporates	*	S
	20	O	B	002	Is line supervisor of	*	O
	30	S	A	008	Holder	*	*

Figure 3.19 Evaluation Path With Nonspecified Target Object

The optimization measures described so far reach their limits when users are authorized to view or edit a large quantity of objects of the structural check. In this case, the structural check, which is carried out online on an ongoing basis, leads to unacceptable response times. For these situations, a procedure is provided by default. It enables you to store the information on the permitted objects of a user in the SAP memory. Then, the accesses to the SAP memory have a high performance.

Buffering large data quantities

As a prerequisite, you must enter the affected users (it doesn't have to and shouldn't include all users) in Table T77UU. There are two possible alternatives:

Manual maintenance in the IMG

You can maintain Table T77UU manually in IMG activity PERSONNEL MANAGEMENT • ORGANIZATIONAL MANAGEMENT • BASIC SETTINGS • AUTHORIZATION MANAGEMENT • STRUCTURAL AUTHORIZATION • SAVE USER DATA IN SAP MEMORY. Here, you enter the number of days that are supposed to pass between the automatic updates of the SAP memory for the respective user. The date of the last update of the system is stored here as well (Figure 3.20).

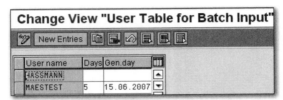

Figure 3.20 Maintaining Table T77UU – User with SAP Memory

Automatic maintenance using RHBAUS02

Instead of maintaining Table T77UU manually, you can also use the RHBAUS02 report (Check and Compare T77UU (User Data in SAP Memory)). In the standard system, you can start the report only via SYSTEM • SERVICES • REPORTING (Transaction SA38). The report maintains Table T77UU by means of a threshold value. The value results from the number of permitted objects that correspond to the structural authorization. When the report is executed (as shown in Figure 3.21), the system enters all users with an object quantity above 1,000 in Table T77UU or deletes users with an object quantity below this value from the table.

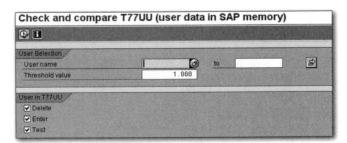

Figure 3.21 RHBAUS02 Report – Check and Compare T77UU

Regardless of your entries in Table T77UU, if the Days field is left empty, the SAP memory is not automatically supplied. Instead, you must ensure that the RHBAUS00 (Regeneration INDX for Structural Authorization) report runs properly. You can start it in batch mode on a regular basis (for example, hourly), or it can run online, if required. It runs for the users that have been defined in the selection screen.

The consequence of all procedures of regular SAP memory updates described previously is that changes to the objects, for example, the organizational structure, for the defined users reach the authorizations with a delay.

> **Tip**   [+]
>
> The online update of the SAP memory is not supported in the standard version. SAP Note 421399 provides information on how you can modify the standard settings.

There are situations in which even the SAP memory reaches its performance limits. This is the case when the SAP memory area provided for authorization purposes gets too small due to a considerably large number of users with a high quantity of permitted objects. In these cases, the structural authorization check must be replaced by a customer-specific authorization check for this user category. For this purpose, you can use the Business Add-In (BAdI) of the structural authorization check, HRBAS00_STRUAUTH. This BAdI is described in greater detail in the following section.

3.10   Extensions

BAdIs enable you to implement requirements for the authorization check that exceed the SAP standard without having to modify it. They also enable you to change the standard coding at places predefined by SAP and implement customer-specific checks. From Release 4.6C onward, the authorization check provides a BAdI for the structural authorization check.

The HRBAS00_STRUAUTH BAdI is called for any structural authorization check before the check is actually executed. Then, the BAdI allows you

If nothing else helps

to issue or reject the structural authorization while avoiding the standard checks.

You can find the BAdI in the IMG via PERSONNEL MANAGEMENT • ORGANIZATIONAL MANAGEMENT • BASIC SETTINGS • AUTHORIZATION MANAGEMENT • STRUCTURAL AUTHORIZATION • BADI: STRUCTURAL AUTHORIZATION. The corresponding documentation is also provided here.

The BAdI is comprised of six methods; two of them are described below as examples:

▶ **CHECK_AUTHORITY_VIEW**
This method serves to check the structural authorization of a user for an object. This method is supposed to reduce runtime problems. As a result of the check in this method, you obtain the information that the user has or doesn't have authorization for a specific object or that a new object to be checked (CHECK_OBJECT_OUT) is transferred. In that case, the standard check with the built-up view is used. You can control this by setting the transferred EXIT_FLAG switch to INITIAL. If you don't want to use the standard coding, you must set the switch to "X."

▶ **CHECK_AUTHORITY_SEARCH**
This method serves to check the structural authorization within the SEARCH FUNCTION or the input help. For this purpose, the hit list is transferred for clean-up purposes. The plan version that is supposed to be checked and the permitted object types are transferred to the method in the PLVAR and OTYPES parameters. In addition, the complete hit list is available in the OBJECTS table that can be changed if required. The check deletes all entries from the hit list for which the user doesn't have a structural authorization.
If you set the SKIP_STANDARD switch to "X" upon return, the search function doesn't execute another structural authorization. If you set the SKIP_STANDARD switch to " " (blank), the standard check of the structural authorization is performed.

Examples

At this point, we want to provide some examples of how you can use BAdIs.

Insufficient SAP memory

For users with central authorizations in Organizational Management, the response times were insufficient although the SAP memory was used. This was probably caused by the large number of this category of users.

Consequently, for a specific user community within the BAdIs, the structural authorization check was deactivated and replaced by a customer-specific authorization check. In the maintenance of the structural profiles, the respective users were identified by a specific profile. Because this profile issues unrestricted structural authorizations, it doesn't fill the table of the permitted objects.

The BAdI recognizes that the structural check hasn't been performed by the name of the profile and navigates to the check of a customer-specific authorization object. This object contains the company codes for which the user is authorized. The BAdI checks whether the object of Organizational Management that is supposed to be checked is linked with a permitted company code.

The company code is a standard object type of OM called IC. The relationship to the company code is written with a customer-specific program, which is continuously running.

To enable administrators or assistants to book a business event for an employee, they require a maintenance authorization for the event. However, if the business event catalog is exclusively maintained centrally, a conflict in the authorization assignment arises. The HRBAS00_STRU-AUTH BAdI must be used in order to allow for access to specific person groups regardless of the action to be performed (for example, booking an event for all employees, analyses and follow-up processing only for a selection of employees). In general, the structural authorization is granted if all actions are allowed for a group of employees. In other cases, the BAdI controls the access to employees depending on the transaction. It may cause problems that different actions in SAP Training and Event Management are sometimes executed with identical transactions. As an alternative, you can define in the BAdI that the structural authorization is only supposed to be assigned to employees with restricted actions, and that the access authorization for these employees is withdrawn for other transactions.

Training and Event Management

Assistants are supposed to maintain business trips for selected persons. However, they don't use Organizational Management. That means, it is no longer possible to check any authorization via the organizational structure. The permitted personnel numbers are assigned

Missing Organizational Management

to the assistant in a Customizing table. This table is queried by BAdI HRBAS00_STRUAUTH.

> **Tip**
>
> For BAdI HRBAS00_STRUAUTH, you must always implement all methods. Immediately after creating the implementation, you can find a sample coding in the menu via GOTO • SAMPLE CODE • DISPLAY or in the CL_EXM_IM_HRBAS00_STRUAUTH class.

3.11 Critical Success Factors

The following section describes some critical success factors that you must take into account when using the structural authorization check:

▶ Keep your Organizational Management reliably maintained and up-to-date. Maintenance is reliable only if Organizational Management is integrated with personnel administration. As soon as the structural authorization is used, the maintenance in Organizational Management can directly affect the authorizations.

▶ In the structural authorization check, you should use as many function modules as possible and simplify the maintenance in this way. For this purpose, it is always useful to use the existing information of Organizational Management via function modules.

▶ Pay attention to the response times, particularly for users that can access multiple objects. If required, use the optimization options described in Section 3.9, Performance Optimization. As your Organizational Management usually grows along with the increasing number of components you implement and the longer it is in use, you should check the performance for critical users carefully at regular intervals.

▶ Cautiously determine which of the variants of handling SAP* described in Section 3.6, Assigning Structural Profiles to the Users, you want to select. In any case, make sure that not too many authorizations are assigned by mistake.

▶ Don't forget to implement appropriate authorization protection for people not integrated with Organizational Management (see Section 3.8, How the Structural Authorization Check Handles Nonintegrated Persons).

This chapter describes how context-dependent authorization checks work and how you can use them efficiently to check where employees perform various activities for their different responsibilities.

4　Context-Dependent Authorization Check

The context-dependent authorization check is an authorization concept that is still quite young even though it was implemented with SAP R/3 4.7 (Enterprise). This check is a specific combination of the general and structural authorization checks. We'll begin the chapter by first defining the context in which this concept is used. Then, the setup and maintenance of the context-dependent authorization check are explained using real-life examples.

4.1　Functionality

At this point, we want to explain once again how the general and structural authorization checks interact. The first thing to consider is that if you use structural authorizations, two authorizations — one general and one structural — must exist for each object accessed by a user. Within both authorizations, it's sufficient that the checked object is permitted at least once.

Interaction of the general and structural authorization checks

But what happens if one person is supposed to carry out several functions for different areas of responsibility?

[Ex]

Example

A team lead has read access to the salary data of her team. At the same time, she processes the time data of her department because she also assumes the role of the time administrator. In this role, she isn't supposed to view any salary data.

Without the context-dependent authorization, the authorizations would look as follows:

General authorization without context   Figure 4.1 shows that the user is authorized to read Infotype 0008 (Basic pay) including the salary data with the first authorization. With the second authorization, the user has write access to Time Management Infotypes 2001 through 2004.

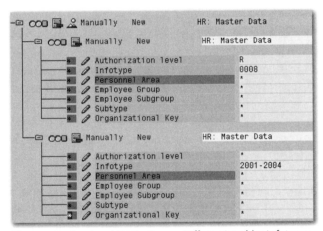

Figure 4.1   Read and Write Access Differentiated by Infotypes

Structural authorizations   This is supplemented by the two structural profiles, ZB_EIGEN for her own team and ZPA01_GESAMT for the entire department. Figures 4.2 and 4.3 show these profiles.

Auth.profile	No.	Plan Vers.	Obj.Type	Object I	Maint.	Eval.path	Function module
ZB_EIGEN	0	01	O		☐	PERSON	RH_GET_ORG_ASSIGNMENT

Figure 4.2   Read Access for One Organizational Unit

The structural profile, ZB_EIGEN (see Figure 4.2), uses a function module that returns the own organizational unit as a root object. In this case, the maintenance flag is not checked, that is, the data can only be viewed.

Auth.profile	No.	Plan Vers.	Obj.Type	Object I	Maint.	Eval.path	Function module
ZPA01_GESAMT	0	01	O	50004001	☑	PERSON	

Figure 4.3 Maintenance Authorization for the Entire Department

In the structural profile, ZPA01_GESAMT (see Figure 4.3), the related persons are determined on the basis of a root object that comprises the entire department of the team lead. The maintenance flag is set, that is, the data can be maintained.

The result of this assignment of authorizations is displayed in Figure 4.4.

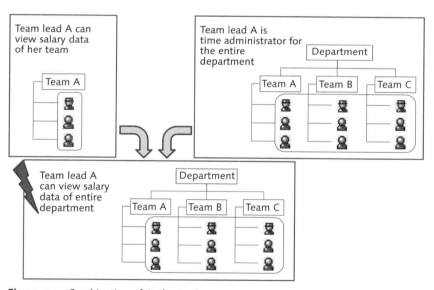

Figure 4.4 Combination of Authorizations

If the two different authorizations, *Display Salary Data* and *Time Data Maintenance*, and the two structural profiles, *Team* and *Department*, are assigned to a single user, the authorizations are combined (see Figure 4.4). Consequently, the user is authorized to maintain the time data and view the salary data for the entire department, because the infotype authorizations illustrated in Figure 4.1 always apply to all structural profiles.

However, such a system behavior is usually not desired and often causes problems in real life scenarios. These problems cannot be solved by using only the structural and general authorization. You would only work around the problem if you assigned two different user IDs.

Differentiation with context-dependent authorization check

The context-dependent authorization check provides a proper solution. It differentiates the interaction of the general and structural authorization checks and links the role with the structural profile in order to avoid their combination. The context-dependent authorization check ensures that the read and write accesses that have been granted with the general master data authorizations for specific infotypes and subtypes no longer apply to each structural profile of the user without restrictions. Instead, the permission for specific master data authorizations is limited to specific structural profiles.

From the technical point of view, this is implemented by introducing a new group of authorization objects that all contain a field that indicates the structural profile to which this authorization is assigned. For example, the context-dependent authorization object, P_ORGINCON, which is shown in Figure 4.5, replaces the master data authorization object, P_ORGIN, from Figure 4.1.

Structural profiles in the authorization object

Figure 4.5 illustrates how the example described previously should be implemented with context authorization objects in role maintenance: The first authorization includes viewing salary data, the second includes editing time data. You can use the new Authorization Profile field to differentiate which authorizations can be used in which part of the organizational structure. The structural profiles entered remain unchanged (see Figures 4.2 and 4.3). Only the usage of the structural profile has been restricted, in this case to a specific master data authorization.

Now you can assign authorizations to the different roles of a user. In our example: The team lead is authorized to view and maintain the time data of the entire department. However, she is only authorized to view the salary data of her own organizational unit. On this technical basis, you can assign various roles to a single user, even if their functions and organizational structures overlap.

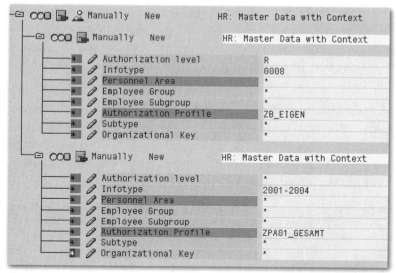

Figure 4.5 Read and Write Access Differentiated by Structural Profiles

The next section explains how you can implement context-dependent authorization checks and adapt your existing roles to the new context-dependent authorization objects.

4.2 Setup and Maintenance

For a context-dependent check of personnel master data, the common authorization object is replaced by a context-dependent object. Table 4.1 lists the objects and the respective authorization switch that is responsible for the corresponding context object.

Object without Context	Object with Context	Authorization Switch with Context	Authorization Switch without Context
P_ORGIN	P_ORGINCON	AUTSW INCON	AUTSW ORGIN
P_ORGXX	P_ORGXXCON	AUTSW XXCON	AUTSW ORGXX
P_NNNNN	P_NNNNNCON	AUTSW NNCON	AUTSW NNNNN

Table 4.1 Context-Dependent Authorization Objects in the Personnel Master Data

In addition, the object that is not context-dependent must be deactivated in the authorization main switches. Even if it is theoretically possible to use two authorization objects of one category (for example, P_ORGIN and P_ORGINCON) simultaneously, you should not do that, because it would involve tedious work and is also error-prone.

The last Customizing configuration to be made is to transfer the values for the AUTSW ORGPD switch to the AUTSW DFCON switch. This concerns the handling of personnel numbers that are not integrated with Organizational Management. See Chapter 3, Structural Authorization Check, for more detailed information.

[!]

Warning

For the P_ORGXXCON object, it is advisable to check in Transaction SU24 (Maintain the Assignments of Authorization Objects) whether the respective context object is actually checked where it is supposed to be checked. Figure 4.6 shows that Transaction PP61 doesn't check P_ORGXXCON, for example. If required, you must add P_ORGXXCON where necessary using the Object button. For more information on this transaction, see Chapter 2, section 2.5, Customizing of the Profile Generator.

	Status	Object	Object Description	Check Ind.	Proposal	
	☐	P_ABAP	HR: Reporting	Check	NO	🗐
	☐	P_ORGIN	HR: Master Data	Check	YS	🗐
	☐	P_ORGINCON	HR: Master Data with Context	Check	NO	🗐
	☐	P_ORGXX	HR: Master Data - Extended Check	Check	NO	🗐
	☐	P_PCLX	HR: Clusters	Check	YS	🗐
	☐	P_PEPSVAR	Shift Planning: User-Independent Sort Variants	Check	NO	🗐
	☐	P_PERNR	HR: Master Data - Personnel Number Check	Check	NO	🗐
	☐	P_TCODE	HR: Transaction codes	Check	YS	🗐
	☐	PLOG	Personnel Planning	Check	YS	🗐

Figure 4.6 Checked HCM Authorization Objects in Transaction PP61

Setting the roles

How do you use your existing authorization roles? This is easy for users with SAP* access. If the roles of these users don't work as they should, you may have to generate the SAP_ALL authorization profile again.

For setting the normal roles, you should leave the authorization objects that are not related to context in the roles and simply add the context-dependent objects. Only then can you configure the switches described previously. If there are major problems with the new objects, this procedure enables you to reset the switches without problems and work with the old objects for now.

Unfortunately, it's not sufficient to enter the structural profiles in the respective authorization object as shown in Figure 4.5, for example. In addition to that, you must assign the profiles to the individual users via Transaction OOSB (User Authorizations), as shown in Figure 4.7 for the MAESTEST user.

Double maintenance of the profiles

Change View "User Authorizations": Overview

User name	Auth.profile	Start date	End date	Exclusion	Display Objects
CHICAGO	CHICAGO	01.01.1900	31.12.9999	☐	ℹ
COMMCLERK_A	COMMCLERK_A	01.01.1900	31.12.9999	☐	ℹ
HASSMANN	ALL	01.01.1900	31.12.9999	☐	ℹ
MAESTEST	ZB_EIGEN	01.01.2001	31.12.9999	☐	ℹ
MAESTEST	ZPA01_GESAMT	01.01.2001	31.12.9999	☐	ℹ

Figure 4.7 Profiles Must Also be Assigned for Context-Dependent Checks in Table T77UA

You can also virtually assign the T77UA profiles using BAdI HRBAS00_GET_PROFL (from SAP Basis Release 6.20 onward). In the sample code provided, the profiles for the P_ORGINCON object are directly read from the authorization object instead of Table T77UA.

Authorization Profile as Organizational Level   [+]

Let's assume numerous users require identical authorizations for different areas of responsibility (results from the authorization profile). In this case, reference roles (see Section 2.2.3, Reference Roles) can considerably simplify the role administration process. You must merely define the authorization profile as the organizational level. For this purpose, use the PFCG_ORGFIELD_CRE-ATE (Profile Generator: Create New Organizational Level Field) report, which must be executed for the PROFL field in all systems.

Then, the PROFL field is available as the organizational level wherever you use context-dependent authorization objects (Figure 4.8).

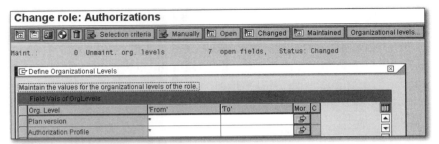

Figure 4.8 PROFL Field as the Organizational Level

4.3 Other Context-Dependent Authorization Objects

Besides the context-dependent authorization objects of the personnel administration already described, there is one additional context-dependent authorization object: P_HAP_DOC (Appraisal Systems: Appraisal). This object maintains one structural profile for each appraisal template (or categories or category groups). This profile defines the persons allowed for this template. The Profile field works in the same way as in the corresponding objects of the personnel administration. For more information, see Chapter 5 on Performance Management.

[+]

> **Tip**
>
> If you use BAdI HRBAS00_GET_PROFL to avoid additional maintenance work for the structural profiles in T77UA, you must add this authorization object to the BAdI when you use P_HAP_DOC.

PLOG_CON doesn't work

Unfortunately, SAP supplied a context-dependent equivalent to PLOG (Personnel Planning), PLOG_CON (Personnel Planning with Context) that is still not free of errors according to SAP's own information. For example, a context-dependent check within Organizational Management, Event Management, Personnel Development, and so on cannot be performed in the standard version. You have to use the HRBAS00_STRU-AUTH BAdI to implement the requirements in this environment.

4.4   Critical Success Factors

To summarize, let's list some critical success factors you need to take into account when using the context-sensitive authorization check:

▶ Focus on the future-proof context check: The more functions you use in SAP ERP HCM, the requirements become more complex for your authorization concept. Without using the context-dependent check, you don't have many options. Therefore, working with the context-dependent authorization objects right from the start provides many advantages, even if they are not required initially.

▶ You can only consider using the context-dependent authorization if you meet all requirements for the use of the structural authorization check. You must, therefore, ensure that Organizational Management is carefully maintained in particular.

▶ Don't use the PLOG_CON object. Even if it is required in many instances — SAP itself recommends not using it. Wherever organizational rules don't provide any help, you must program customized context-dependent checks in BAdI HRBAS00_STRUAUTH.

▶ Use meaningful profile names. Unfortunately, there are often numerous structural profiles, which the system doesn't arrange specifically. Consequently, only a transparent naming convention helps you to keep your overview during maintenance.

You can refer to this chapter if you need to select an appropriate authorization tool for a specific HCM area. The chapter will help you understand what options are available, what makes sense for your projects, and which aspects should be considered? Additionally, you'll be introduced to a selection of the roles provided by SAP and their usability in real life.

5 Authorization Roles in SAP HCM Components

(Satish Bagdi, chapter co-author)

Because we described the different tools of the authorization check in previous chapters, we'll now apply this knowledge to the individual SAP HCM components, which we've sorted alphabetically.

This chapter begins by introducing the standard roles provided by SAP. SAP offers a wide range of roles that you can usually use as templates for your individual roles. The analysis of the *Roles* by Complex Selection Criteria provides an overview of all of the roles that are relevant for the SAP HCM system. You can access this analysis from the SAP Easy Access menu via TOOLS · ADMINISTRATION • USER MAINTENANCE • INFORMATION SYSTEM • ROLES. In this menu, you can search by using the placeholder *SAP*HR** (Figure 5.1). If you use the *SAP*RCF** placeholder, you'll find roles for E-Recruiting, and *SAP*TV** searches for travel management roles.

SAP roles

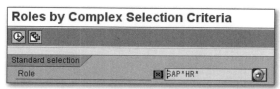

Figure 5.1 Searching for SAP Roles That Are Relevant for the SAP HCM System

Menu entries in
the SAP roles

The SAP roles usually contain a wide range of useful entries in the menu that you have to customize according to your requirements. Refer back to Chapter 2, section 2.3.1, Transaction Authorizations, if you need to obtain information on the functions of the authorization objects, S_TCODE and P_TCODE, which are linked to the menu entries.

Authorizations for
master data in SAP
roles

Most of the SAP roles contain additional entries for authorizations for master data. They focus on the P_ORGIN authorization object and sometimes also on P_PERNR. The authorizations provided are usually incomplete, because the SAP system can't decide which criteria you use to assign your authorizations here. So you usually need to revise these authorizations, particularly if you use different authorization objects for the master data (discussed in Chapter 2, Section 2.3.2, Infotype Authorizations in Personnel Administration)..

Throughout the next sections, we'll analyze the SAP roles for each component, but we'll only mention authorizations for transaction and master data as required.

5.1 Payroll and Subsequent Activities

The SAP roles for payroll follow the naming convention SAP_HR_PY*. In this section we'll describe the SAP_HR_PY_US_PAYROLL-ADM (Payroll Administrator United States) role as an example.

"Payroll (US)
Administrator
United States"

In the Payroll Administrator (US) United States role, you can find the following authorization object:

- **Cluster authorizations**
  Despite small redundancies, the clusters proposed provide a good overview of all the elements you might require. The payroll driver or, for example, the preliminary data medium exchange program, mainly writes the clusters. The clusters in detail include:
  - B2 (time evaluation results)
  - CU (payroll cluster directory)
  - L1 (individual incentive wages)
  - PC (personal calendar) (essential for attendances/absences)

- ▸ PS (payroll schema)

- ▸ PT (time evaluation schema)

- ▸ RU (payroll results (USA))

- ▸ U1 (tax reporter form cluster (USA))

- ▸ ZL (time wage types/work schedule)

If required, you may have to add organizational management authorizations (PLOG and structural authorization). These are necessary if the payroll administrators also read or maintain Infotype 0001 as well as qualifications. We'll cover this in more detail later in section 5.10, Organizational Management (OM).

TemSe is another critical authorization object for payroll administrators: S_TMS_ACT (Actions on TemSe Objects). It enables you to write on objects with temporary sequential data and is used in subsequent programs for payroll.

So let's look at several special authorizations for payroll and its environment.

5.1.1 Authorizations for Controlling Payroll and Its Subsequent Activities

The personnel control record (Transaction PA03) is the central control tool for the actual payroll (Figure 5.2). The P_PCR authorization object (HR: Personnel Control Record) checks the rights to display and maintain the elements. It checks the payroll area and the activities (add, change, display, delete) permitted.

Personnel control record

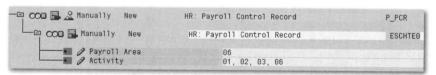

```
─☐ OOO 🖫 ♟ Manually    New        HR: Payroll Control Record              P_PCR
   └☐ OOO 🖫 Manually    New        HR: Payroll Control Record              ESCHTE0
      ├─■ 🖉 Payroll Area            06
      └─■ 🖉 Activity                01, 02, 03, 06
```

Figure 5.2 Authorization Object for Transaction PA03

The central reports for processing the payroll, RPCALC*, require numerous infotype authorizations for master data. The PLOG authorization

Payroll driver

object is additionally needed. It is required for Infotype 1018 (Cost distribution).

The following authorization objects assign authorizations for updating in FI/CO:

- ▶ **P_PYEVRUN (HR: Posting Run)**
  It checks several activities (add, change, display, delete, post, release, reverse), the simulation indicator, and the run type.

  The following run types are relevant for payroll processes:

  - ▶ PM (Payment Posting)
  - ▶ PP (Payroll Posting)
  - ▶ TP (Posting of Third Party Remittances)

- ▶ **P_PYEVDOC (HR: Posting Document)**
  This object checks several activities with regard to posting documents (display, delete, post, display line items, release) based on the company code.

[!]

> **Warning**
>
> If SAP HCM and SAP FI/CO run on separate systems, refer to SAP Note 926726 (Authorizations with transfer of payrolls) for additional RFC authorizations.

The accounting payment medium program checks the P_ABAP (HR: Reporting) authorization object. Although common, this object is usually optional, (see Section 5.16.3, The Authorization Object P_ABAP), it's required in this case. The *ABAP Program Name* field must contain the name of the payment medium program, and in the *Degree of Simplification* field, the value "2" (or "*") must be entered.

The Process Workbench Engine (also referred to as *Payroll Process Manager*) is a tool for payroll controlling. If you use the Process Workbench Engine, you'll need the P_PBSPWE (Process Workbench Engine (PWE) authorization) authorization object, which assigns authorizations for specific activities for:

- ▶ Personnel action types (subtypes of Infotype 0716 according to Table T591A, infosubtype characteristics)

- Personnel actions (Table T7PBSWB2J)

- Personnel subactions (Table T7PBSWB2B)

- Subtasks (Table T7PBSWB2L)

The B2A Manager is responsible for the data transfer to authorities or   **B2A Manager**
social insurance agencies. The B2A Manager has its own authorization
object as well: P_B2A (HR-B2A: B2A Manager), which is shown in Figure 5.3.

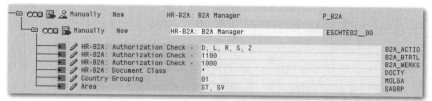

Figure 5.3 Authorization Object for the B2A Manager

The P_B2A (HR-B2A: B2A Manager) authorization object checks the fol-   **P_B2A fields**
lowing fields:

- B2A Manager Actions
  Detail view of messages, delete messages, reorganize messages, execute processes, implement message statuses

- Personnel Subarea
  Allowed personnel subareas

- Personnel Area
  Allowed personnel areas

- **Document Class**
  Compilation of documents according to B2A Customizing, for example, statement of earnings for health insurers

- Country Grouping
  Allowed country grouping

- Area
  Tax, social insurance, for example

[+]

> **Tip**
>
> The system also requires the S_OC_SEND (Authorization Object to Send Documents) authorization object for the B2A Manager.

US Payroll

Because US payroll has functionality in the areas of benefits, garnishments, and taxes, SAP has provided a specific role SAP_HR_PY_US_PAYROLL-PROC-ADM (Payroll Process Administrator United States). The role menu allows the user to work in the Payroll, Benefits, and Taxes, as well as Garnishments areas. In addition, SAP has also provided a role SAP_HR_PY_US_PS_PAYROLL-PROC (Payroll Processor USA Public Sector).

It's worth mentioning the object P_USTR (US Tax reporter), because the US has specific requirements to run the tax reporter using transaction PU19, and the roles need to include the transaction with this associated authorization object.

US Benefits

The US Benefits Administration functionality comes with a standard role SAP_HR_BN_US_HR-ADMINISTRATOR (HR Administrator Benefits United States). This role uses most of the HRBEN* transactions that are applicable for US benefits administration.

P_BEN (Benefit area) is also an important authorization object used in benefits administration.

5.1.2 Authorizations for Maintaining and Displaying Forms

In addition to the general and structural checks of the data contents, the following special authorization checks apply to all forms that have been created with HR Forms.

Displaying forms on the screen

Every user that calls a form created with HR Forms requires at least one display authorization for the P_HRF_INFO (HR: Authorization Check Infodata Maintenance for HR Forms) object.

In addition, this object checks changes in the form using the country grouping, InfoSet name (applies automatically to the related subobjects, such as InfoStars, InfoDimensions, InfoFields, and InfoFigures), and activity (change, display, activate) field.

The change authorization in the P_HRF_INFO object only refers to the form itself. P_HRF_META (HR: Authorization Check Metadata Maintenance for HR Forms), however, assigns the authorization to maintain metadata. This authorization object runs checks when metadata is displayed or processed in HR Metadata Workplace, when metadata is displayed in the HR Forms Workplace, and when a form is called for tests. In addition, the read authorizations for the respective content data must be assigned.

Authorization object for metadata

The documentation of this object contains more information on fields that are checked by the P_HRF_INFO (HR: Authorization Check Infodata Maintenance for HR Forms) authorization object. You can call the documentation using Transaction SU21 (Maintain the Authorization Objects).

5.1.3 Authorizations for Auditors

For auditors, SAP has provided a few roles that can be used along with Audit Information Systems (AIS) functionality in SAP (e.g., SAP_AUDITOR_BA_HR and SAP_AUDITOR_BA_HR_A). You can search the roles under SAP_AUDITOR*. They contain several templates, particularly for system authorizations and also include Transaction TPC6 (Change View "Periods for Authorization Check"), which is an essential transaction. You can use this transaction to maintain a table that restricts the auditor's access in specific reports (payroll account, for example) to defined periods.

5.1.4 Authorization for Deleting Payroll Results

Transaction PU01 (Delete Current Payroll Result) enables you to delete the current payroll result for individual personnel numbers in the Rx cluster (x refers to the country grouping) of Table PCL2. After the payroll result has been successfully deleted, the previous payroll result is provided as the current payroll result.

You can use the BAdI, HR_PY_AUTH_PU01, to implement customer-specific authorization checks.

5.2   Appraisal System

From Release 4.7 onward, you can replace the "old" appraisal system with the new Performance Management. Basically, it's not possible to use both in the standard version in most cases. Icon HAP00 REPLA in Table T77S0 is decisive for the selection between the "old" appraisal system and performance management.

[+]   The AdManus newsletter from October 2007 (*www.admanus.de/int/index. php Newsletter* • Online *Archive*) describes how you can use both components in parallel and, for example, use the old appraisal system for event management and the new performance management functions for personnel appraisal at the same time.

Infotypes for persons   In the appraisal system, the read authorization for displaying the appraisee is checked for the following infotypes:

▶ 0002 (Personal data)

▶ 0024 (Qualifications), only for active integration of the qualifications – see switch PLOGI QUALI in T77S0

▶ 0025 (Appraisals), only for active integration with the appraisals – see switch PLOGI APPRA in T77S0

This check must be assigned by one of the authorization objects for infotypes, for example, by P_ORGIN (Figure 5.4).

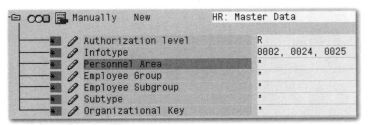

Figure 5.4   Read Authorization for Master Data of the Appraisal System

You can deactivate the check for Infotype 0002 in the HRPDV00APPR AISAL0005 BAdI using the EXIT_FLAG parameter. If the parameter is set to "A," this authorization check is deactivated for the appraiser. If it's set to "X," the check is neither run for the appraiser nor the appraisee.

In addition, the object types and infotypes of the appraisal system itself must be checked. To do this, use the PLOG (Personnel Planning) object and the structural authorization for the object types. The following elements are used:

Object types, infotypes, and subtypes

- ▶ **Object types**
  - ▶ BA (Appraisal)
  - ▶ BG (Criteria Group)
  - ▶ BK (Criterion)
  - ▶ BS (Appraisal Model)

  Depending what and who you appraise, additional object types are: P (Person), AP (Applicant), E (Event). BG and BK belong to Customizing, that is, normal users have only read authorizations for these objects. BA, however, can usually be assigned with a complete write authorization, BS only for the relationship to BA (003).

- ▶ **Infotypes**
  - ▶ 1000, 1001, 1043 (Appraisal Model Info)
  - ▶ 1044 (Result Definition)
  - ▶ 1045 (Rating)
  - ▶ 1047 (Processing Modules)
  - ▶ 1048 (Proficiency Description)

- ▶ **Subtypes of Infotype 1001**
  - ▶ 003 (Belongs to/Incorporates)
  - ▶ 045 (Created/Was created by)
  - ▶ 046 (Receives/Was created for)
  - ▶ 047 (Contains/Is an element of)
  - ▶ 057 (Has participant appraisal model/Is participant appraisal model for)
  - ▶ 058 (Has event appraisal model/Is event appraisal model for)
  - ▶ 0710 (Fulfils/Is fulfilled by)
  - ▶ 0711 (Requires/Is required by)

If you use the appraisal system to appraise events or attendees for event management, you must authorize Relationships 045, 047, 057, and 058 to Object Types E (Event) and D (Event type).

Because no hierarchical structures exist within the object types of the appraisal system, only the individual object types need to be structurally authorized. You can assign specific authorizations to individual keys, particularly for appraisal models, by making entries in Object I.

Write authorizations for Object Types BA and BS (due to the relationship to BA) must also be structurally authorized in order to process appraisals. Figure 5.5 illustrates an example that allows for accessing object types of the appraisal system and appraising persons of a specific organizational unit.

Auth.profile	No.	Plan Vers.	Obj.Type	Object I	Maint.	Eval.path
BEURTEIL	10	01	BA		☑	
BEURTEIL	20	01	BG		☐	
BEURTEIL	30	01	BK		☐	
BEURTEIL	40	01	BS		☑	
BEURTEIL	50	01	O	50123456	☑	PERSON

Figure 5.5 Example of a Structural Authorization for the Appraisal System

[+]

Tip

ZGET_APPRAISALS is a useful function module for structural authorizations. For a manager authorization, the module provides all appraisals for employees for which he is responsible. You can download this module via SAP Note 668962 (Authorization to See Appraisals from Managed Employees Only).

5.3 Position Budgeting and Control

Position budgeting and control is an essential development of position management and is supposed to replace it in the long run. The new position budgeting and control is comprised of the following SAP HCM components, which you must use to set up your roles in the planning process phase:

- **Personnel administration**
  The authorizations in personnel administration are assigned in the same way as in all other SAP HCM components that access this data. Section 5.12, Personnel Administration and Time Management, provides detailed information on this topic.

- **Organizational management**
  Like the other HCM processes, position budgeting and control uses the organizational plan of the SAP organizational management, including the PLOG authorization object and structural authorization (see Section 5.10, Organizational Management (OM)). In addition to Object Types O (Organizational unit), P (Person), and S (Position) as well as their infotypes, you also require:

  - Object Type BU (Budget structure element)

  - Relationships 003 (For the hierarchy of the budget structure elements), 300 (Is financed by/Finances), 301 (Increases/Is increased by), 310 (Is responsible for/Is responsibility of), 312 (Belongs to (reclassif.)/Incorporates (re-valuatn)), 313 (Reclassified from/Reclassified into), 314 (Is to be financed by/Is earmarked for), and 315 (Responsible for Financing) between BU and O, S and P

  - Infotypes 15xx
    For structural authorizations, you can either assign unlimited authorizations to Object Type BU, or you can limit specific areas of the hierarchy of the budget structure elements by entering a root object and the BU-BU evaluation path.

- **Payroll (simulation)**
  Section 5.1, Payroll and Subsequent Activities, described payroll authorizations in detail.

- **Personnel cost planning, including transferring the results into controlling and from there to funds management**
  In section 5.17, Personnel Cost Planning, we'll provide more information on personnel cost planning.

Unfortunately, the roles for position budgeting and control provided by SAP are rather incomplete. Only the SAP_HR_PBC_PAYSIM_RESPON-

SIBLE (Responsible for Payroll Simulation) role provides a useful basis for this task area.

Specific
authorization
objectsBut there are some specific authorization objects in position budgeting and planning, which apply solely there.

▶ **P_EXMGRP (HR: PBC – Exceptions for Financing Rules)**
This authorization object restricts the usage of check exceptions. Only the Grouping of check exceptions field is checked.

▶ **P_ENGINE (HR: PBC – Authorization for Automatic Commitment Creation)**
This object assigns an authorization for the generation of an automatic commitment in position budgeting and control. Only the Activity field with the only possible value, "Generate," is checked.

▶ **P_ENCTYPE (HR: PBC – Financing)**
Here, earmarked funds categories are permitted. Figure 5.6 shows the checked fields and their possible values.

▶ **P_FINADM (HR: PBC – Changes in the Financing Past)**
This authorization object enables you to change financing before the date that has been defined in the Customizing of the IMG activity under Personnel Management • Position Budgeting and Control • Personnel budget plan Management • Settings for financing persons/positions • Maintain Period Allowed For Changes in the Past. The Changes in the Past Allowed field may contain the values "X" or " " (space).

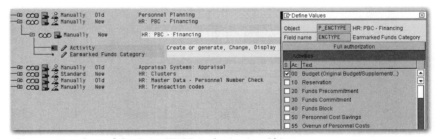

Figure 5.6 Values of the P_ENCTYPE Authorization Object

When you determine the required full-time equivalents in the transactions of the job index management, the authorization check can be deactivated using the T77S0 switch HRFPM NOPAU (see SAP Note 796357 – Org Man for PS: Authorization management for PA infotypes).

5.4 Cross Application Time Sheet (CATS)

There are no preconfigured roles provided by SAP for the Cross Application Time Sheet (CATS), so you need to set up new CATS roles using two components.

First, you must define for all CATS profiles whether a user may use the respective profile. For this purpose, CATS uses the SAP HCM authorization object, P_ORGIN (HR: Master Data), or the related context-dependent P_ORGINCON object.

In this object, the following virtual infotypes are entered for working in CATS

▶ Infotype 0316 for reading and maintaining data

▶ Infotype 0328 for reporting and approvals

These two infotypes are virtual infotypes, that is, they don't exist on the database. They are only part of the authorization role of the CATS users.

For Infotype 0316, you must additionally enter a subtype. This subtype indicates the data entry profile for which the user has an authorization. The subtype of the virtual Infotype 0316 contains the four-digit profile authorization group, which is entered in the Authorization field of the Customizing table for the data entry profile (Figure 5.7). You can navigate to this view in the IMG via CROSS-APPLICATION COMPONENTS • TIME SHEET • SETTINGS FOR ALL USER INTERFACES • AUTHORIZATIONS • CREATE AUTHORIZATIONS FOR DATA ENTRY PROFILES • MAINTAIN DATA ENTRY PROFILES

| Warning | [!] |

There must always be an authorization group in the data entry profile, even if "*" is entered in the Subtype field for the authorization.

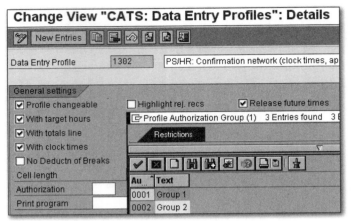

Figure 5.7 CATS Data Entry Profile with Authorization Group

Component 2: The second component provided in each CATS authorization refers to
Authorizations for the data. Here, all authorizations of the SAP components involved are
data content valid. For the SAP HCM system, this refers to the following authorization objects:

- ▶ P_ORGIN/P_ORGINCON (HR: Master Data, with or without Context)

- ▶ P_PERNR (HR: Master Data – Personnel Number Check)
  This object is particularly important for decentral data entry scenarios
  that are typical in CATS. For more information, refer to Section 2.3.3,
  Additional Authorization Objects for Master and Time Data.

- ▶ P_ORGXX/P_ORGXXCON (HR: Master Data – Extended Check, with
  or without Context)

- ▶ P_PCLX (HR: Cluster)

For master data objects, consider the CATS-specific Infotype 0315 (Time
Sheet Defaults). This infotype is — in contrast to the infotypes described
previously — not virtual but actually filled with data. You should also
consider the structural authorizations, if they affect persons.

BAdI for CATS In IMG, under Cross-Application Components • Time Sheet • Specific
regular Settings for CATS regular • CATS regular • Approve working time •
BAdI: Refine Settings for Approval, you can find an extension option
that enables you to add additional authorization checks.

A third component must be taken into account for the time sheet for service providers. In this case, the P_CATSXT (HR: Time Sheet for Service Providers Type/Level Check) authorization object is used (Figure 5.8). So, the authorization check for task level and activity type is carried out in the time sheet for service providers.

Time sheet for
service providers

Figure 5.8 CATS: Time Sheet for Service Providers

The following fields are checked:

▶ **Activity**
Add, change, display, delete, analyze

▶ **Company Code**
Permitted actions for these company codes only

▶ **Personnel Number Check**
Processing the own personnel number, processing an external personnel number

▶ **Cost Center**
As in the company code and the following four fields, Infotype 0001 is checked here.

   ▶ Organizational Unit
   Permitted organizational units

   ▶ Personnel Area
   Permitted personnel areas

   ▶ Employee Group
   Permitted employee groups

   ▶ Employee Subgroup
   Permitted employee subgroups

▶ **Task Level**
Appraisal levels maintained in the time sheet for each activity level (Table CATSTCATX_LEVELS)

▶ **Activity Type**
For example, consultation, instructor function (Table TCATX_TASKTYPES)

5.5 E-Recruiting

High demands on data protection Data protection in E-Recruiting goes far beyond the requirements within the scope of SAP HCM authorizations. The system architecture places high requirements on security, especially when internal and external candidates can access the same system. As in the previous sections, let's now focus on SAP HCM aspects.

5.5.1 SAP Roles

SAP offers a wide range of authorization roles for E-Recruiting. They correspond to the preconfigured E-Recruiting roles, which control the user and working interfaces. The SAP authorization roles of the E-Recruiting are updated via support packages on a regular basis.

SAP roles of E-Recruiting The authorization roles in detail:

▶ **SAP_RCF_BUSINESS_ADMINISTRATOR**
Administrator

▶ **SAP_RCF_CONTENT_SERVER**
Access to the *Search and Classification* (TREX) search engine

▶ **SAP_RCF_DATA_TYPIST (Data Entry Clerk)**
This role contains the authorization to make minimum data entries for incoming paper applications.

▶ **SAP_RCF_DECISION_MAKER (Decision Maker)**
The decision maker answers queries on candidates that are assigned to requisitions. These queries include questions on the decision maker's opinion.

▶ **SAP_RCF_EXTERNAL_CANDIDATE (External Candidate)**
This role is only authorized to display and change its own data. It can only display the job postings that you have published via external posting channels.

▶ **SAP_RCF_INTERNAL_CANDIDATE (Internal Candidate)**
This role is only authorized to display and change its own data. It can only display the job postings that you have published via internal posting channels. It is not authorized to access data of requisitions, job postings, applications, and selection processes.

▶ **SAP_RCF_MANAGER (Manager)**
This role is required to enable access to E-Recruiting from the *Manager Self-Service* portal.
The manager wants to fill the vacant positions. For this purpose, it creates requisitions in the processing status, which are then processed by recruiters. When accessing candidates and requisitions, this role can only display data for which it's responsible. The role also contains the authorization to answer queries on candidates that are assigned to the respective requisitions.

▶ **SAP_RCF_MANAGER_ASSISTANT (Manager's Assistant)**
This role is only used in the career portal and no longer in the SAP E-Recruiting standard.

▶ **SAP_RCF_RECRUITER (Recruiter)**
This role provides access to all candidate data from the talent pool, all publications, all requisition data, all application data, and all selection process data. This role contains the authorization to make minimum data entries for incoming paper applications.

▶ **SAP_RCF_REQUISITION_REQUESTER (Requester)**
This role creates requisitions and forwards them to a recruiter in the processing status. The recruiter then completes the requisition, creates the job posting, and releases both.

▶ **SAP_RCF_RESTRICTED_RECRUITER (Restricted Recruiter)**
This role is not authorized to release requisitions.

▶ **SAP_RCF_REST_SUCCESSION-
PLANNER (Restricted Succession Planner)**
This role is not authorized to release requisitions.

- ▶ **SAP_RCF_SUCCESSION_PLANNER (Succession Planner)**
  This role provides access to all candidates from the talent pool, all requisitions of the succession planning area, and all candidacies regarding succession planning. Applications, job postings, and publications are not required here.

- ▶ **SAP_RCF_TALENT_CONSULTANT (Talent Consultant)**
  This role is only used in the career portal and no longer in the SAP E-Recruiting standard.

- ▶ **SAP_RCF_UNREGISTERED_CANDIDATE**
  (Unregistered Candidate – Service User)
  This is important for logons without registration in order to display publications

Front end and back end run on different systems

If you use a separated system (front end and back end run on different systems) and user interfaces with Web Dynpro for ABAP, the following roles are added:

- ▶ **SAP_RCF_EXT_CANDIDATE_CLIENT**
  Front-end authorizations for external candidates

- ▶ **SAP_RCF_EXT_CANDIDATE_SERVER**
  Back-end authorizations for external candidates

- ▶ **SAP_RCF_INT_CANDIDATE_CLIENT**
  Front-end authorizations for internal candidates

- ▶ **SAP_RCF_INT_CANDIDATE_SERVER**
  Back-end authorizations for internal candidates

- ▶ **SAP_RCF_UNREG_CANDIDATE_CLIENT**
  Front-end authorizations for unregistered candidates

- ▶ **SAP_RCF_UNREG_CANDIDATE_SERVER**
  Back-end authorizations for unregistered candidates

5.5.2 Authorization Objects

Before we describe the authorization objects for E-Recruiting in detail, we want to help you understand the central structures of E-Recruiting as the basis for the authorizations. To do this, we'll provide preliminary information on the data model. For persons, the candidate is the central E-Recruiting object type (Object Type NA). The following object types and the respective relationships are always created when a candidate is created:

Data model

▶ CP (Central Person)

▶ BP (Business Partner)

▶ US (User)

The business partner not only represents an object in the SAP HCM system, it's also stored in the SAP business partner component.

Business partners

In E-Recruiting, the SAP business partner is used for personal data of all persons involved (candidates, employees, for example) and for the addresses of the individual branches of your enterprise. You can find the corresponding settings in IMG under SAP E-RECRUITING • TECHNICAL SETTINGS • SET SYSTEM PARAMETERS for the following entries:

▶ **CPERS PROLE**
  Defines the role that is assigned to an SAP business partner that the system uses as an employee.

▶ **RECFA BRARO**
  Defines the role that is assigned to an SAP business partner that the system uses as a branch.

▶ **RECFA AGYRO**
  Defines the role that is assigned to an SAP business partner that the system uses as an agency.

SAP recommends not to change these entries.

Figure 5.9 provides an overview of the entire E-Recruiting data model, including its object types, relationships, and additional infotypes.

Overview of the data model

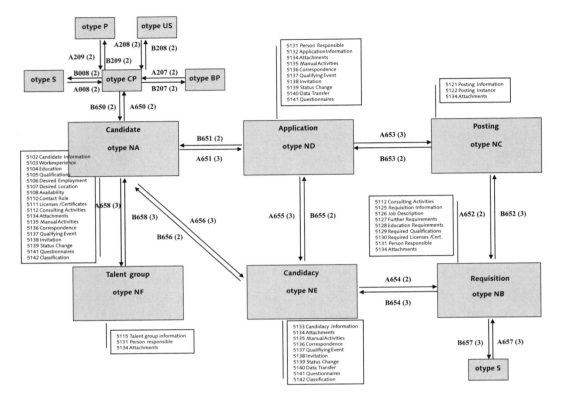

Figure 5.9 E-Recruiting Data Model

The following sections will explain the E-Recruiting authorizations using the administrator role as an example, because it represents the most comprehensive role. Figures 5.10 and 5.11 illustrate the most important values of this SAP role.

Figure 5.10 shows the authorizations of the administrator role outside the SAP HCM system:

- **B_BUPA_ATT (Business Partner: Authorization Types)**
  This authorization object is optional and only necessary for specific requirements.

- **B_BUPA_FDG (Business Partner: Field Groups) and B_BUPA_GRP (Business Partners: Authorization Groups)**
  These two authorization objects are optional and are only used when you maintain field groups or authorization groups.

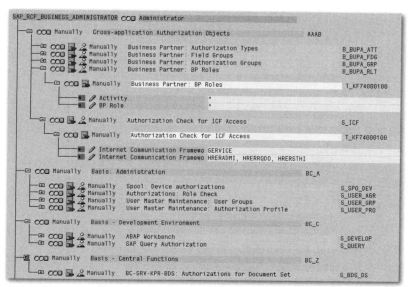

```
SAP_RCF_BUSINESS_ADMINISTRATOR OOO Administrator
  └─⊡ OOO Manually   Cross-application Authorization Objects                    AAAB
     ├─⊡ OOO ⬛🔑 Manually   Business Partner: Authorization Types              B_BUPA_ATT
     ├─⊡ OOO ⬛🔑 Manually   Business Partner: Field Groups                     B_BUPA_FDG
     ├─⊡ OOO ⬛🔑 Manually   Business Partner: Authorization Groups             B_BUPA_GRP
     └─⊡ OOO ⬛🔑 Manually   Business Partner: BP Roles                         B_BUPA_RLT
        └─⊡ OOO ⬛ Manually   Business Partner: BP Roles                       T_KF74000100
           ├─⬛ 🖊 Activity                                      :
           └─⬛ 🖊 BP Role                                       :
     └─⊡ OOO ⬛🔑 Manually   Authorization Check for ICF Access                 S_ICF
        └─⊡ OOO ⬛ Manually   Authorization Check for ICF Access             T_KF74000100
           ├─⬛ 🖊 Internet Communication Framewo SERVICE
           └─⬛ 🖊 Internet Communication Framewo HRERADMI, HRERRQDO, HRERSTHI
  └─⊡ OOO Manually   Basis: Administration                                      BC_A
     ├─⊡ OOO ⬛🔑 Manually   Spool: Device authorizations                      S_SPO_DEV
     ├─⊡ OOO ⬛🔑 Manually   Authorizations: Role Check                        S_USER_AGR
     ├─⊡ OOO ⬛🔑 Manually   User Master Maintenance: User Groups              S_USER_GRP
     └─⊡ OOO ⬛🔑 Manually   User Master Maintenance: Authorization Profile    S_USER_PRO
  └─⊡ OOO Manually   Basis - Development Environment                            BC_C
     ├─⊡ OOO ⬛🔑 Manually   ABAP Workbench                                    S_DEVELOP
     └─⊡ OOO ⬛🔑 Manually   SAP Query Authorization                           S_QUERY
  └─⊡ OOO Manually   Basis - Central Functions                                  BC_Z
     └─⊡ OOO ⬛🔑 Manually   BC-SRV-KPR-BDS: Authorizations for Document Set   S_BDS_DS
```

Figure 5.10 Administrator Role in E-Recruiting: System Authorizations

▶ **B_BUPA_RLT (Business Partner: BP Roles)**
This authorization object is mandatory for accessing business partners. TR0640 (Applicant), BUP003 (Employee), and BUP004 (Organizational Unit) are business partner roles that are interesting for
E-Recruiting.

▶ **S_ICF (Authorization Check For Internet Communication Framework Access**
This object enables you to use services (see entry in the first field) in
the Internet Communication Framework. Transaction SICF (Maintain
Services) provides more information on this. Please refer also to SAP
Note 1017866 (Consulting note: Candidate scenarios using Web Dynpro ABAP).

▶ **Basis Administration and Basis Development Environment**
The spooler authorization and the authorizations for the authorization management are not E-Recruiting-specific. They may belong
to any administrator role. The same applies to display access in the
workbench and query access.

▶ **S_BDS_DS (BC-SRV-KPR-BDS: Authorizations for Document Set)**
This authorization object is particularly critical for E-Recruiting,

because it is required to use the E-Recruiting search engine. The S_BDS_D (BC-SRV-KPR-BDS: Authorizations for Accessing Documents) object is to be added to the object in the role.

▶ **Other RFC authorizations**
The two RFC authorizations, S_RFC (Authorization Check for RFC Access) and S_RFCACL (Authorization Check for RFC User (e.g., Trusted System)), are additional system authorizations that are essential for E-Recruiting but are not included in this role. Please refer to SAP Note 1017866 (Consultating note: Candidate scenarios using Web Dynpro ABAP).

SAP HCM authorizations   In E-Recruiting, the HR authorizations (see Figure 5.11) are the following:

▶ **PLOG (Personnel Planning)**
As the E-Recruiting data is also stored in the HRP* tables, the PLOG (Personnel Planning) authorization object is of particular importance. You only require the object types listed in Table 5.1:

BP	Business partner
C	Job
CP	Central person
N*	E-Recruiting object types
O	Organizational unit
P	Person
Q	Qualification
QK	Qualification group
S	Position
US	User
VA	Appraisal template
VB	Criteria group
VC	Criterion

Table 5.1 Object Types Required for E-Recruiting

You need Infotypes 1000, 1001, 50* for performance management and 51* for E-Recruiting.

The subtypes relevant for Infotype 1001 are 0605 – 0607 for performance management as well as 0207 – 0209, 0291, and 0650 – 0657 for E-Recruiting.

The structural authorization must also be considered. For Object Types C, O, P, Q, and QK, hierarchical structural authorizations (including evaluation path or function module) are required and useful. Structural authorizations are not necessary for Object Types N*. All other object types are assigned with general authorizations.

▶ **P_HAP_DOC (Appraisal Systems: Appraisal)**
As parts of performance management are used in E-Recruiting (for example, queries on appraising candidates), the P_HAP_DOC (Appraisal Systems: Appraisal) authorization object is required. For more information, refer to Section 5.11, Performance Management.

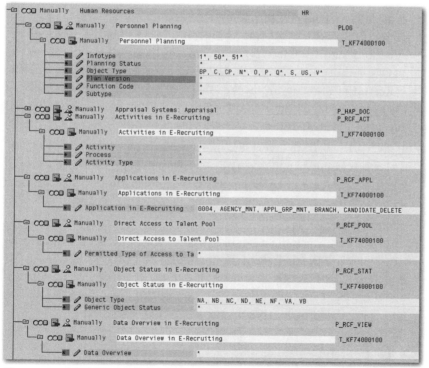

Figure 5.11 Administrator Role in E-Recruiting: Human Resources Authorizations

▶ **P_RCF_ACT (Activities in E-Recruiting)**
This authorization object checks the activities, such as add, change, delete, for specific processes (e.g., Preselection or Candidate appraisal) and activity types (e.g., Inform manager or Letter: Offer on hold).

▶ **P_RCF_APPL (Applications in E-Recruiting)**
This object checks the access to E-Recruiting applications (for example, Delete external candidates or Release of Profile) and the BSP application of E-Recruiting Web pages.

▶ **P_RCF_POOL (Direct Access to Talent Pool)**
This authorization object controls the permitted types of direct access to candidates in the talent pool for a user. Such a type may be, for example, the recognition check for candidates that are already stored in the talent warehouse in the context of the manual applicant entry. Only the Permitted Type of Access to Talent Pool field is checked.

▶ **P_RCF_STAT (Object Status in E-Recruiting)**
Here, the access to E-Recruiting objects is checked based on the object type and status. Object types include only the object types of the PLOG authorization object here. Via Generic Object Status, specific E-Recruiting statuses are checked that don't correspond to the statuses checked in PLOG, for example, the requisition status for restricted recruiters.

▶ **P_RCF_VIEW (Data Overview in E-Recruiting)**
This object defines which data overviews a user can access, for example, the overview of equal employment information or the overview of publications.

▶ **P_RCF_WL (Access to Worklists)**
If you want to use the analytical dashboard in an E-Recruiting role, you must add the SAP HCM authorization object, P_RCF_WL (Access to Worklists). This object controls the to-do lists that can be called in the dashboard using only the Identifier of Work List field. For example, these could be MNWENA (new external candidates).

5.5.3 User Types

In addition to the roles for "normal" users, you must also maintain some specific roles in E-Recruiting.

The reference user concept serves generally to simplify the authorization maintenance. First, you define a user as the reference user (Figure 5.12). Then, you assign a different user to the reference user. This user inherits all attributes of the reference user.

Reference user

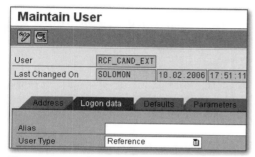

Figure 5.12   Defining a Reference User in SU01

E-Recruiting uses this concept for the external candidates. As soon as the candidates register, a user is assigned to them in the background. This user is then linked to the reference user.

In the Customizing (SAP E-RECRUITING • TECHNICAL SETTINGS • USER ADMINISTRATION • ROLES IN E-RECRUITING • DEFINE ROLES IN E-RECRUITING), you define which reference user is assigned to the user of an external candidate during the registration (Figure 5.13).

Change View "Roles in E-Recruiting": Overview

Role	Name	Reference User
1	Candidate (internal)	RCF_CAND_INT
2	Manager	RCF_MANAGER
3	Talent Consultant	RCF_TC
4	Assistant Manager	RCF_MGRASS
5	Candidate (external)	RCF_CAND_EXT

Figure 5.13   Assigning the Reference Role to External Candidates

When accessing documents of the document area, you require a technical user for a communication with the SAP NetWeaver Application Server, that is, a communication user. You assign it to the CONTENTSERVER

Communication user

service via the IMG activity, SAP E-RECRUITING • TECHNICAL SETTINGS • SEARCH ENGINE • SET UP ACCESS TO DOCUMENTS.

Service user
Some scenarios can only be accessed by registered users, and some can also be accessed by non-registered users (for example, registration, job postings). You must assign a service user to these services so that non-registered users can use the services. This can be done in the IMG under SAP E-RECRUITING • TECHNICAL SETTINGS • SAP WEB APPLICATION SERVER • DETERMINE E-RECRUITING SERVICES.

Background user for workflow
The WF-BATCH system user must be created in the standard version in order to use the workflow functions. In E-Recruiting, you must also assign a candidate to this user.

Create a candidate for the WF-BATCH user. For this purpose, use the RCF_CREATE_USER report. This report also creates an email address. Maintain printer and authorization profiles, particularly the authorization for status changes to E-Recruiting objects (P_RCF_STAT).

More information are provided in the IMG under: SAP E-RECRUITING • TECHNICAL SETTINGS • WORKFLOW • Workflow in E-Recruiting.

5.6   SAP Expert Finder

SAP Expert Finder roles
The SAP Expert Finder is a web-based tool to search and find experts within an enterprise. The roles provided by SAP for this tool are the following:

- SAP_HR_PA_XF_ADMIN (HR Expert Finder: Administrator)
- SAP_HR_PA_XF_DESIGNER (HR Expert Finder: System Designer)
- SAP_HR_PA_XF_EXPERT (HR Expert Finder: Expert)
- SAP_HR_PA_XF_SERVICE_USER_DOC (HR Expert Finder: Service User for Accessing Search Engine)

The first two roles are provided for component supervisors and system administrators. The last of the roles mentioned is required for the service user, which is always used if the search engine service is called from anywhere.

The SAP_HR_PA_XF_EXPERT role is authorized to change the own data (profile and picture) and use the search engine. Figure 5.14 shows this role.

Descriptions for the role illustrated in Figure 5.14:

▶ **Basis Administration and Basis – Central Functions**
At this point, we only mention the system authorization objects, S_LDAP (Authorization to Access LDAP Directory), S_BDS_D (BC-SRV-KPR-BDS: Authorizations for Accessing Documents), and S_BDS_DS (BC-SRV-KPR-BDS: Authorizations for Document Set), without further explanations.

▶ **PLOG (Personal Planning)**
PLOG differentiates between display and maintenance authorizations. Object Types XG (Expert group) and XP (Expert) as well as Infotypes 5030 (Expert basic data), 5031 (Profile type, Search scenarios), and 5032 (qualification export EF) are new here.

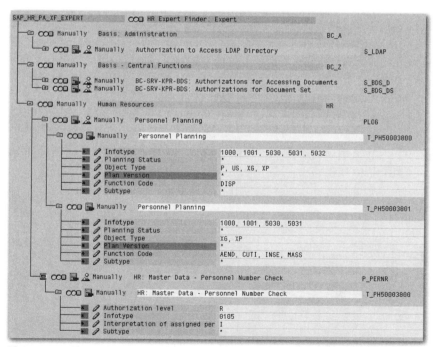

Figure 5.14 The "HR Expert Finder: Expert" Authorization Role

When you use the qualification exports from the qualification catalog (Infotype 5032) in the SAP Expert Finder, Object Types Q and QK are to be added.

The object types, including XG and XP, don't have to be authorized structurally.

- ▶ **P_PERNR (HR: Master Data – Personnel Number Check)**
  Here, the P_PERNR authorization object checks the master data and permits read access to Infotype 0105 (Communication) in order to convert the SAP user into a personnel number.

5.7 HR Administrative Services

The HR Admin (HR Administrative Services) role is part of the SAP NetWeaver Portal. Based on forms, it enables you to maintain personnel master data from any infotype and to store workflows for forms or individual fields.

Unfortunately, this book cannot discuss the required system authorizations in detail. From the SAP HCM viewpoint, you initially need all authorizations that are required in the transactions for the maintenance of infotypes in order to use HR Admin. These are mainly the authorization objects for master data described in Section 5.12, Personnel Administration and Time Management. However, in individual cases, authorizations for objects of the organizational management and qualification catalog may be added if you maintain transfers or qualifications using the HR Admin role.

Specific authorizations for HR Admin

Every *HR Admin* user requires additional accesses in the P_ASRCONT (Authorization for Process Content) object. Figure 5.15 shows an example.

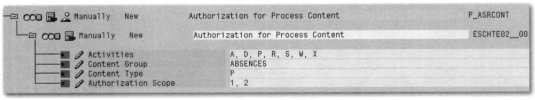

Figure 5.15 Sample Authorization for Process Content

The following fields are checked in the P_ASRCONT authorization object (see Figure 5.15):

▶ **Activities**
Allowed actions, such as read, approve form (Table T5ASRACTIVITY)

▶ **Content Type**
Allowed content types, such as attachment, form, and so on (Table T5ASRCONTENTTYPE)

▶ **Content Group**
Permitted content groups (process group for processes, form groups for forms)

▶ **Authorization Scope**
Authorization for the own objects/authorization for all objects except the own objects

You can restrict the effect of the authorizations described in the Customizing of HR Admin via the IMG path, PERSONNEL ADMINISTRATION • HR ADMINISTRATIVE SERVICES • AUTHORIZATIONS • DEFINE AUTHORIZATION METHODS FOR ACTIVITIES. You can use this path to control the authorization check for each activity and if required for each process group as follows (Figure 5.16):

▶ Only P_ASRCONT is checked.

▶ Only application-specific checks are carried out (P_ORGIN etc.).

▶ Both is checked.

Appl. Type	Personnel

Personnel Administration

Methods of Authorization Check for Activities

Activiti	Method
A	Only Application-Specific Checks
D	Only Application-Specific Checks
P	Only Application-Specific Checks
R	Application and Content-Specific
S	Application and Content-Specific
W	Application and Content-Specific
X	Only Application-Specific Checks

Figure 5.16 Customizing the HR Admin Authorization Check

[+]

Tip

Even if you only use the P_ASRCONT authorization object for checks, the users require a minimum authorization for the Person object type. This means that the user roles must contain an active HR authorization object.

Options for enhancement

Finally, you can program customized authorization checks using a business add-in (see in the IMG under PERSONNEL MANAGEMENT • HR ADMINISTRATIVE SERVICES • AUTHORIZATIONS• CONTENT GROUPS FOR AUTHORIZATION CHECK • BADI: IMPLEMENT OWN LOGIC FOR GROUPS FOR AUTHORIZATION CHECK).

5.8 Management of Global Employees

Management of global employees enables you to maintain two or more employment contracts for the same person. In this context, "Employment contract" technically refers to the personnel number.

[Ex]

Example

An employee that is posted abroad can keep his or her personnel number and additionally receive a new personnel number to which the data of the global assignment is allocated. The new central personnel number links both numbers, and it applies to both employment contracts, that is, both personnel numbers of the employee.

As soon as you have activated the Management of Global Employees FUNCTION (CCURE GLEMP switch in Table T77S0), an object of the CP type (Central person) and Relationship 209 (Is filled by/Has employment contract) are automatically created when a new personnel number is created.

PLOG and structural authorization

With respect to authorizations, this leads to additional entries in the PLOG (Personnel Planning) object and a structural authorization for the CP object type.

Within personnel administration, numerous infotypes are added, which you can find via the IMG path PERSONNEL MANAGEMENT • MANAGEMENT OF GLOBAL EMPLOYEES.

PA infotypes

5.9 Manager's Desktop

The Manager's Desktop (MDT) is a global user interface for managers. It offers an entire range of transactions and reports. These are preconfigured so that the managers are only provided with exactly the persons, positions, organizational units, and so on they are responsible for.

The authorizations required for managers are different regarding the functions provided in the Customizing — from position maintenance to the evaluation of payroll results. Please refer to the respective sections of this chapter for more information.

Only one additional authorization object is checked specifically in the MDT: S_MWB_FCOD (Allowed Function Codes for Manager's Desktop). As the functions in the MDT are usually called directly via function modules and not via transactions, this authorization object serves to protect these calls. Managers can only use the function codes that are entered in Table T77MWBFCD. Figure 5.17 shows an example.

Allowed function codes

Figure 5.17 Allowed Function Codes in the MDT

To assign authorizations for transfers in the MDT beyond responsibility boundaries is not that easy. The transfer to a position outside authorizations must be possible, but should be allowed for this action only. For this purpose, SAP provides Workflow 01000014, whose relationship to the authorizations is described in SAP Note 551973 (WF 01000014 and Structural Authorization) in detail.

Authorizations for transfers

Example

In the standard Customizing, persons manager positions can only access the MDT for their own department. In real life, substitutes or secretaries often require access to the MDT as well. You can integrate these persons by:

▶ Creating a specific relationship, Is Assistant For

▶ Copying the SAP_MANG evaluation path and integrating the new relationship type

▶ Assigning the evaluation path to the MDT scenario

▶ Linking the positions of the secretaries or substitutes to the organizational unit via the new relationship

5.10 Organizational Management (OM)

The SAP roles (SAP_HR_OS*) for OM provide useful tips for the structure of the menus but don't contain enough authorizations.

PLOG (Personnel Planning)

The PLOG (Personnel Planning) authorization object in connection with the structural authorization is sufficient for display and maintenance processes in the organizational management. The following object types are used:

▶ O (Organizational unit)

▶ S (Position)

and, depending on the usage,

▶ A (Work center)

▶ C (Job)

▶ T (Task)

There are numerous infotypes and subtypes; therefore, they are not listed individually. You can find the necessary information in the IMG via Personnel Administration • Organizational Management • Basic Settings • Data Model Enhancement.

Please refer back to Chapter 3, Structural Authorization Check, for more information on the structural authorization check, which is essential in OM.

Personal data

Object Type P and at least minimum read access in one of the authorization objects of personnel administration are added to display information on personal master data. As a minimum, Infotypes 0000, 0001, and 0002 are sufficient. In PPOME, for example, read access for Infotype 0024 (Qualifications) (including the rights for the respective relationship — see Section 5.15, Personnel Development) is also to be added to display the qualifications of a person.

> **Tip**
>
> Because the name is also displayed in its formatted form (i.e., usually in connection with the first name) in Infotype 0001 (Organizational assignment), you can neglect read access for Infotype 0002 (Personal data) in OM.

[+]

You only require write access to Infotype 0001 (Organizational assignment) in order to change Relationships P-S from OM. However, if you trigger an actual personnel action from PPOME (Organization and staffing change), the respective authorizations for this personnel action must be assigned when the batch-input sessions are processed after the RHINTE30 (Transfer org. assignment in batch input folder for Infotype 0001) report is completed.

Please note that maintenance transactions that use structures, for example, PPOME (Organization and staffing change), branch to other transactions for individual maintenance. PPOME branches to Transaction PP01 (Maintain object) or PA30 (Maintain personal master data — Figure 5.18), for example. If you want to allow for this, you must enter these transactions in the P_TCODE authorization object and, for PA30, also in S_TCODE. If there are only rights for PA20 in S_TCODE, PPOME navigates to Transaction PA20.

Transactions

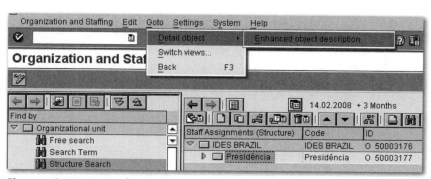

Figure 5.18 Navigating from PPOME to PP01 or PA20/PA30

[!]

> **Warning**
>
> If you work with an integration between OM and Personnel Administration, you should pay particular attention to carefully assign authorizations for HR administrators. Otherwise, vacancies, for example, may not be written due to missing authorizations. This leads to unnecessary research and maintenance work with regard to OM. For more information, refer to section 5.12 coming up shortly.

5.11 Performance Management

The SAP roles for performance management are according to the naming convention SAP_HR_HAP*. In this section, we'll explain the required authorizations for the most comprehensive role, SAP_HR_HAP_ADMINISTRATOR (Figure 5.19).

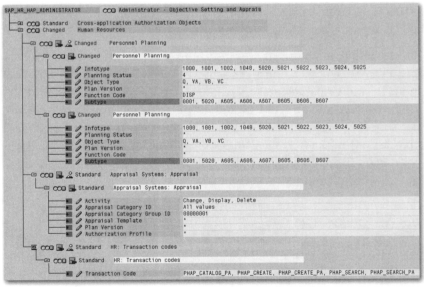

Figure 5.19 "Administrator Performance Management" SAP Role

The two most critical authorization objects for the administrator role and the overall performance management are PLOG (Personnel Planning) and P_HAP_DOC (Appraisal Systems: Appraisal).

In the PLOG authorization object (Personnel Planning) you always require Object Types VA (Appraisal Template), VB (Criteria Group), and VC (Criterion). If OM objects are appraised during an appraisal (frequently qualifications (Q), but also course types (D)), these object types need to be (read) authorized when the appraisal is created.

PLOG

As always for PLOG, they must have an additional structural authorization. Because no hierarchical structures exist here, only the individual object types are structurally authorized. For status-dependent template control, if, for example, a button is supposed to be visible only for a specific person/role, Object Type AC (Rule) is used. This must also be authorized in PLOG to enable access to the respective buttons.

Infotype 5026 (Status Switch) is not included in the infotypes.

The Subtypes 0001 (General description) and 5020 (Description in Web) relate to Infotype 1002. All others are relationships from Infotype 1001 between the object types of the appraisal.

The planning status in the performance management is either 3 (Submitted) or 4 (Approved).

Only the administrators require write access for the PLOG authorization object described here. For the appraisers and appraisees, read authorization is sufficient.

In the second, critical P_HAP_DOC authorization object (Appraisal Systems: Appraisal), you can permit templates that may be processed. In this authorization object, the access to persons is controlled via a structural profile (context dependency).

P_HAP_DOC

The following fields are checked (see Figure 5.19):

Fields of P_HAP_DOC

▶ **Activity**
Change/Display/Delete

▶ **Appraisal Category ID**
Technical key for the appraisal categories. The appraisal categories are created for the specific customers using Transaction PHAP_CATALOG_PA (Catalog for Appraisal Templates) and stored in Table T77HAP_C.

▶ **Appraisal Category Group ID**
ID of the appraisal category groups. For personnel appraisals, SAP has determined the ID 00000001.
If you want to use the performance management in other ways, you are provided with additional appraisal category groups (Figure 5.20).

▶ **Appraisal Template**
Used to maintain the customer-specific ID of the appraisal template in Transaction PHAP_CATALOG_PA (Catalog for Appraisal Templates). The template is an object of the VA type (see PLOG authorization object).

▶ **Plan Version**
Plan version for appraisals

▶ **Authorization profile**

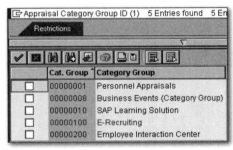

Figure 5.20 Appraisal Category Groups in the Performance Management

Context-dependent authorization

The *Authorization Profile* field is handled just like the analog fields in the other context-dependent authorization objects (see Chapter 4, Context-dependent Authorization Check). It includes a structural profile that must be assigned to the respective users in the OOSB user maintenance (provided that you don't use the BAdI described in Section 4.2, Setup and Maintenance).

In the SAP role (see Figure 5.19) no structural profile has been defined yet. If you use the BEURTEILER (APPRAISER) structural profile (displayed in Figure 5.21) this means that the owner of this authorization can process all persons whose manager he is. Moreover, he requires the display authorization for Object Types VA, VB, VC, and Q. The user can have multiple authorizations, also with different structural profiles. However, we recommend mapping the structural authorization in a profile and, if applicable, mapping extensions (for example, authorized to appraise all subordinate managers) in a separate function module.

Auth.profile	No.	Plan	Obj.Type	O	Maint.	Eval.path	S	Function module
BEURTEILER	5	01	0		☑	PERSON	1	RH_GET_MANAGER_ASSIGNMENT
BEURTEILER	10	01	VA		☐			
BEURTEILER	15	01	VB		☐			
BEURTEILER	20	01	VC		☐			
BEURTEILER	25	01	Q		☐			

Figure 5.21 Structural Profile for Appraiser

Preformance Management Without Context-dependent Authorization **[+]**

If you don't use the context-dependent authorization and if you assign a second (different) profile using Transaction OOSB to a manager for creating appraisals, the profiles add for other applications (e.g., Manager's Desktop).

As a prerequisite for using the Authorization Profile in P_HAP_DOC, you need to activate the HAP00/AUTHO switch in Table T77S0 (Figure 5.22).

Activation switch

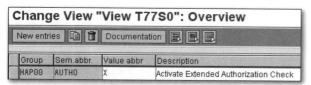

Group	Sem.abbr.	Value abbr	Description
HAP00	AUTHO	X	Activate Extended Authorization Check

Figure 5.22 Activating the Context-Dependent Check in P_HAP_DOC

Tip **[+]**

Category group and category are table entries not object types. Consequently, they are not checked via PLOG and structural authorization but exclusively using the P_HAP_DOC authorization object.

Additionally, the standard checks the read authorization for Infotype 0001 to display the template, the header, and the formatted name (ENAME).

Infotype authorizations

187

This authorization must be assigned by one of the P_ORGIN(CON) or P_PERNR authorization objects.

The system can display the name and other information from the organizational assignment in the template. This primarily refers to the appraisee, but also to the appraiser or roles participating in the process. You generally must assign the read access to all of these people.

Transaction assignment per processing role

In template customizing, you determine which processing roles may see and maintain which template fields at which stage of the appraisal process, and which status they may set in the appraisal process (Infotype 5023 (Column access)). In the HRHAP00_COL_ACCESS and HRHAP00_COL_OWNER BAdIs you can further refine the customizing.

The authorization for the appraisee must always be assigned, both for master data access and in P_HAP_DOC via the structural profile. In order to avoid that an authorization check is implemented for the appraiser when the appraisee accesses the template, in the template maintenance you can check the No Authorization Check For Appraiser flag in Infotype 5025 (Processing) (Figure 5.23).

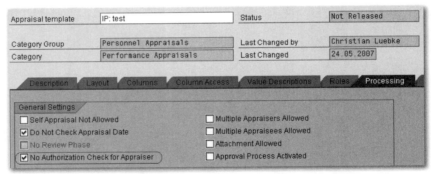

Figure 5.23 Deactivating the Authorization Check for Appraiser in the Template

Figure 5.24 gives an overview of the structure and function of the individual elements within the performance management.

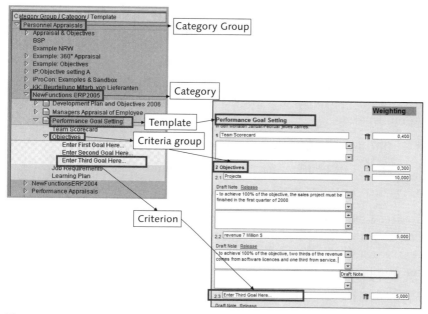

Figure 5.24 Data Model of the Performance Management

You have the option of using workflows in performance management (for control of who is permitted to carry out status changes, or for sending of notifications). In this case, you must be assigned with the corresponding workflow authorizations.

Workflow

In principle, the users of the performance management work in the portal, either via Employee Self Services or Manager Self Services. Regardless of whether you require it for authorizations, the Infotype 0105, Subtype 0001, must be maintained for the personnel number of each portal user. In the authorizations context, this entry is required for the P_PERN authorization object and the function module of the MANAGER structural profile.

Call via the portal

In the HRHAP00_AUTHORITY BAdI you can define customer-specific authorization checks for the performance management, and also deactivate the standard checks.

Extension of the authorization check

5.12 Personnel Administration and Time Management

The infotypes for Personnel Administration and Time Management are an integral part of the SAP HCM system. For this reason, we already discussed the authorizations objects required for their protection back in Chapter 2, section 2.3.2, Infotype Authorizations in Personnel Administration:

▸ P_ORGIN/P_ORGINCON (HR: master data)

▸ P_PERNR (HR: master data – personnel number check)

▸ P_ORGXX/P_ORGXXCON (HR: master data - extended check)

To access infotypes of the personnel administration, you usually need cluster authorizations for the PC (personal calendar) and TX (infotype texts) clusters. In this context, refer to Section 2.3.4, HR: Cluster – Cluster Authorization Object (P_PCLX).

Moreover, the structural authorization (see Chapter 3, Structural Authorization Check) and the test procedures of Infotype 0130 (see Section 2.7, Test Procedures (Infotype 0130)) play a significant role, if you use these tools.

Possible extensions of the authorization check of the personnel administration data can be:

▸ the customer-specific P_NNNNN or P_NNNNNCON authorization object developed by SAP (see Section 2.8.1, The Authorization Object P_NNNNN)

▸ the HRPAD00AUTH_CHECK BAdI (see Section 2.8.3, BAdI for General Authorization Checks)

OM relationships in Infotype 0001 · If the integration between administration and organizational management (OM) is activated, data of the OM are read in Infotype 0001 (Organizational assignment) by clicking the ORGANIZATIONAL STRUCTURE button. Changes in the POSITION field result in a relationship to OM.

Employees that work with Infotype 0001 require read and possibly write access in the PLOG authorization object (personnel planning) and, if applicable, structural authorizations. You can see the necessary minimum authorizations in Figure 5.25.

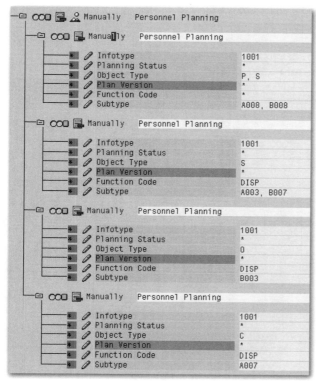

Figure 5.25 PLOG Authorizations for Infotype 0001

The first authorization in Figure 5.25 enables changing the *Position-Person* assignment. The others are required to read the organizational management by means of the Organizational Structure button.

When using the structural authorization check for the personnel administration, there are additional structural authorizations for the object types displayed in Figure 5.25. For the P and S object types the maintenance checkbox must be checked in the structural profile.

Another interface from Infotype 0001 (Organizational Assignment) to the organizational management is the OM Infotypes 1007 (Vacancy) and 1014 (Obsolete). For all changes, which refer to the relation between position and person, and provided that OM-PA is integrated, pop-ups are displayed that request the maintenance of the two OM infotypes within the administration (see Figure 5.26). This will only work correctly if the

Vacancies and flags obsolete

HR administrators have the write access for the Infotypes 1007 and 1014 in PLOG.

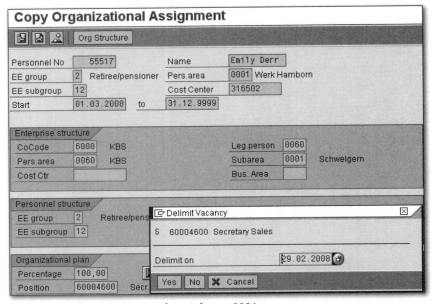

Figure 5.26 Writing Vacancies from Infotype 0001

The pop-up displayed in Figure 5.26 only appears if you activated the use of the Infotype *Vacancy* in OM. The corresponding IMG path is PERSONNEL MANAGEMENT • ORGANIZATIONAL MANAGEMENT • INFOTYPE SETTINGS • ACTIVATE/DEACTIVATE "VACANCY" INFOTYPE. However, you can't deactivate the pop-ups for the OBSOLETE (Infotype 1014 (Obsolete)) flag.

Structure search and object manager

At many points in personnel administration, you can use the structures of organizational management to systematically search for persons. For this purpose, we would like to mention the object manager and the structure search in the value help (F4). Administration users who want to use these options must be assigned with display access in the PLOG authorization object for Object Types O, S, and P, and with the corresponding read access in the structural authorization.

Special role of qualifications

Qualifications play a special role. If the integration between personnel administration and personnel development is activated, the qualifications of an employee are stored as relationships between the *Person* and *Qualification* object types. The IMG path is as follows: PERSONNEL MANAGEMENT • PERSONNEL DEVELOPMENT • INTEGRATION • SET UP INTEGRATION WITH PERSONNEL ADMIN. AND RECRUITMENT. For further information on the authorizations required here, refer to Section 5.15, Personnel Development.

Whereas the task distribution in personnel administration is usually very enterprise-specific and the SAP standard roles are useful only to a minor extent, the time management processes are often comparable. Therefore, it is worth taking a look at the SAP roles delivered for the SAP_HR_PT_TIME* namespace:

> SAP roles for time management

▶ The SAP_HR_PT_TIME-ADMINISTRATOR (time administrator) role comprises authorizations for the time data maintenance in TMW and PA transactions, and for CATS and incentive wages including the associated reporting.

▶ The SAP_HR_PT_TIME-LABOR-ANALYST (time and labor analyst) role shows the minimum of infotypes required for displaying the time data (Figure 5.27).

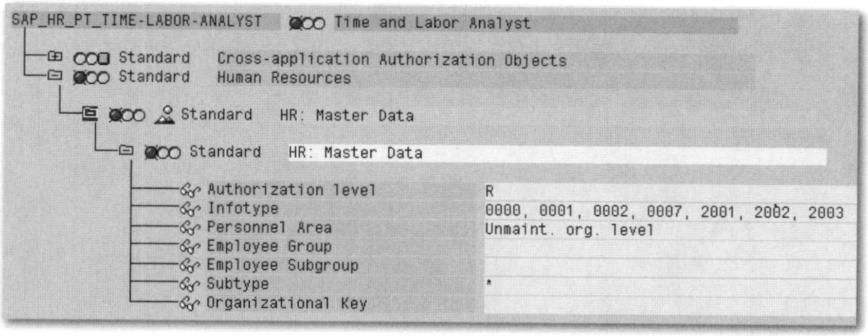

```
SAP_HR_PT_TIME-LABOR-ANALYST    ⊗CO Time and Labor Analyst

 ┌─⊞ CCⓄ Standard    Cross-application Authorization Objects
 └─⊟ ⊗CO Standard    Human Resources

    └─⊟ ⊗CO ⚇ Standard    HR: Master Data

       └─⊟ ⊗CO Standard    HR: Master Data

          ├──⅋ Authorization level        R
          ├──⅋ Infotype                   0000, 0001, 0002, 0007, 2001, 2002, 2003
          ├──⅋ Personnel Area             Unmaint. org. level
          ├──⅋ Employee Group
          ├──⅋ Employee Subgroup
          ├──⅋ Subtype                    *
          └──⅋ Organizational Key
```

Figure 5.27 SAP Role "Time and Labor Analyst"

Because time management is often maintained decentrally, the authorization concepts provided for this purpose play a significant role:

> Authorization concepts

▶ The structural authorization check (see Chapter 3, Structural Authorization Check)

▶ The organizational key field in the P_ORGIN and P_ORGINCON authorization objects (see Section 2.3.2, Infotype Authorizations in Personnel Administration)

▶ The administrator field in the P_ORGXX and P_ORGXXCON authorization objects (see Section 2.3.3, Additional Authorization Objects for Master and Time Data)

5.13   Recruitment (Classic)

The "classic" recruitment has been superseded by the new components *e-recruiting* (see Section 5.5, E-Recruiting). However, it is still in use and is subject to maintenance.

SAP provides two roles for the *recruitment* component: SAP_HR_RC_HR-MANAGER (HR manager recruitment) and SAP_HR_RC_RECRUITER (recruiter). We will use the latter as a template (Figure 5.28).

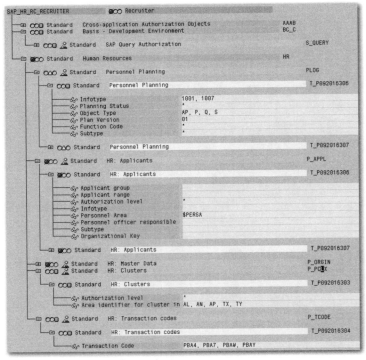

Figure 5.28 SAP Role for Applicant Management

The authorizations assigned in PLOG assume that the recruiter is permitted to work with internal persons (Object Type P). You can enter more detailed specifications in Object P_ORGIN or in any other authorization objects used for master data authorizations.

PLOG

In addition, the authorization to access the qualifications for using the applicant management is assigned here. A prerequisite is the integration of the qualifications in the personnel administration and recruitment (in IMG, see PERSONNEL MANAGEMENT • PERSONNEL DEVELOPMENT • INTEGRATION • SET UP INTEGRATION WITH PERSONNEL ADMIN. AND RECRUITMENT).

For the authorizations for the PLOG object shown in Figure 5.28, the INFOTYPE field, which already contains the Infotypes 1001 (Relationships) and 1007 (Vacancy), is to be supplemented with the Infotype 1000 (Object).

The Object P_APPL (HR: Applicant) is the only object that checks the access to tables of the "classic" applicant data administration, in the technical sense, the tables with the PB prefix.

P_APPL object

The following fields are checked:

▶ INFOTYPE of the applicant data administration

▶ SUBTYPE of the corresponding infotype

▶ AUTHORIZATION LEVEL, corresponds to the authorization levels of the HR: Master Data object described in Chapter 2, General Authorization Check

▶ PERSONNEL AREA, here and in the three fields below the Organizational Assignment infotype of the applicant data administration is checked.

▶ APPLICANT GROUP

▶ APPLICANT RANGE

▶ ORGANIZATIONAL KEY

▶ PERSONNEL OFFICER RESPONSIBLE as stipulated in Customizing of the applicant data administration

Clusters of the SAP role

The clusters of the SAP role mean:

- ▸ AL (Letters for applicant activities)
- ▸ AN (Note pad for applicant activities)
- ▸ AP (Applicant activities (replaced by Infotype 4003))
- ▸ TY (Infotype texts)

The clusters LB (long-term documents) and SB (short-term documents) may also be included, if the user is supposed to evaluate the change documents of the applicant data administration.

Transaction codes

The entries in the P_TCODE authorization object (HR transaction code) are proposed reliably by the Profile Generator in compliance with your entries in the menu.

Structural authorization

You can initiate the structural authorization check in the "classic" applicant data administration by activating the PPVAC STRAU switch in Table T77S0.

A structural authorization check in recruitment is useful if the applicants are assigned to a vacant position. Because the positions belong to the organizational structure, you can, for example, ensure that managers can only view applicant data assigned to positions of their respective department. Structural profiles are implemented by means of evaluation paths that comprise Relationship 048 (Application by) and Object Type AP (Applicant). Figure 5.29 shows an example. Additional useful evaluation paths would be O-AP and O-VS-PAP.

Evaluation Path	O-S-AP	Applicants along organizational structure			
No.	Obj.Type	A/B	Relat'ship	Relationship name	Priority	Rel.obj.type
10	O	B	003	Incorporates	*	S
20	S	A	048	Application by	*	AP
30	O	B	002	Is line supervisor of	*	O

Figure 5.29 Evaluation Path for the "Recruitment" Structural Profile

Unsolicited applications

How do you handle applications that can't be assigned to a vacancy initially, for example, unsolicited applications? You have two options here:

You either define a structural profile with which you can process all applicants by permitting Object Type AP without any limitations. Applications without vacancy assignment would then be maintained only by those users.

Or you program a function module for the structural profiles that provides all applicants not related to a vacancy. This function module must read all available applicants, for example, by means of Table PB0001. Then, all applicants related to a vacancy are removed. The remaining applicants are transferred as a table of non-related applicants. You can see an example of a structural profile in Figure 5.30.

New Entries: Overview of Added Entries

Dialog Structure	Auth.profile	No.	Plan Vers.	Obj.Type	O	Maint.	Eval.path	Function module
▽ ☐ Authorization profiles	AP_WITHOUT_V	5	01	AP		☑		Z_GET_BEWERBER_OHNE
☐ Authorization profile

Figure 5.30 Profile for Applicants Without Vacancy Assignment

> **Problems with the Structural Authorization for the Initial Recording of Applicants** **[!]**
>
> Problems occur in all structural profiles during the initial recording of applicant data. Here, the standard unfortunately checks the structural authorizations at a point in time when the applicant number is not yet known. This means that there is neither a record in the applicant database nor a vacancy relationship. As a result, the authorization check always fails and saving the applicant data is rejected.

There are two solutions to bypass this problematic system behavior:

The initial recording is implemented by users without a restricted structural profile (only AP without evaluation path). As soon as the data is stored, all described structural profiles can be used. **Organizational solution**

Or you extend the function module for applicants not related to a vacancy, which we've just described, by one routine that determines available applicant numbers and transfers them to the table of the authorized objects. **Technical solution**

The programming is as follows: Prior to removing the applicants that are already assigned to a vacancy, you need to import the Table NRIV (Number ranges) for the Object RP_PAPL (Number ranges applicant number) from the NUMAP characteristic using the number range key (NRRANGENR field). (An example code for importing the characteristic can be found in Program MP400040.) In Table NRIV you can then query the current numbers (Field NRLEVEL). Because the applicant data administration always reserves a block of five numbers, you should supplement the *Applicants* internal table with five numbers before the current number and five numbers after the current number. This ensures that the number assigned to the applicant by the system is available in the table of authorized objects.

5.14 Shift Planning

In shift planning, we can use the SAP_HR_PT_SHIFT-PLANNER SAP standard role, which is a very useful template.

[!]

> **Warning**
>
> However, the menu does not comprise the transactions for requirement maintenance. If the shift planners also maintain the requirements, you need to add this function.

Object types in shift planning

The role entries for the PLOG authorization object (Personnel planning) contain all standard object types that are possible for personnel planning (Figure 5.31).

Infotypes and subtypes in PLOG

If required, you can add the Infotypes 1027 (Site-Dependent Info) and 1222 (General Attribute Maint.) provided that they are managed decentrally.

If the shift planners also have access to the transactions of the organizational management, the number of proposed authorizations is far too high. In SAP Note 496993 (Authorization objects of shift planning) you can obtain detailed information about the object types and infotypes and their respective use. This note also include a list of the relationships used in shift planning.

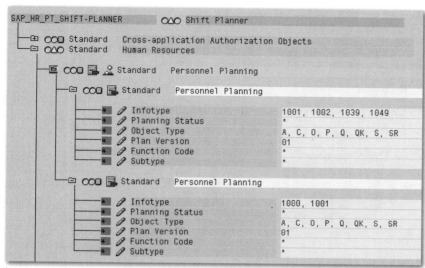

Figure 5.31 PLOG Authorizations for Shift Planners

You can set up the structural authorizations for the object types displayed in Figure 5.31 parallel to the authorizations in the Object PLOG. If you assign structural authorizations to persons, you must pay special attention to the temporary assignment. For this purpose, the shift planner only requires a read authorization for the area he is temporarily assigned to. Writing the assignment is done in the program without any authorization check. For the temporary assignment, the PLOGI ADAYS switch in Table T77S0 (see Section 3.4, Period of Responsibility and Time Logic) defines how long the shift planner can access the persons assigned to him beyond the temporary assignment period.

Structural authorization

For the infotype authorizations in the shift planning, you use the same object(s) as in personnel administration and time management. In shift planning, you require read access for a range of master data (minimum: 0000, 0001, 0002, and 0007) and write access for most of the infotypes in time management.

Master data authorization

In the P_PCLX authorization object (HR: Cluster), the first entry of the standard role comprises (more than) all maximum required clusters (Figure 5.32).

Cluster authorization

The clusters abbreviations stand for:

- B1 (PDC Data)
- B2 (Time evaluation results)
- PC (Abbreviation of attendances/absences)
- PS (Payroll schema) (not required in shift planning)
- PT (Time evaluation schema)
- TX (Infotype texts)

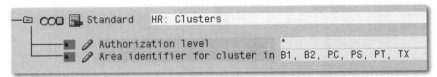

Figure 5.32 Clusters in Shift Planning

Special transaction authorizations

The P_TCODE (HR: Transaction Code) object is also correctly maintained in the standard role. Additions of transactions to the menu are copied to this object as required by means of the Profile Generator.

[+]

Shift Planning Authorization for Time Management Transaction PA61

Transaction PA61 (Maintain Time Data) plays a significant role in shift planning. It is used in the background for writing time data via a CALL TRANSACTION. It is only difficult if your shift planner is not supposed to receive the authorization for Transaction PA61 (Maintain Time Data) in the time management.

In older releases (up to at least R/3 4.6c) this problem was solved by entering Transaction PA61 in P_TCODE, but not in S_TCODE. As of ECC 6.0, this is no longer possible. The entry in the P_TCODE authorization object has no impact any longer. Now, Transaction SE97 (Maintain Transaction Call Authorization in CALL TRANSACTION) decides whether the called Transaction PA61 is to be checked from the calling Transaction PP61 (Shift Plan: Entry Screen).

Currently, the tables belonging to Transaction SE97 are set in such a way that Transaction PA61 is not checked when called from shift planning (Transaction PP61). SAP, however, reserves the right to change this in future releases. Where applicable, you then need to change the check indicator in Transaction SE97.

Extended authorization check switch

The PEINS AUTH switch in Table T77S0 enables you to deactivate the following system behavior in the shift plan (Transaction PP61): Upon entering the change mode it is checked whether the maintenance authorizations are available for the affected objects:

- of the organizational management, for instance, the organizational unit and the requirement.

- of the time management infotypes (here which time infotypes are permitted in the shift group is checked precisely).

Only when all these maintenance authorizations are available, can you enter the target plan. SAP Note 492112 (Authorization check during the call of shift planning) describes in detail which infotype and subtype authorizations are checked upon startup provided that you haven't deactivated the switch mentioned earlier. If you deactivated this switch the checks are implemented when changes for the target plan are stored.

Locked records are generally not imported in shift planning. Persons, however, for whose time data the planner has authorization for locked write access (authorization level = E or S), are available in the shift plan.

Authorizations for locked write access

To conclude this section on shift planning, let's briefly discuss the authorization object that enables the maintenance of user-independent sorting variants. A prerequisite here is the use of the *Sort Employees in Shift Plan* functionality taken from the public sector. In the P_PEPSVAR authorization object (Shift planning: user-independent sorting variants) you assign the right to maintain sorting variants that is available to all users.

User-independent sorting variants

5.15 Personnel Development

In the personnel development area, we focus on the SAP standard role SAP_HR_PD_DEVELOPMANAGER (personnel development manager). Because the Profile Generator in PLOG has overdone his work like in so many other cases, we've copied the SAP role to a separate role. We've also changed it slightly for better comprehension so that you can use the authorizations displayed in Figure 5.33 as a template. The SAP role provides you with very good proposals for the required menu.

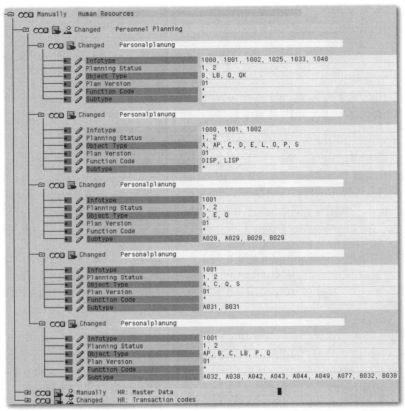

Figure 5.33 Corrected PLOG entries of SAP Role "Personnel Development Manager" (SAP_HR_PD_DEVELOPMANAGER)

Personnel planning (PLOG) The first authorization in PLOG assumes that the personnel development manager is allowed to fully maintain all infotypes of Object Types B (Development plan), LB (Career), Q (Qualification), and QK (Qualification group), including their relationships, for instance, for the qualifications catalog. You can store associated restrictions in the structural authorization.

This is followed by the display authorization for other object types whose maintenance — according to our assumption — is not the task of the personnel development manager.

The next three authorizations in the PLOG object in Figure 5.33 focus on the maintenance of relationships, namely:

- ▶ the link of the business event catalog to the qualifications including Relationships 028 (Imparts) and 029 (Has prerequisite)
- ▶ to Relationship 031 (Requires) with sample object types
- ▶ to Relationships
  - ▶ 032 (Fulfills) for AP (Applicant) and P (Person) to Q
  - ▶ 038 (Has potential for), in this example for P to C (Position) and Q
  - ▶ 042 (Interests and preferences) like 038
  - ▶ 043 (Dislikes) like 038
  - ▶ 044 (Consists of), in this example for B to C and Q
  - ▶ 049 (Is developed by), in this example for P to C and Q
  - ▶ 077 (Passes through), in this example for P to B and LB

You also need an additional structural authorization check for all object types mentioned here. You can restrict this check to parts of the business event or qualification catalog as required.

Structural authorization

In the structural profiles you need to assign maintaining access to Object Types P and Q for the relationship from P to Q (assignment of qualifications to a person).

Figure 5.34 shows an example that enables the write access to the qualification catalog restricted to a subcatalog (and read access for the remaining parts). The authorizations for development plans and careers are not restricted here. Moreover, the access to persons is restricted to a specific part of the organizational structure. So if a user wants to assign qualifications to the persons managed by him for which he only has read authorization, this is not possible. But if you use the HRBAS00_STRUAUTH BAdI you can bypass this problem. More information can be found in Section 3.10, Extensions.

Auth.profile	No.	Plan Vers.	Obj.Type	Object I	Maint.	Eval.path	Status vec
PE	5	01	B		☑		
PE	10	01	LB		☑		
PE	15	01	QK	50023467	☑	QUALCATA	12
PE	16	01	QK	50001000	☐	QUALCATA	12
PE	20	01	O	51000032	☑	PERSON	12

Figure 5.34 Structural Profile for the Personnel Development Manager

Recruitment | You require the P_APPL authorization object (HR: Applicant) if you:

1. work with the "classic" applicant data administration

2. this is integrated in personnel development

If your personnel development managers are supposed to integrate applicant qualifications and their evaluations, they require read access to the applicant Infotypes 0001 (Organizational assignment), 0002 (Personal data), and 4000 (Applicant actions).

When using E-Recruiting, the work of the personnel development manager (gradually) shifts to this application, including its "new" career and succession planning. For information on the authorizations in this subcomponent, refer back to Section 5.5, E-Recruiting.

Master data authorization | A minimum characteristic of any object in the personnel administration using read access to the Infotypes 0000, 0001, and 0002 is mandatory. For the integration of personnel development and personnel administration you additionally require authorizations for Infotype 0024 (Qualifications), namely change accesses for maintaining relationships to persons.

HR: Transaction code | Some transactions are not called in the menu and neither requires the System Object S_TCODE. Nevertheless, entries in P_TCODE are necessary if you want to assign the following tasks:

- OOQ4 (Career Maintenance)
- PPDPIS (Individual Development) (even if PPDPIM is in the menu)
- PPLB (Evaluate Careers)
- OOQA (Catalog: Change qualification(s))
- OOEC (Change Development Plan Catalog)

Qualification catalog in other subcomponents | The qualification catalog of personnel development is used in various subcomponents of the SAP HCM system. For all these uses, you require read access for the catalog and parts thereof, and write access for selected relationships. This happens in the PLOG authorization object in connection with the structural authorization.

In personnel administration, you call transactions of personnel development PPPD (Display Profile) and PPPM (User: Change Profile) via Transactions PA30 (Maintain HR Master Data) and PA20 (Display HR Master Data), as soon as the integration of the personnel development is activated (Figure 5.35). One of these transactions needs to be authorized. The necessary relationships depend on the functions used in personnel development. Earlier in this section, we've already described the subtypes of the Infotype 1001 (Relationships) required for this purpose.

Personnel
administration

This also includes the relationships of the "classic" appraisal system that are also maintained in PPPM. Refer back to Section 5.2, Appraisal System, for the details.

With active integration of personnel development in personnel administration (IMG path PERSONNEL MANAGEMENT • PERSONNEL DEVELOPMENT • INTEGRATION • SET UP INTEGRATION WITH PERSONNEL ADMIN. AND RECRUITMENT) the authorization for Infotype 0024 (Qualifications) is checked by means of one of the objects in master data authorizations (see Section 5.12, Personnel Administration and Time Management).

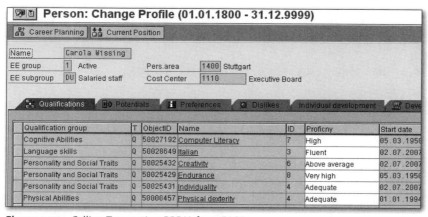

Figure 5.35 Calling Transaction PPPM from PA30

In performance management, qualifications are related with criteria and criteria groups (Relationship 607 is described by/Descriptive element of). Moreover, relationships of qualifications with persons, are read.

Performance
management

Training and event management/ SAP Learning Solution

Training and Event Management and SAP Learning Solution use Relationships 028 (Imparts), for example, between an event type and a qualification, and 029 (Has prerequisite), for example, between a curriculum type and a qualification. For this purpose, you require:

▶ Read access to the catalog

▶ Structural write access to objects of the Training and Event Management/SAP Learning Solution, and to qualifications

▶ Write access to Relationships 028 and 029 in connection with the required object types in PLOG

Employee Self Service

If an employee is allowed to change his qualifications in Employee Self Service, he requires:

▶ Read access to the catalog or a subcatalog

▶ Structural write access to P and Q

▶ Write access in PLOG to Relationship 032 (Fulfills) of P to Q

▶ Write access to Infotype 0024 for his own personnel number

Shift planning

In shift planning you can relate requirements (Object Type SR) to qualifications. For this purpose, the requirements planner needs:

▶ Read access to the catalog

▶ Structural write access to SR (Requirements) and Q

▶ Write access in PLOG to Relationship 031 (Requires) of SR to Q

The shift planner only requires display access to qualifications (in PLOG and structural).

Collaboration Projects

The *Collaboration Projects* components that are available outside the SAP HCM system can use the qualifications of the SAP HCM system via Object Type QB (Qualification Block) and Infotype 1055 (Qualification Management). Customizing is implemented in IMG path COLLABORATION PROJECTS • RESOURCE MANAGEMENT • QUALIFICATION MANAGEMENT.

SAP Expert Finder

The SAP Expert Finder uses the HR qualification catalog via Infotype 5032 (Qualification Export EF) that can belong both to a qualification and a qualification group.

5.16   Human Resources Information System/Reporting

As a basic rule, the same authorization checks are used in reporting as in the display and maintenance transactions in the SAP HCM system.

5.16.1   Logical databases

The main part of the authorization check is implemented in *logical databases*. These comprise:

▶ **PAP for classic recruitment**
It checks the P_APPL authorization object and, if required, the structural authorization (see Section 5.13, Recruitment (Classic)).

▶ **PCH for all applications that work using the database tables HRP***
It checks the PLOG authorization object and the structural authorization.

▶ **PNP for personnel administration**
It checks all authorization objects of the personnel administration and the structural authorization (see Section 5.12, Personnel Administration and Time Management).

▶ **PNPCE for personnel administration using global employee management**
PNP is supplemented by the structural authorizations for managing global employees (refer back to section 5.8, Management of Global Employees).

Assigning Infotypes to Reports   [+]

Assigning infotypes to reports can be very tedious. You can facilitate this process by calling the source code of the program to search for the INFOTYPES declaration there. The infotypes contained therein are read in the report and must be authorized accordingly.

In reports that work with evaluation schemes (RPCALCx0, RPTIME00) you can avoid the reading of tables through corresponding functions. For example, in RPTIME00, Infotype 0008 (Basic Pay) is only read when you call the CHECK function by means of Parameter BP.

The P_PCLX authorization object is not checked in the logical databases, but only in places where clusters are accessed. The clusters are assigned

Cluster authorizations

to the several HCM subcomponents and are discussed in the corresponding sections.

Additional authorizations for reports are also described for the respective subcomponents.

5.16.2 SAP Reports Without Logical Database

You should pay special attention to SAP reports without logical databases. In general, you shouldn't provide them to end users, because the authorization checks stored in the logical databases don't exist here. You can see an example of such a report in Figure 5.36.

The Report RPCLSTB2 displayed in Figure 5.36 checks the cluster authorization using the P_PCLX object, but no other authorization object. Therefore, you can display cluster data of the time management for all persons in the enterprise.

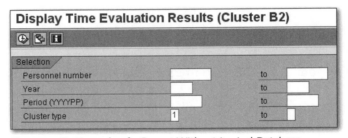

Figure 5.36 Example of a Report Without Logical Database

Report RPTBAL00   Use the Report RPTBAL00 (Cumulated Time Evaluation Results: Time Balances/Wage types) in time management to display the most critical cluster tables.

[!]   **Warning: Gaps in the Authorization Check in Case of Absences**

The Time Statement report (RPTEDT00) runs in the PNP logical database and additionally checks the cluster authorization for time management. Within the B2 cluster there is the AB table, including all absences. If the user executing the time statement report has no infotype authorization for absences, he could still see it in the output of the time statement, if these are provided in the form via customizing. To solve this problem you must program your own authorization check in the user exit of the time statement.

5.16.3 The Authorization Object P_ABAP

Because the process of checking read authorizations for master data uses a lot of computing time, especially in the running of reports, you are provided with the P_ABAP authorization object (HR: Reporting). This enables you to restrict or completely deactivate the check for certain reports.

Simplification of the authorization check

The object does not replace the basic authorization required to start a report. Rather, P_ABAP simplifies and speeds up the process of checking the reported data. If you assign full authorization for this object, a user will be able to view all the HR master data in the associated reports, even if he does not have authorization for the relevant infotypes and personnel numbers.

The P_ABAP authorization object (Figure 5.37) has an effect only in reports that use the personnel administration logical database (PNP). Exceptions are the reports of the payment medium programs for financial accounting and evaluation of logged changes in the infotype data. Here, the P_ABAP authorization object is active, although the PNP logical database is not used.

P_ABAP for PNP only

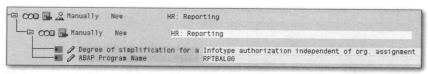

Figure 5.37 Authorization Object P_ABAP

The following fields are checked (see Figure 5.37):

Fields in P_ABAP

- **ABAP Program Name**
  Report(s) for which a simplified authorization check is supposed to be run

- **Degree of simplification for an authorization check**

  - 1 – Infotypes and organizational assignment are checked independently of each other. In other words, users can view all infotypes for all personnel numbers to which they have access. This approach speeds up the authorization check.

▸ 2 – When the report is run without checks, no checks of HR master data or structural checks are carried out. This approach makes sense for "uncritical" reports, such as a room directory, and for users who already have full read access to HR master data.

> **Tip Simplification Degree 1**
>
> It can be used for report authorizations to infotypes that an administrator is not allowed to see. To do this, you need to assign a non-existing employee subgroup for this infotype in P_ORGIN (or a corresponding master data object) and the simplification degree "1" for this report in P_ABAP. By authorizing the infotype for a non-existing employee subgroup, it is only accessible if it's read in a report where the authorization check is reduced by means of simplification degree 1.

5.16.4 Reporting Basics

Calculation of time specifications

A tool is provided to customize the calculation of the time specifications at various places in the SAP HCM system and can be found under Personnel Management • Personnel Administration • Evaluation Basis • Calculation of Employment Period. The Calculation Process• Override Attributes for Calculation Process activity enables you to deactivate the authorization check for reading relevant data in selected calculation processes (Figure 5.38).

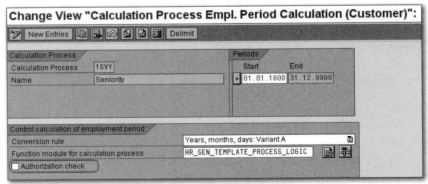

Figure 5.38 Deactivating the Authorization Check for the Employment Period Calculation

5.17 Personnel Cost Planning

The SAP roles provided for personnel cost planning are according to the naming convention SAP_HR_CP*. Unfortunately, they contain many errors and redundancies, so that you must set up new authorizations using the following objects. We'll exclusively refer to the new personnel cost planning as of SAP R/3 Release 4.7.

Because the cost planning of the SAP HCM system is based on the organizational structure, the personnel cost planners require access (in PLOG and structural) to the organizational structure or parts thereof including Object Types O, C, and S. In addition to the Infotypes 1000 (Object) and 1001 (Relationships), you must authorize the Infotype 5010 (Planning of Pers. Costs).

PLOG and structural authorization

The structural authorizations are very complex for this area, if the personnel cost planning work is implemented de-centrally by superiors. For more information refer back to Chapter 3, Structural Authorization Check.

In the personnel cost planning, you work with the authorization objects typically used in personnel administration (see Section 5.12, Personnel Administration and Time Management). In addition to Infotype 0008 (Basic Pay) and other infotypes relevant for remuneration, you should remember Infotypes 0027 (Cost Distribution) and 0666 (Planning of Pers. Costs). Infotypes 0000 (Actions), 0001 (Organizational assignment), and 0002 (Personal data) are always required.

Master data

You can use the following clusters:

Clusters

- CB (Personnel Cost Planning: Data basis from payroll results)
- CC (Personnel Cost Planning: Source document for CO Posting)
- CP (Personnel Cost Planning: Planning run data)
- PS (Payroll schema)

If you use the live payroll results for planning, you need to check the PROVIDE COST PLANNING parameter in the COST PLANNING pop-up when transferring the payroll results to FI/CO (Report RPCIPE00). As a rule, no special authorizations must be assigned for personnel cost planners.

Using the payroll results

This usually needs to be done retroactively during the go-live of cost planning. A test run for the Posting Program RPCIPE00 (type of the document creation = T) is sufficient to fill the Cluster CG relevant for cost planning. This run is often implemented by the cost planner, who requires the authorization in Object P_PYEVRUN (HR: Posting run) using Run type PP and Simulation Indicator X (Figure 5.39).

Generally P_PYEVRUN checks several activities (add, change, display, delete, post, release, reverse), the simulation indicator, and the run type.

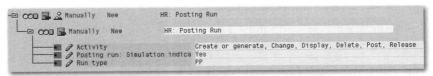

Figure 5.39 Example Authorization for Cost Planners in P_PYEVRUN

If you use the payroll simulation, the payroll is simulated from the posting run, and the relevant results are transferred to Cluster CB. Here as well, a test run is sufficient. However, this procedure has a very long runtime, because generally at least 12 months per personnel number are simulated. If you use this option, the cost planner requires the Authorization P_PYEVRUN with RUN TYPE PP and SIMULATION INDICATOR X for the Report RPCIPE00.

Transferring to CO   For transferring the results of the personnel cost planning (Transaction PHCPADCO, Report RHHCP_PLAN_ADMIN) to the financial account, you also require access to the Object P_PYEVRUN (HR: Posting run). Here, the RUN TYPE for the cost planning is called CP.

5.18   Self Services

As a rule, Self Services applications are called from the SAP NetWeaver portal.

Authorization check in HCM   The SAP NetWeaver portal doesn't have its own authorization check. Instead, the authorization is always checked in the back-end system. In the portal, you are only provided with the menu entries. The respective back-end system (in the case of ESS usually SAP ERP HCM) decides whether they may be executed. Already for read access, for example, to his own address data, the user requires the read authorization for Infotype 0006 (Addresses).

For Self Service applications the P_PERNR authorization object (HR: Master data – personnel number check) plays a significant role. If an employee is provided with the menu entry for ESS in the portal, although the respective user ID does not exist in the SAP HCM back-end system, the SAP HCM back-end system displays an error message when calling the entry.

To ensure that you don't have to assign a menu to each user ID in the SAP NetWeaver portal, you can use groups (for example, employees, managers, external persons). These groups are then assigned to corresponding menus (Figure 5.40).

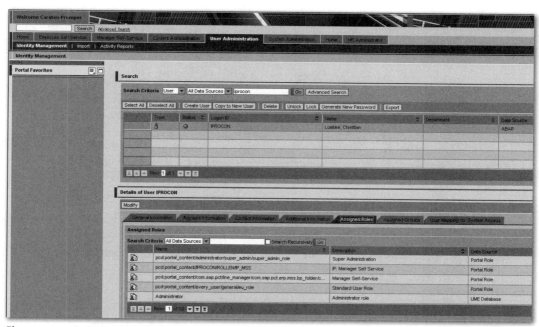

Figure 5.40 Assigning User Actions to a Role in the Portal

An employee can only access ESS in the SAP HCM system, if his user ID is related with a personnel number. This is done by using the Infotype

0105 (Communication), where you can enter the user ID in Subtype 0001 (System user name (SY-UNAME)).

This is valid for all user interfaces that access SAP HCM data from outside the SAP ERP system either with or without the SAP NetWeaver portal. Among these user interfaces are:

- Employee Self Service (ESS)
- Manager Self Service (MSS)
- Duet: Access to SAP HCM data from Microsoft® Outlook®
- HR Admin: *HR administrator* role in the portal
- HCM Processes & Forms: process-oriented forms, including workflows and using Adobe Interactive Forms

User administration

The user must be available in the portal. If you want to access downstream systems from the portal, then the users of the same name must be created in the respective downstream systems.

The user administration is controlled by the *User Management Engine* (UME) in the portal. The UME can:

- be used as a separate user database. This means a redundant maintenance of the users in all systems.
- display the user administration of an ABAP stack (constitutes the SAP NetWeaver Application Server together with the Java stack) and consequently can use the user administration there. Users must only be maintained once.

Single sign-on
- use the user administration of a non-SAP system (Single sign-on). For example, this can be a Microsoft Active Directory. In this case, the user and password from the Microsoft Windows network login would be used for the portal.

To enable the creation of users in the SAP NetWeaver portal, the Communication User SAPJSF must enter the SAP Role, SAP_BC_JSF_COMMUNICATION, and the corresponding profile in his user master records (see SAP Note 899912 – Logging messages from the UME/ABAP connection).

5.19 Travel Management

SAP provides multiple roles for travel management, starting with SAP_ FI_TV*. The roles depend on the tasks the employee must fulfill:

▶ **Travel management administrator**

His task is to check and approve travel requests, book travel plans, approve travel costs, enter travel expenses, and settle travels for all travelers in the enterprise.

▶ **Traveler**

He may generate travel requests and plans, request trip advance, book travel services, and enter travel expenses himself.

▶ **Travel assistant**

He may implement all tasks of the traveler, however, not just for himself, but also for other travelers in his department.

▶ **Approving manager**

As a manager, he is allowed to approve travel requests, plans, and expense accounting, and to implement evaluations in the travel management.

▶ **Travel expense manager/Travel system manager**

His task is to maintain the HR master data of all travelers in the enterprise that is required for travel management, to maintain and settle travels, to create posting runs, to set up the travel customizing, and to execute travel evaluations.

▶ **Advance payer**

He may document the cash payment of the approved trip advances of all travelers.

▶ **Travel policy administrator**

In Customizing, he maintains tables with travel policies.

Let's assume that you use the travel management de-centrally, that is, all employees may maintain their own travels. The role of the traveler SAP_FI_TV_TRAVELER is very unclear and contains more information than necessary. Therefore, we create a new role and the system proposes authorizations based on Transaction TRIP (travel manager). The traveler is supposed to create a travel request in the travel manager and, upon approval, create the travel expenses.

Role for decentral maintenance

Authorization
object F_TRAVL

In the authorization proposal for Transaction TRIP only the F_TRAVL authorization object is missing. The check could be added in Customizing of the Profile Generator (Transaction SU24) (see Section 2.5, Customizing of the Profile Generator). The name and the description of the F_TRAVL authorization object (Travel Planning) doesn't intuitively imply the necessity of this authorization object as long as no travel planning is used. Nevertheless, the authorization object is checked in the *Travel Manager* transaction. Authorize for reading (R) and writing (W) of data records and the check of the own personnel number (O). For travel assistants who also maintain travels for other employees, you must enter a "*" in the Personnel Number Check field (Figure 5.41). By doing so the user may view all travelers. Therefore, another restriction must be made via the structural authorization.

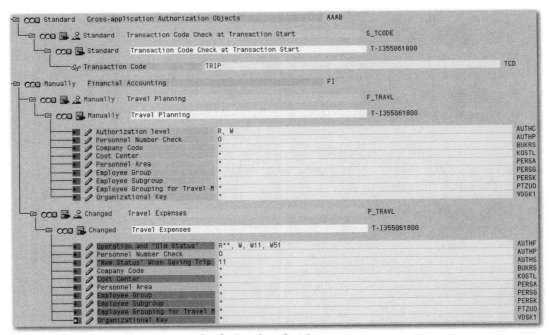

Figure 5.41 Role of a Traveler – Part 1

Object P_TRAVL

The P_TRAVL (Travel Expenses) is the central authorization object of travel management. It enables you to control the dialog process between the traveler and the approver or the travel management administrator.

For the PERSONNEL NUMBER CHECK field the same description applies as for F_TRAVL. In the OPERATION AND "OLD STATUS" field you determine which activities may be executed for which request and settlement status. In the "Status New" WHEN SAVING TRIP field you establish which status the request or travel expenses have when saving. The permissible statuses are only determined in the role, there is no additional customizing.

In the first authorization object of P_TRAVL (Figure 5.41) you authorize the following:

P_TRAVL – 1

► R** (Reading of travel data)

► W (Writing a new trip)

► W11 (Changing a request that has not been approved yet)

► W51 (Changing a request to be corrected)

► 11 (Saving in the "Request to be accounted/Trip to be accounted" status)

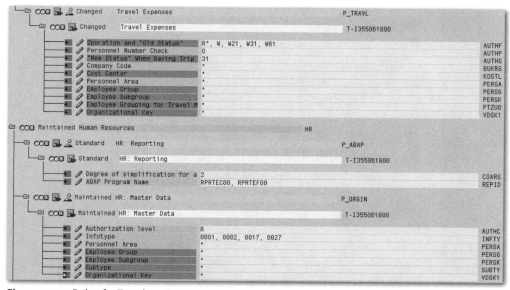

Figure 5.42   Role of a Traveler – Part 2

In the second authorization object of P_TRAVL (see Figure 5.42) you authorize the following:

P_TRAVL – 2

- ▸ R* (Reading of trip data)
- ▸ W (Writing a new trip)
- ▸ W21 (Writing travel expenses in the "Request approved/Trip to be accounted" status)
- ▸ W31 (Changing travel expenses that have not been approved yet)
- ▸ W61 (Changing a trip to be corrected)
- ▸ 31 (Saving in the "Trip to be accounted" status)

This ensures that the traveler can't change approved requests or travel expenses. He can only change requests and expenses for which the authorized person (e.g., the travel management administrator) has set the ON HOLD status (W51, W61). Further information and possible field values are available in the field documentation ([F1] help).

P_ABAP Another authorization object to be checked is P_ABAP (HR: Reporting) that includes the Reports RPRTEC00 (Travel expenses) and RPRTEF00 (Standard form for travel expenses). This will be proposed correctly. The reports are required because a simulation of the travel costs is implemented when saving the trip, which can be displayed using the RESULTS button.

Finally, the traveler needs read authorization to the Infotypes 0001 (Organizational Assignment), 0002 (Personal Data), 0017 (Travel Privileges), and 0027 (Cost Distribution).

5.20 Training and Event Management/ SAP Learning Solution

In the *Training and Event Management/SAP Learning Solution* components most of the roles provided by SAP (namespace SAP_HR_LSO*) are not useful. Often, they are unclear and generally incomplete. Simply, the menu allocation can provide you with good ideas. We, therefore, explain the necessary authorization objects individually. In Section 5.20.2, Major Standard Roles, we'll detail two major standard roles.

5.20.1 Overview of the Authorization Objects

Users that are supposed to book, cancel, or mark from the Learning Portal, don't need menu entries for SAP Learning Solution (LSO). For those working in the back end, transaction authorizations are required, both via the S_TCODE system authorization object and P_TCODE. You can find the necessary transaction codes in the SAP menu. The Profile Generator reliably proposes the entries for P_TCODE.

Transaction authorizations

> **Warning: Calling PP01 from the Master Data Catalog**   **[!]**
>
> Calling Transaction PP01 (Maintain Object) from the master data catalog (PVCT or LSO_PVCT) plays a major role for changing the event groups and event types (Figure 5.43). So if you are permitted to maintain in PVCT/LSPO_PVCT you may also do so in PP01, as long as you want to move in the standard. This requires increased care for the PLOG authorization object: Which object types and relationships are permitted here?

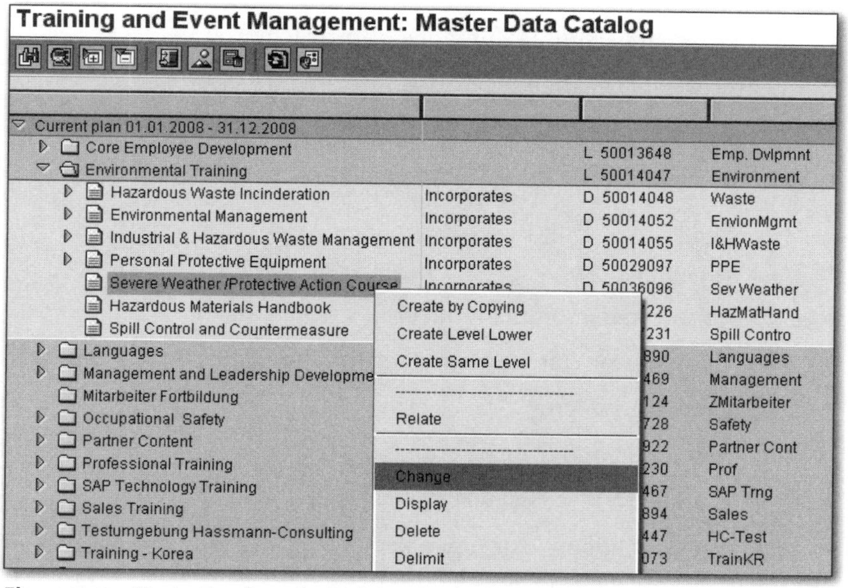

Figure 5.43 Navigating from the Training Catalog to Transaction PP01

Training and Event Management (TEM) and SAP Learning Solution (LSO) require the Object PLOG and the structural authorization for the authorization check. This includes the following object types:

PLOG and structural authorization

► D   (Business event type) (TEM and LSO)

► DC   (Curriculum Type) (LSO)

► E   (Course) (TEM and LSO)

► EC   (Curriculum) (LSO)

► EK   (Training program) (as of ECC 6.0, Enhancement Package 2)

► ET   (e-Learning) (LSO)

► L   (Business event group) (TEM and LSO)

► OJ   (Learning objective)

Depending on the use, this also includes:

► AP   (Applicant) (as attendee)

► BU   (Budget Structure Element) (for Budgeting)

► F   (Location) (Event location)

► G   (Resource)

► H   (External person) (as attendee or instructor)

► KI   (Prospect) (as attendee or organizer)

► KU   (Customer) (as attendee or organizer)

► M   (Material) (for material procurement)

► O   (Organizational unit)

► P   (Person)

► PT   (Contact person) (as attendee)

► Q   (Qualification) (as a prerequisite for attendance or as a result)

► QK   (Qualification group)

► R   (Resource type)

► U   (Company)

► US   (User) (as attendee or organizer)

► VA   (Appraisal template)

► VB   (Criteria group)

► VC   (Criterion)

In the structural authorization, you can authorize the following object types hierarchically combined that means using evaluation paths or function modules:

- D, E, and L in the event catalog
- D, DC, E, EC, ET, and L in the training catalog of LSO
- QK and Q in the qualification catalog
- O, S, P, and possibly C in the organizational structure

This enables you to restrict the access right to specific parts of the respective structure, if required, and to differentiate according to write and read accesses.

Example   **[Ex]**

You want to permit a de-central maintenance of your event catalog. The de-central users are supposed to have read access to the entire catalog. The necessary structural authorizations are displayed in Figure 5.44. The Evaluation Path LSOCATDO includes Object Types L, D, E, DC, EC, and ET. If you use additional customer-specific relationships and/or object types, you must integrate them in the evaluation path.

Auth.profile	No.	Plan Vers.	Obj.Type	Object I	Maint.	Eval.path	Status vec
TCAT_DEZENTR	5	01	L	10	☐	LSOCATDO	12
TCAT_DEZENTR	10	01	L	10004560	☑	LSOCATDO	12

Figure 5.44 De-central Maintenance of the Training Catalog

For the PLOG authorization object in the example displayed in Figure 5.44 you require:

- Write access for Object Types D, E, ET, L (or more, as required) without restriction for infotypes and subtypes (usually not necessary)
- Write access for Relationships P to E, ET, D

Booking, Canceling, Prebooking of Events Not to be Maintained by the User   **[+]**

In the example displayed in Figure 5.44, booking, canceling, prebooking, and so on (relationships from P to E and ET, possibly to D) are only possible for event types and events that the owner of these structural authorizations can maintain himself. If he is also supposed to book, cancel, or prebook events of the entire catalog, he needs a maintenance authorization for these object types of the entire catalog. Because the authorizations here are not context-dependent unfortunately, you can only use the BAdI for structural authorization in these cases. Its use is described in Section 3.10, Extensions.

Infotypes of the administration

Additional authorizations are required for the access to persons. They are assigned via the authorization procedures of the personnel administration (see Section 5.12, Personnel Administration and Time Management).

The minimum authorization for working in the Training and Event Management or SAP Learning Solution includes read authorization for Infotypes 0000 (Actions), 0001 (Organizational assignment), and 0002 (Personal data). Often, Infotype 0006 (Addresses) is also required. If you want to omit these minimum authorizations for personal data, you must use the HRPAD00AUTH_CHECK BAdI (see Section 2.8.3, BAdI for General Authorization Checks).

If you use the integration with personnel time management, you require write access to Infotype 2002 and the respective subtypes, and write access to the Cluster PC.

System authorizations

The following system authorization objects are required:

▶ RFC authorization objects: S_RFC (authorization check for RFC access) and S_RFCACL (authorization check for RFC users, for example, trusted system). These objects are essential for learners when accessing the Learning Portal.

▶ CA_POWL (authorizations for POWL iViews) for the instructor (see Note 1073907 – Learning Solution: Changes to role templates) as of ECC 6.0, Enhancement Package 2

Performance management

The SAP Learning Solution uses the performance management for training and attendee appraisals. For these activities, you require authorizations in the P_HAP_DOC object (Appraisal Systems: Appraisal). There, the Category Group 00000010 is reserved for LSO. For more information, refer to Section 5.11, Performance Management.

Ultimately, we would like to draw your attention to two authorization objects for special activities in the SAP Learning Solution:

In the *authorization for LSO content management* (P_LSO_TU) you check the authorization for the processing of learning content in the SAP Learning Solution. The only field is LSO: Activity for course content that controls the access to the type of processing of training content (such as publishing, releasing).

The *authorization object for participation follow up* (P_LSO_FOUP) checks with Yes or No, whether the users may follow up participations in SAP Learning Solution. This object is relevant both for the administrator and the learner. Following up in Learning Solution can be executed by the learner in case of e-trainings.

5.20.2 Important Standard Roles

Figure 5.45 shows the technical role of the Course Content Player. It is assigned to the Technical User EL_USER and is responsible for the communication of e-learning or Course Content Player and the back end. The S_RFC authorization object (authorization check for RFC access) contains the technical authorizations for accesses. The HR objects must be customized based on the information mentioned earlier, if required.

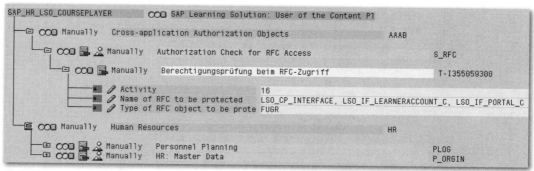

Figure 5.45 Technical Role for the Course Content Player

Authors also work with the Course Content Player; however, they must implement other functions than the regular user of the Course Content Player. These functions can be found in the author role as is displayed in Figure 5.46.

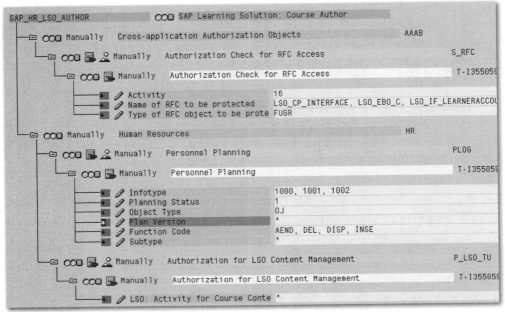

```
SAP_HR_LSO_AUTHOR                    ∞ SAP Learning Solution: Course Author
  ├─ ∞ Manually   Cross-application Authorization Objects              AAAB
  │   └─ ∞ ▦ ⛀ Manually   Authorization Check for RFC Access           S_RFC
  │       └─ ∞ ▦ Manually   Authorization Check for RFC Access        T-I355059
  │           ├─ ■ ⫽ Activity                    16
  │           ├─ ■ ⫽ Name of RFC to be protected LSO_CP_INTERFACE, LSO_EBO_C, LSO_IF_LEARNERACCOU
  │           └─ ■ ⫽ Type of RFC object to be prote FUGR
  ├─ ∞ Manually   Human Resources                                      HR
  │   └─ ∞ ▦ ⛀ Manually   Personnel Planning                          PLOG
  │       └─ ∞ ▦ Manually   Personnel Planning                       T-I355059
  │           ├─ ■ ⫽ Infotype                   1000, 1001, 1002
  │           ├─ ■ ⫽ Planning Status            1
  │           ├─ ■ ⫽ Object Type                OJ
  │           ├─ ▣ ⫽ Plan Version               *
  │           ├─ ■ ⫽ Function Code              AEND, DEL, DISP, INSE
  │           └─ ■ ⫽ Subtype                    *
  └─ ∞ ▦ ⛀ Manually   Authorization for LSO Content Management         P_LSO_TU
      └─ ∞ ▦ Manually   Authorization for LSO Content Management      T-I355059
          └─ ■ ⫽ LSO: Activity for Course Conte *
```

Figure 5.46 SAP Roles for Authors in LSO

The author role also contains the S_RFC authorization object (authorization check for RFC access) with the technical authorizations for accesses. For HR objects, Object Type OJ (learning objective) in PLOG is essential, and the already described P_LSO_TU authorization object (*Authorization for LSO Content Management*).

5.21 Summary

If you read the entire chapter, you've probably noticed that working out the details of authorizations is the tricky part. This ranges from classic authorization objects via various SAP HCM-specific authorization tools (explained in Chapters 2 to 4) to a multitude of switches and other customizing tools that all impact the authorization check in the individual components of the SAP HCM system.

We hope that we've provided you with valuable information and reference material that will support you in accomplishing the tasks in your authorization work.

This chapter describes the System settings that are required for the initial implementation of an authorization concept. In addition, it introduces an efficient procedure — from the implementation to the actual Go Live.

6   Implementing an Authorization Concept

So far, you've created the authorization concept and taken administrative and technical restrictions into account. In addition, you considered the control mechanisms used in your enterprise to ensure auditing security. You've described the employees' tasks as explained in Chapter 1, Process-Oriented Authorization Concept, created an overview of them, and determined the areas of responsibility and data accesses for each task. You derived the necessary authorization tools from the requirements for the future authorization concept, which means you know whether you have to use the structural or context-dependent authorization check in addition to the general authorization check. And, you've thought about which concepts you want to use to keep the number of roles and structural profiles to a minimum.

Before implementing the concept, you should also define a naming convention for the roles and profiles. In addition, it's useful to distinguish between the names of single and composite roles to keep a good overview. If necessary, you can find more information on this in Chapter 1.

So, if all of the prerequisites are met, you can start to implement your authorization concept with a clear conscience.

6.1 Preparations in the System

Before you start maintaining the first role, you must prepare the system accordingly. The following sections describe which settings you have to use when, and where you can configure them.

6.1.1 Central User Administration

If your enterprise works with several SAP systems and clients, you should use the Central User Administration (CUA). This enables you to maintain the user master records and role assignment in a central system, manage them centrally, and distribute them across the child systems via *Application Link Enabling* (ALE). The benefit of this is that:

▶ User data is maintained in a uniform manner.

▶ The transparency and consistency of existing users is higher, particularly with regard to audits.

Setting up the CUA

To implement the central user administration, you must perform the following steps:

1. Create an administration user and assign an administration role to it in order to perform the following steps (Transaction SU01 (User Maintenance)).

2. Configure the logical systems in the central system and assign them to the clients of the SAP systems (Transaction SALE: BASIC SETTINGS • LOGICAL SYSTEMS • DEFINE LOGICAL SYSTEM/ASSIGN LOGICAL SYSTEM TO CLIENT).

3. Create system users, assign roles, and configure RFC destinations for the internal communication of the systems in all logical systems (Transactions SU01, PFCG, Transaction SALE: Communication • Create RFC Connections).

4. Create the central user administration (Transaction SALE: MODELLING AND IMPLEMENTING BUSINESS PROCESSES • CONFIGURE PREDEFINED ALE BUSINESS PROCESSES • CROSS-APPLICATION BUSINESS PROCESSES • CENTRAL USER ADMINISTRATION • SELECT MODEL VIEW FOR CENTRAL ADMINISTRATION).

5. Determine the fields of the user master that are supposed to be globally and locally maintained (Transaction SCUM (User Distribution Field Selection), Figure 6.1).

6. Synchronize and distribute the company addresses in order to ensure that the central system contains all valid company addresses, transfer existing users from child systems, and distribute the users from the central system across the child systems (Transaction SALE: MODELLING AND IMPLEMENTING BUSINESS PROCESSES • CONFIGURE PREDEFINED ALE BUSINESS PROCESSES • CROSS-APPLICATION BUSINESS PROCESSES • CENTRAL USER ADMINISTRATION • TRANSFER USERS AND COMPANY ADDRESSES FROM NEW SYSTEMS).

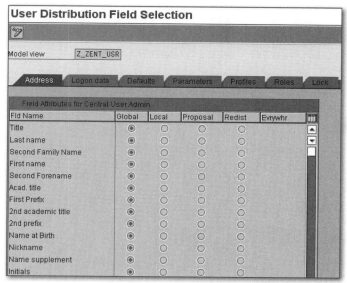

Figure 6.1 Transaction SCUM

The following changes are made to the authorization administration if you use the central user administration:

User administration for the CUA

In the central system, Transaction SU01 (User Maintenance) additionally displays the Systems tab (Figure 6.2) where you specify across which systems the user is supposed to be distributed. You can also specify the system in the Roles and Profiles tabs to be able to determine which system the role or profile has been assigned to. In the S_USER_SYS (User

Master Maintenance: System for Central User Maintenance) authorization object, the Activity and Receiving System for Central User Administration fields enable you to define which child systems the user administrator can assign to the user.

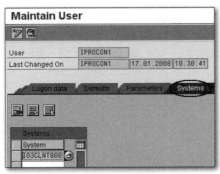

Figure 6.2 Transaction SU01 When Using the Central User Administration

▶ In the initial screen of Transaction SU01, you can change or deactivate the password for several systems (across which the user is distributed) using the ⬛ icon.

▶ The user information system (Transaction SUIM, see Chapter 7, Reports for the Authorization System) of a child system enables you to analyze global user data (Figure 6.3).

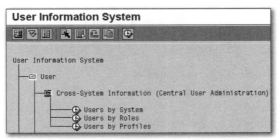

Figure 6.3 Transaction SUIM When Using the Central User Administration

You must take the following aspects into account when using the central user administration:

▶ You must schedule the SUSR_ZBV_GET_RECEIVER_PROFILES (CUA: Text Comparison from Child Systems) report as a regular background job to send the roles and profiles that are maintained in child systems to the central system.

▶ If required, the report can also run in the central system, for example, to clean up the assignment of roles and profiles to users if roles or profiles have been deleted during the import from child systems (Figure 6.4).

CUA: Text Comparison from Child Systems

Receiving system   I03CLNT800   to

☐ Delete Invalid Assignments

Figure 6.4   Selection Screen of the SUSR_ZBV_GET_RECEIVER_PROFILES Report When the Report is Executed in the Central System

To distribute structural profiles, you can distribute Tables T77UA (User Authorizations) and T77PR (Authorization Profiles) across the child systems via ALE. If you use fixed root objects, you should make sure that the object IDs have also been entered in the child systems, because no check is performed during the maintenance of the root object under OBJECTID in Table T77PR. However, it is possible to distribute the Organizational Management components of the child systems into the central system. If you use only function modules that determine the system dynamically, as Schaeffler KG does (see Chapter 10, Section 10.1, Organizational Management Authorizations (Schaeffler KG)), for example, you're always on the safe side.

Distributing structural profiles

6.1.2   Authorization Administrators

The authorization administrators require the respective authorizations in order to work with the system. It is usually necessary to distribute the tasks of the authorization administration across several administrators (double-verification principle). For example, one authorization administrator maintains the roles, another generates the profiles, if required, and a third administrator assigns the roles to the users.

Double-verification principle

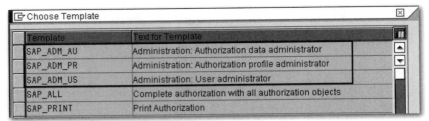

Figure 6.5 Templates for the Role Maintenance of the Authorization Administration

SAP provides templates for maintaining the administrator roles. To use them, you need a user with the predefined S_A.SYSTEM (System Administrator (superuser)) profile.

1. As the superuser, start Transaction PFCG (Role Maintenance) and create a new role.

2. Then select the Change Authorization Data button in the AUTHORIZATIONS tab. A table containing templates now displays, as shown in Figure 6.5.

3. Select the required template and click on the ADOPT REFERENCE button. The selected authorizations are added and can be customized respectively. Initially, a profile name that starts with T is proposed during the generation (Figure 6.6). Select a profile name that doesn't start with T, because only the administrator role is supposed to be authorized for profiles whose names start with T. This ensures that he cannot change his own authorizations.

4. Finally, enter the user name of the authorization administrator in the USER tab.

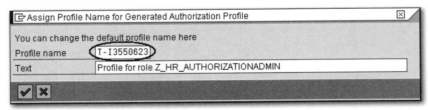

Figure 6.6 Changing Profile Names in Authorization Administrator Roles

The three templates include the following tasks:

▶ **Authorization data administrator**

  ▶ Creating and changing roles

  ▶ Changing the menus or the roles as well as authorization data

  ▶ Using the user information system

▶ **Authorization profile administrator**

  ▶ Viewing roles and the corresponding data

  ▶ Generating authorizations and profiles (whose names start with T) of roles with existing authorization data using Transaction PFCG (Role Maintenance) or SUPC (Roles: Mass Generation of Profiles)

  ▶ Using the user information system

▶ **User administrator**

  ▶ Creating and changing user master records

  ▶ Assigning roles to users

  ▶ Assigning profiles (whose names start with T) to users

  ▶ Viewing authorizations and profiles

  ▶ Using the user information system

Usually, the double-verification principle, which involves the distribution across — one user administrator and one authorization administrator who also generates the profiles — is sufficient.

You can differentiate between the authorizations of the administrators using the following authorization objects:

▶ **S_USER_AUT (User Master Maintenance: Authorizations)**
The ACTIVITY, AUTHORIZATION NAME IN USER MASTER, and AUTHORIZATION OBJECT fields are supposed to be checked. This object checks which actions (e.g., creating, changing, or deleting authorizations) are permitted for which authorization objects and authorization profiles (here: AUTHORIZATION NAME).

▶ **S_USER_AGR (Authorizations: Role Check)**
The ACTIVITY and ROLE NAME fields are supposed to be checked. This authorization object enables you to set up a decentralized user admin-

istration (e.g., depending on components). Consequently, the different user administrators are only provided with the authorizations to assign roles with the respective name (for example, Z_HR_VM*, Z_HR_OM*, and so on).

▶ **S_USER_TCD (Authorizations: Transactions in Roles)**
Here, the TRANSACTION CODE field is supposed to be checked. This object enables you to restrict the permitted transaction codes for authorization administrators that these are authorized to assign.

▶ **S_USER_VAL (Authorizations: Field Values in Roles)**
The FIELD NAME, AUTHORIZATION VALUE, and AUTHORIZATION OBJECT fields are supposed to be checked. This authorization object enables you to restrict which authorization objects the authorization administrators are authorized to add to roles and which field values they are authorized to enter in the respective objects.

▶ **S_USER_PRO (User Master Maintenance: Authorization Profile)**
The ACTIVITY and AUTHORIZATION PROFILE IN USER MASTER MAINTENANCE fields are supposed to be checked Here, you can restrict which profiles can be created and modified (authorization administrator) as well as assigned (user administrator) depending on the name.

▶ **S_USER_GRP (User Master Maintenance: User Groups)**
This authorization object uses the ACTIVITY AND USER GROUP IN USER THE MASTER MAINTENANCE fields. It enables you to restrict the authorization of the user administrator for specific user groups and so distribute the maintenance of the users across different user administrators. You can (but don't have to) enter the user group in the user maintenance (SU01) in the Logon data tab (Figure 6.7). User groups are created in the user maintenance menu via ENVIRONMENT • USER GROUPS • MAINTAIN.

[+] **Tip**

For administrators, enter "SUPER" in the User Group field in the LOGON DATA tab in Transaction SU01 (User Maintenance) to prevent user administrators from changing their own user master records or those of other administrators. In the S_USER_GRP authorization object, you must then enter a blank, for example, instead of "*" if no other user groups are distinguished.

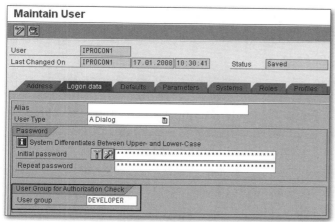

Figure 6.7 Assigning Users to a User Group

Simplifying the Authorization Maintenance for Administrators   **[+]**

You can replace the S_USER_GRP, S_USER_AGR, S_USER_PRO, and S_USER_SYS authorization objects with one authorization object. The S_USER_SAS (User Master Maintenance: System-Specific Assignments) object comprises all fields of the authorization objects mentioned. Before you can use S_USER_SAS, you need to set the Customizing switch in table PRGN_CUST, CHECK_S_USER_SAS, to "YES."

6.1.3   Initial Installation of the Profile Generator

To maintain each authorization separately for every authorization object that is checked in a transaction would require a great deal of effort, so the Profile Generator is provided. When you create roles, the Profile Generator proposes most of the required authorization objects, partly filled with default values for the transactions that are entered in the roles.

You can customize the default values of the Profile Generator. This process is described in great detail in Chapter 2, General Authorization Check. To use this option, you must first enter the SAP default values in the customer tables of the Profile Generator, for which SAP provides the USOBX and USOBT tables.

Default values

**Filling in customer
tables**

To initially fill in the customer tables, proceed as follows:

1. Start Transaction SU25 (Profile Generator: Upgrade and Initial Installation).

2. Select item 1. INITIALLY FILL THE CUSTOMER TABLES (Figure 6.8). First, the system displays a warning message that indicates which existing settings in the Profile Generator (Transaction SU24) will be overwritten. When you confirm the message, the SAP table values are copied into Customer Tables USOBX_C and USOBT_C.

3. Then select item 3. TRANSPORT THE CUSTOMER TABLES. Changes to the customer tables of Transaction SU24 are transported, too.

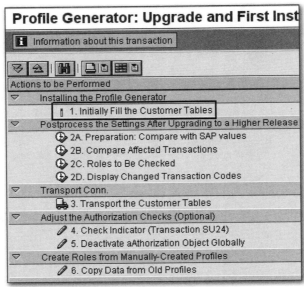

Figure 6.8 Initial Installation of the Profile Generator

**Deactivating
authorization
objects**

In item 5 of Transaction SU25, you can deactivate the check of authorization objects globally to reduce the scope of the check. In this case, the Profile Generator no longer proposes the authorization objects. However, you can't deactivate HR and system authorization objects, that is, objects whose names start with P_ and S_. In addition, you can only deactivate the objects if the system profile parameter, AUTH/OBJECT_DISABLING_ACTIVE, has the value "Y." This is the default setting. Figure 6.9 shows the parameter's setting for the RSPARAM (Display Profile Parameter) report.

To make sure the authorization objects cannot be deactivated, a system configurator with the respective authorization must set the value to "N" in Transaction RZ11 (Maintain Profile Parameters) (Figure 6.10).

	Parameter Name	User-Defined Value	System Default Value	N	Comment
	auth/object_disabling_active		Y	Y	Value 'N' prohibits disabling of authorization objects

Figure 6.9 This Profile Parameter Allows for the Deactivation of Authorization Objects

Figure 6.10 Profile Parameter Maintenance with Transaction RZ11

The following sections introduce a Customizing switch that can change the behavior of the Profile Generator as well as two additional switches that affect Transaction PFCG:

Switches in Table PRGN_CUST

▶ **Generating the SAP_ALL profile without customer authorization objects**
The RSUSR406 (Automatically Generate Profile SAP_ALL) report creates a new SAP_ALL profile in the current client, while the AGR_REGENERATE_SAP_ALL (Regenerate SAP_ALL Profile in all Clients) report generates the SAP_ALL profile in all clients. If you want to make sure, for example, that generally no customer-specific authorization objects (starting with Y or Z) can be added to the SAP_ALL profile, you must set the ADD_ALL_CUST_OBJECTS switch in Table PRGN_CUST (Transaction SM30) to "NO" (Figure 6.12).

▶ **Hiding the button for indirect user assignment via Organizational Management in Transaction PFCG**
If you generally don't want to permit indirect user assignments, you can hide the Organizational Management button setting the HR_ORG_ACTIVE switch to "NO" (Figure 6.11). In this case, users can no longer unhide the button in Transaction PFCG via the menu (initial

screen of PFCG: GOTO • SETTINGS). (Chapter 2, General Authorization Check, describes the indirect user assignment via Organizational Management.)

▶ **Deactivating the "Organizational Management" and "User Comparison" buttons in the display mode of Transaction PFCG**
If specific users are supposed to be assigned only with the display authorization for Transaction PFCG, it may not be desired that these two buttons are activated in the USER tab in display mode. You can deactivate the buttons by setting the USRPROF_IN_DISP_MODE switch to "NO" (Figure 6.11).

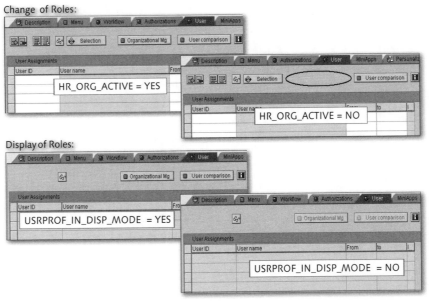

Figure 6.11 Effects of the Customizing Switches

You can find additional switches by calling the F4 help in the Name column of Table PRGN_CUST.

Name	Val	Text
ADD_ALL_CUST_OBJECTS	NO	YES (default), NO - Give full authorization for customer authorization objects (namespace Y, Z) in the profile SAP_ALL
HR_ORG_ACTIVE	NO	YES (default), NO - HR Org Management for Role Assignment Active
USRPROF_IN_DISP_MODE	NO	YES (default), NO - Display pushbuttons for user master record reconciliation in display mode in PFCG

Figure 6.12 Customizing Switches in Table PRGN_CUST for the Authorization System

6.1.4   Creating Organizational Levels

Your specific requirements may make it necessary to use the reference role. This role supports an efficient role administration and is used if several users carry out identical functions with identical authorizations, but for different areas of responsibility (for example, personnel areas). In SAP ERP HCM, only the PLAN VERSION field is defined as an organizational level for the reference role. Consequently, you have to specify at least one other field as an organizational level. This is the only way to use the reference role efficiently, because the organizational level is the only field that isn't passed on and is the only distinguishing criterion in derived roles. You should define the new organizational level(s) before creating the first role. This process was described in greater detail in Chapter 2, General Authorization Check.

Reference role

6.2   Creating and Testing Roles

In addition to what we covered in Chapter 2 on the general authorization check, there are some aspects that you need to consider to make this process run as efficiently as possible.

For comprehensive authorization concepts, it's not useful to implement all roles right away. There will be some roles that only distinguish themselves through a few authorizations. In this case, it makes sense to create some general roles and then test them in greater detail. Only if the tests are successful should you copy and customize the verified roles. This way you can avoid having to correct multiple roles even several times, if errors occur.

Don't create everything immediately

To carry out the tests, a comprehensive test environment must be available in a separate quality assurance (QA) system. The QA system should contain a realistic organizational management with a corresponding level of complexity. Frequently, it's not sufficient to test single roles separately, because the interaction of various roles that are supposed to be assigned to one user at a later stage can indeed lead to negative test results, even if each single role has been tested successfully.

When testing authorizations, it is important that ...

[Ex]

Example

If a user is authorized to maintain objects of SAP Training and Event Management, you should create a role with Transaction PP01 (Maintain Object) and allow access only to object types of SAP Training and Event Management. In an additional role, the user can use Transaction PA30 (Maintain HR Master Data) with change authorization for Infotype 0001 (Organizational Assignment) as well as the object types, *Person*, *Position*, *Job*, and *Organizational Unit*. If the two roles were combined, the user would be authorized to maintain event objects as well as positions, jobs, and organizational units in Transaction PP01.

If you use the structural authorization, you should test the roles together with the corresponding structural profiles.

Who carries out the tests? In addition, the question usually arises about who is best suited to test the roles. In most cases this would be the end users themselves. If they know which functions they are authorized to carry out, they can best assess if something is missing. However, an additional person should check the authorizations to analyze whether the user is authorized to carry out too many functions.

After the tests have been performed, the test results should be included in the authorization concept and documentation, if the results involved changes to the concept. This is necessary to keep the concept, implementation, and documentation consistent.

Training as a crucial test Finally, it's advisable to complete the work related to creating authorizations some time ahead of the system Go Live. You also should have created them before the training starts so that the "real" roles can be used in the trainings — a last crucial test for the authorization concept.

After the roles and profiles have been created and successfully tested, you can transfer them to the live system. So let's consider the issues you need to take into account in this context.

6.3 Transport

Role maintenance transaction There are two different ways you can transfer the roles into the quality assurance system and live system. In both cases, you have to start Transaction PFCG (Role Maintenance):

▶ Select ROLE • TRANSPORT from the menu. Only the selected role — optionally with or without profile, for composite roles with or without single roles — is included in the transport request.

▶ To transport several roles, you can also select UTILITIES • MASS TRANSPORT from the menu. This starts the PFCG_MASS_TRANSPORT (Mass Transport of Roles) report (Figure 6.13).

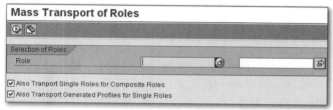

Figure 6.13 Selection Screen of Report PFCG_MASS_TRANSPORT

When you execute the PFCG_MASS_TRANSPORT report, a dialog window enables you to additionally transport the user assignment. Please note that, in this case, existing user assignments are overwritten in the target system. If you want to use the central user administration, you should generally transport user assignments only from the central system.

Locking the System Against the Import of User Assignments	[+]
The transport of user assignments is an additional option provided during the creation of a transport request. When user assignments are imported, they're overwritten in the target system. If you want to prevent user assignments from being imported into a system, you can set the USER_REL_IMPORT switch to "NO" in Table PRGN_CUST (Transaction SM30).	

If you transport authorizations, consider that some additional actions that are not transported are required in both the QA system and live system. These include:

▶ User master records (Transaction SU01), provided that you don't use the central user administration

▶ Assignment of roles to users (Transaction PFCG or SU01, see Chapter 2, General Authorization Check)

Required actions in the target system

     ▶ Assignment of users to structural profiles (Transaction OOSB (User Authorizations), see Chapter 3, Structural Authorization Check)

     ▶ SAP memory (buffer) for structural authorization check using report RHBAUS02 (Check and compare T77UU) (see Chapter 3)

The maintenance tasks should be performed immediately after the roles have been transported. Depending on the structure of the SAP* profile, some structural profiles may be unintentionally accessed if the respective assignments are missing (see Chapter 3).

User master comparison   If the target system now contains all roles, user master records, and user assignments, you need to compare the user master as a last step. For this purpose, you should schedule the RHAUTUPD_NEW (User Master Data Reconciliation) report as a daily job (Figure 6.14). It enters the roles and profiles into the user master of the user and additionally restricts assignments to time limits. To directly carry out the user master comparison, you can also select UTILITIES • MASS COMPARISON from the menu in the initial screen of Transaction PFCG.

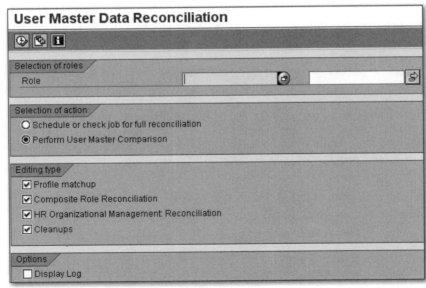

Figure 6.14 Selection Screen of Report RHAUTHUPD_NEW

> **Tip** [+]
>
> SAP Notes 571276 (PFCG: Transporting roles) and 511200 (Role assignment and profile comparison) provide detailed and helpful descriptions that you should take into consideration in any case.

6.4 Documentation and Redesigning

Comprehensive documentation that is always up-to-date can help you recognize optimization potentials at an early stage. You can usually implement minor changes to a concept much more quickly and flexibly than having to redesign a complete authorization concept after several years of operation. This would be especially important for a large project involving a high budget that needs to be approved first, requires more resources, a great deal of effort, and so on. Therefore, we once again recommend to always maintain useful documentation.

Documentation simplifies redesigning

Chapter 1, Process-Oriented Authorization Concept, already described what the documentation may look like, which has been derived from the concept for implementing the authorizations. Section 6.2, Creating and Testing Roles, also pointed out that it's essential to include test results in the documentation that have led to changes. Even if it appears to be a matter of course, the action of documenting gets shifted more and more to the background the longer time elapses after the implementation of the concept. However, changes are made on an ongoing basis, for example, because a position has been eliminated and another user is supposed to perform this task or because the use of the SAP ERP HCM system is continuously extended and so new functions are added that need to be authorized. Consequently, the authorization concept blossoms like a tree in spring. To enable the tree to grow as desired — widespread, high, or dense — you must frequently prune it. You should also check whether the authorization concept is growing out of control so that administration and maintenance work don't get out of hand or it becomes more and more difficult to implement the new requirements with the "old" concept. In this case, you must prune the authorization concept. Depending on which authorization tools you already use, additional instruments may help minimize the number of roles and simplify the role maintenance.

Better: create new roles

In general, it's advisable to create new roles instead of adapting existing roles, if major changes are supposed to be implemented. By doing so , you can ensure that the running operation isn't interrupted if the new authorization concept doesn't work as it should. But if you are unsure, you can assign the old role again and check the new roles.

Now let's move on to discuss some tips regarding the required redesign:

Changing over to the reference role

Let's assume you have only used the general authorization check so far and now want to extend the system usage to decentralized units. For example, time administrators in the branch offices are now supposed to be authorized to post times by themselves. You assign the same role, which only contains different areas of responsibility (e.g., personnel area), to all time administrators. In this case, it may be useful to use the reference role (see Chapter 2, General Authorization Check). To do so, you must define at least one new organizational level field, and you need to maintain some of the already existing roles again. You can estimate the customizing requirements by starting the PFCG_ORGFIELD_CREATE (Profile Generator: Create New Organizational Level Field) report in test mode. This creates a detailed log that indicates the customizing requirements. However, the customizing requirements are not usually as extensive as you might think.

Changing over to the structural authorization check

Before the structural authorization check is implemented, the VDSK1 (Organizational Key) field in the P_ORGIN authorization object is often used to distinguish between the different areas of responsibility. This leads to a very large number of roles that usually can be considerably reduced by implementing the structural authorization. Of course, it's not useful to replace the number of roles by the same number of structural profiles because that only shifts the maintenance work. Instead, as we mentioned in Chapter 3, the start object should be determined as dynamically as possible using function modules. This allows you to make do with a very small number of profiles. But, pay particular attention to the naming convention for the profiles so that you can prevent profiles from being assigned to the wrong users. When you change over to the structural authorization, you should first create the structural profiles and then set the VDSK1 field in the roles to "*."

It makes sense to use the context-dependent authorization check, if you have users with different functions for different areas of responsibility (see Chapter 4, Context-Dependent Authorization Check). The following procedure works well for changing over to the context-sensitive authorization check:

Changing over to the context-dependent authorization check

1. First, add the additional context authorization objects to the existing roles (see Chapter 4, Context-Dependent Authorization Check), and maintain them accordingly.

2. Transport the roles and carry out the user comparison. At this point, nothing changes for the users.

3. In Table T77S0, deactivate the authorization objects that are not context-dependent and activate the context-dependent objects. If major problems occur after the context-dependent authorization objects have been activated, you can reset the Customizing configurations so that each user is provided with proper authorizations again.

4. If everything works as it should, you can eliminate the authorization objects that are not context-sensitive in the roles.

6.5   Critical Success Factors

This completes the chapter, so let's review the critical success factors you should consider when implementing an authorization concept:

▶ When you define the responsibilities of the authorization administrators, ensure that auditing security is provided.

▶ Use the Profile Generator as well as all of the options provided to customize the functionality of the Profile Generator. In addition, check and document the Customizing settings.

▶ Schedule sufficient time to test the roles. In a large project, you should perform all integration tests and trainings for the roles that are used in the production environment at a later stage.

▶ Don't forget to include the test results in the documentation of the authorization concept.

The User Information System is comprised of several reports that you can use to simplify the management of users and roles. In this chapter, you'll learn how you can identify users with critical authorizations, and how you can obtain an overview of the general and structural authorizations of a user.

7 Reports for the Authorization System

For reporting of authorization and user data, you're provided with a comprehensive information system. You can find the User Information System in the SAP Easy Access menu under TOOLS • ADMINISTRATION • USER MAINTENANCE • INFORMATION SYSTEM or as a separate menu tree via Transaction SUIM (Figure 7.1).

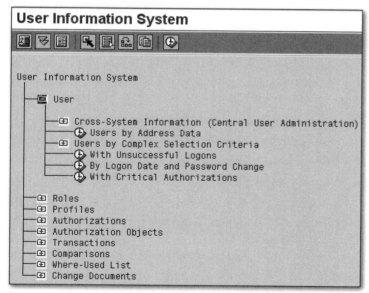

Figure 7.1 Transaction SUIM — User Information System

The following sections describe the evaluations that we — based on the authors' consulting experience — consider the most vital and valuable. These include:

▸ Analysis of users with critical authorizations (RSUSR008_009_NEW)

▸ Overview of the most vital authorizations of a user (RHUSERRELATIONS)

▸ Overview of all authorization objects of a user (Transaction SU56)

▸ Roles by complex selection criteria

▸ Assignment of single roles to composite roles

7.1 Analysis of Users with Critical Authorizations

Due to auditing and data protection issues, you might have to identify users with critical authorizations. As of SAP Basis Release 6.20 you are provided with Report RSUSR008_009_NEW, which replaces the former reports, RSUSR008 and RSUSR009. You can find this report in Transaction SUIM under USER • WITH CRITICAL AUTHORIZATIONS (see Figure 7.1). In this report, you determine which authorizations are to be considered as critical. If you created variants with critical authorizations, you can start the report for a variant or a combination of variants to obtain a list of users that meet these criteria. The following sections detail the evaluation based on two examples.

Example: user with developer authorization

The first example involves the identification of all users with developer authorization.

In order to maintain critical authorizations, you must first start the report as described previously.

1. In the initial screen, select the CRITICAL AUTHORIZATIONS button (Figure 7.2). In the subsequent MAINTENANCE view (Figure 7.3), you can create variants of your selection. The variants consist of multiple IDs of critical authorizations that you defined yourself. They in turn comprise the critical authorization data (authorization objects with characteristics).

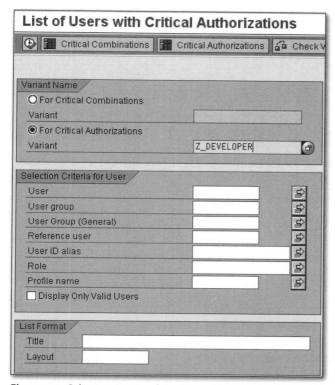

Figure 7.2 Selection Screen of the User with Critical Authorization Report

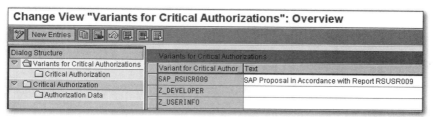

Figure 7.3 Creating Variants of Critical Authorizations for Selection

2. Select the CRITICAL AUTHORIZATION folder. Here, you can find some entries predefined by SAP. You can add your own customer-specific critical authorizations (Figure 7.4). Specify an ID, a descriptive text, and the color in which the critical authorization is to be displayed in the results list. You can also enter a transaction code. The authoriza-

tion data to be checked is then automatically transferred to the authorization data after saving it.

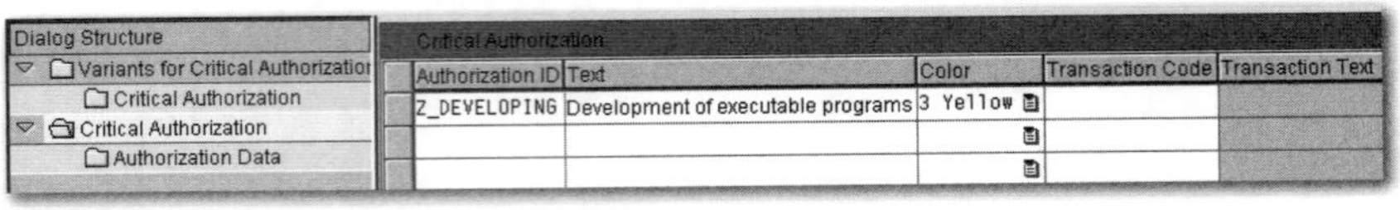

Figure 7.4 Adding Critical Authorizations

3. In the next step, you define the composition of the critical authorization (Figure 7.5). The required entries can be found in Transaction SU24 (Maintain the Assignments of Authorization Objects) and in your enterprise-specific requirements.

The example shown in Figure 7.5 defines the following authorizations for ID Z_DEVELOPING:

- ► S_TCODE (Transaction Rights) for SE37, SE38, or SE80
- ► S_DEVELOP (Development Rights) for Object Type PROG (Programs) and Activity 02 (Change)

[+] **Tip**

For the definition of critical authorizations, note the descriptions in the SAP documentation available under **Users and Roles • User Information System • Determining Users with the Users Node • with Critical Authorizations** (new version, RSUSR008_009_NEW).

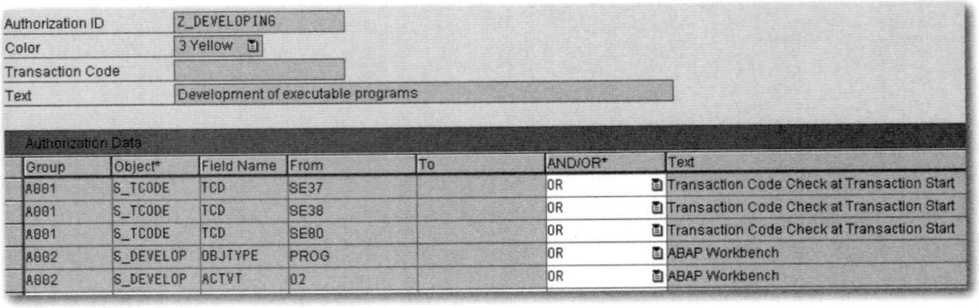

Figure 7.5 Maintaining Authorization Data for Z_DEVELOPING

4. Finally, you need to combine the critical authorizations into one selection variant, which in turn is used to implement the report. To do this, create the variant in the VARIANTS FOR CRITICAL AUTHORIZA-

TIONS view, and assign one or more critical authorizations to the variant in the CRITICAL AUTHORIZATION view (Figure 7.6).

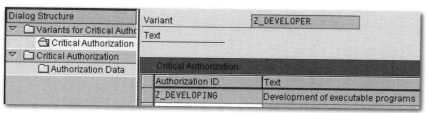

Figure 7.6 Assigning Critical Authorizations to a Variant

5. Then return to the SELECTION screen (see Figure 7.2), and carry out the report using an existing variant. Each AUTHORIZATION ID is displayed in the selected color and with the corresponding users identified (Figure 7.7). Click on the ID OF THE CRITICAL AUTHORIZATION to navigate to the DISPLAY/MAINTENANCE section of the critical authorization data.

List of Users with Critical Authorizations								

ID of CA	Text of Critical Authorization (CA)	User Name	Complete name	User group	Valid from	Valid to	Account no	User Type
Z_DEVELOPING	Development of executable programs	ESCHM	ESCHM	TRAINING_08				A Dialog
		HASSMANN	Richard Hassmann	PIKON				A Dialog
		IPROCON	Christian Luebke	PIKON				A Dialog

Number of Selected Users for Variant Z_DEVELOPER: 3

Figure 7.7 Three users have the authorization to develop programs.

Figure 7.7 shows three users who have at least one of the critical authorizations displayed in Figure 7.5.

Combinations of authorizations

In addition, you can arbitrarily combine the IDs of critical authorizations and create variants (similar to multiple selection). Within a combination, the authorizations are checked by means of an AND link. The user must have all authorizations contained in the combination in order to be selected.

Example: authorization proof

In our second example, you're supposed to prove that no employee is allowed to simultaneously create roles and users, and assign roles. To do this, you initially define the authorization IDs for role and user maintenance, as described in the first example. Then proceed as follows:

249

1. Return to the initial screen of the report, and then click on the CRITICAL COMBINATIONS button.

2. In the COMBINATION folder, enter an ID of the critical combination, select a color, and enter a description for the combination.

3. Go to the Critical Authorization folder, and assign the authorization IDs specified in step 1 to the combination. (Note: These IDs are now checked as AND link.)

4. In the VARIANTS FOR CRITICAL COMBINATION OF AUTHORIZATIONS folder, create a (selection) variant and assign one or more combinations to the variant below this folder. Multiple combinations within a variant are checked separately or as an OR link!

5. In the initial screen of the report (see Figure 7.2), select CRITICAL COMBINATIONS and enter your variant. The combinations are displayed in the specified colors and with the identified users.

[+] **Tip**

Use the 🗒 button (Display Details) to display the results list for a selected user and roles assigned to him as well as the authorization data.

7.2 Overview of the Most Vital Authorizations of a User

The authorizations of a user are assigned by means of various transactions. To obtain an overview of the most vital authorizations of a user, you are provided with Report RHUSERRELATIONS. You can't find this report in the User Information System, but you can start it by selecting SYSTEM • SERVICES • REPORTING from the menu. Among other things, this program provides you with the authorization switches of Table T77S0 (Figure 7.8). For the selected user, you are additionally provided with:

▶ the person and the validity period of the user in Infotype 0105.

▶ the organizational units to which the user is assigned or which he manages.

▶ the structural profiles to which the user is assigned.

▶ the roles and standard profiles to which the user is assigned via the role maintenance, via Infotype 1016 or via Infotype 1001, Subtype 007.

▶ the field values of the selected authorization objects from the user master record.

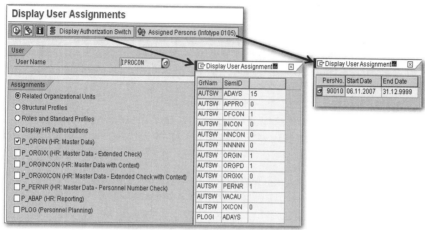

Figure 7.8 Selection Screen of Report RHUSERRELATIONS

[+]

The disadvantage of this report is that you don't obtain a general overview of all assigned authorization objects. To do this, you can use the transaction described in the next section.

7.3 Overview of all Authorization Objects of a User

Transaction SU56 provides you with a good general overview of which authorization objects are assigned to a user with which characteristics. When calling the transaction, you're provided with a list of all authorizations for the logged-on user that are entered in the buffer (Figure 7.9).

[!]

> **Warning**
>
> The buffer is refilled after each logon, so it's not up-to-date when the authorizations have been changed via the role maintenance after you logged on to the system.

You can use the button to select another user. You can also use this button to limit the display of the authorization objects to P_*, for example.

[Ex]

> **Example**
>
> If you want to know, for example, whether a user has the P_TRAVL authorization object, via which role or profile it is assigned, and which characteristics it has, we recommend starting this transaction.
>
> This application is also useful if you want to check authorization errors. For example, if you think that a specific authorization object has not been assigned to a user, because you can't find it in any of the roles provided in the user master record, you can look it up in the buffer (Transaction SU56). It's possible that an old assignment between profile and user still exists that derives from the time before the change from profiles to roles.

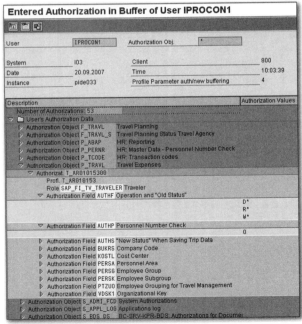

Figure 7.9 All Authorization Objects of a User

7.4   Roles by Complex Selection Criteria

Having dealt only with the user-related evaluations so far, well now focus on the analysis of roles. By selecting TOOLS • ADMINISTRATION • USER MAINTENANCE • INFORMATION SYSTEM • ROLES in the SAP EASY ACCESS menu you can access the reports provided by SAP for this purpose. The first report is comprised of all options of the other reports in one single selection screen. Because this screen is very complex, we'll describe it step by step. Figure 7.10 shows the upper part of the screen.

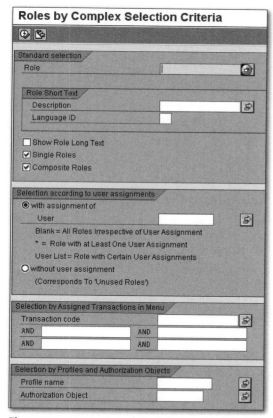

Figure 7.10 Upper Part of the Selection Screen

The first selection options of the report shown in Figure 7.10 are as follows:

- **Role**
  Search for specific roles, also partially qualified

- **Selection according to user assignments**
  Only roles are selected that are assigned to specific users or no user at all.

- **Transaction**
  Selection of roles with specific transactions in the menu

- **Profile name**
  Selection of roles with specific profiles

- **Authorization Object**
  Selection of roles with specific authorization objects

As you can see in Figure 7.11, you can display the fields for a specific, preselected authorization object (here: PLOG) using the Entry Values button.

In Figure 7.11, under Selection According to Authorization Values, you can enter the required field values, for example, in the Plan version field, to receive a list of all roles that contain the authorizations of the determined field values of the selected authorization object.

The additional selection fields displayed in Figure 7.11 are comprised of the following:

- **Selection by Field Name**
  Here you can enter a field name and value independent of a specific authorization object, for instance, the AUTHC (Authorization level) field that can be found in authorization objects P_ORGIN, P_ORGIN-CON, P_ORGXX, P_ORGXXCON, and P_PCLX.

- **Selection by MiniApps**
  Search according to roles that are assigned to specific MiniApps in the MiniApps tab of the role maintenance.

- **Additional selection criteria**
  Selection according to change information about the role

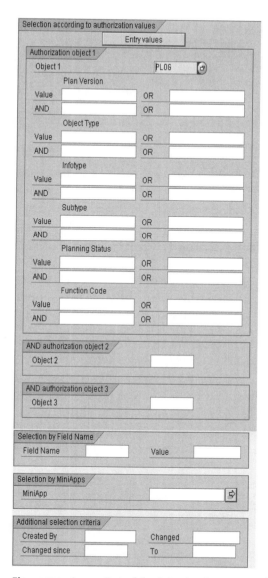

Figure 7.11 Lower Part of the Selection Screen — Values for Authorization Object PLOG, Expanded

Figure 7.12 shows the first part of a list of the roles after the selection by specific field values has been carried out. Double-click on the ROLE to obtain detailed information about it.

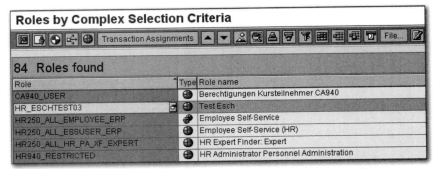

Figure 7.12 List with Roles for Specific Field Values of an Authorization Object

7.5 Assignment of Single Roles to Composite Roles

In Chapter 2, General Authorization Check, we described when it makes sense to combine single roles into composite roles. There are two options available to get an overview about which single roles were combined into which composite roles:

1. Start Transaction PFCG (Role Maintenance). Select Roles in COMPOSITE ROLES in the dropdown menu of the Views button. Initially, the system displays all composite roles (⊕), which you can expand using the small triangle (Figure 7.13). The single roles (⊕) are listed underneath. Use the SHOW DOCUMENTATION button to view the online documentation of the selected (standard) role on the right side of the screen.

Roles in Comp. Roles	Description
▽ ⊕ SAP_EMPLOYEE_ERP	Employee Self-Service
⊕ SAP_BC_EMPLOYEE	Employee Self-Service (BC)
⊕ SAP_BC_ENDUSER	Non-critical Basis Authorizations for All Users
⊕ SAP_ESSUSER_ERP	Employee Self-Service (HR)
⊕ SAP_HR_EMPLOYEE_DE_ERP	Employee Self-Service Germany
⊕ SAP_HR_EMPLOYEE_US_ERP	Employee Self-Service USA
⊕ SAP_HR_PA_XF_EXPERT	HR Expert Finder: Expert
▷ ⊕ SAP_EMPLOYEE_ERP05	Composite role for all country-specific functions
▷ ⊕ SAP_FMCA_ALL	공공 부문에 대한 계약 회계
▷ ⊕ SAP_ICC_KOREA_SUPER	Korea Super User
▷ ⊕ SAP_ICM_C_AGENT	Commissions: Composite Role - AGENT
▷ ⊕ SAP_ICM_C_AUDITOR	Commissions: Composite Role - AUDITOR

Figure 7.13 Transaction PFCG: Roles in Composite Roles

2. Call Transaction SE16 (Data Browser: Initial Screen) and enter the table name, AGR_AGRS. The AGR_NAME column lists the composite roles, while the CHILD_AGR column lists all assigned single roles (Figure 7.14).

MANDT	AGR_NAME	CHILD_AGR	ATTRIBUTES
800	SAP_EMPLOYEE_ERP	SAP_BC_EMPLOYEE	
800	SAP_EMPLOYEE_ERP	SAP_BC_ENDUSER	
800	SAP_EMPLOYEE_ERP	SAP_ESSUSER_ERP	
800	SAP_EMPLOYEE_ERP	SAP_HR_EMPLOYEE_DE_ERP	
800	SAP_EMPLOYEE_ERP	SAP_HR_EMPLOYEE_US_ERP	
800	SAP_EMPLOYEE_ERP	SAP_HR_PA_XF_EXPERT	
800	SAP_EMPLOYEE_ERP05	SAP_EMPLOYEE_ERP05_AR	
800	SAP_EMPLOYEE_ERP05	SAP_EMPLOYEE_ERP05_AT	

Figure 7.14 Transaction SE16: Roles in Composite Roles

7.6   Additional Reports

To conclude this chapter, we'll present three very interesting additional reports.

The *List of Users According to Logon Date and Password Change* report is available in the SAP Easy Access menu under TOOLS• ADMINISTRATION • USER MAINTENANCE • INFORMATION SYSTEM • USER. The report provides information about when a user last logged on and whether he changed his password on that occasion. The comprehensive selection screen enables you to make selections according to days since the last logon or password change. Additionally, you can select according to:

"Users According to Logon Date and Password Change"

▶ the validity of the user.

▶ the lock of the user.

▶ users with failed logon attempts.

▶ user type.

▶ status of the password (valid, initial password, inactive).

The *Comparisons* report (TOOLS • ADMINISTRATION • USER MAINTENANCE • INFORMATION SYSTEM • COMPARISONS • FROM USERS) enables you to compare users from different systems.

"Comparisons"

"Change Documents for Users"

Changes to the authorization system are automatically documented. Figure 7.15 shows the report that evaluates the documentation. In the *Change Documents for Users* report (TOOLS • ADMINISTRATION • USER MAINTENANCE • INFORMATION SYSTEM • CHANGE DOCUMENTS • FOR USERS) you can make selections according to both the user who implements the changes (CHANGES BY field) and the user to be changed (USER field).

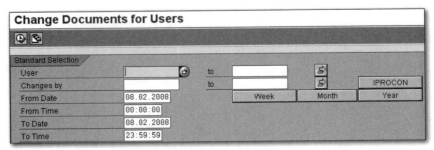

Figure 7.15 "Change Documents for Users" Report

7.7 Summary

The numerous examples detailed in this chapter show that the reporting of the authorization system is very comprehensive in the standard version, and that it covers a large part of the requirements. So, it's always worth thoroughly checking the options of the standard report in this work area before you start programming customer-specific reports. The structural authorizations constitute an exception to this rule. If you want to learn more about the structural profiles of the users beyond the assignment analysis, such as in which structures you can find specific object types (see Section 7.2, Overview of the Most Vital Authorizations of a User of a User), you must use customer-specific reports.

How do programmers proceed if they want to implement correct authorization checks in customer-specific reports? This chapter provides information about the technical means available for this purpose. And, we'll give you some tips regarding authorizations for program developers.

8 Authorizations in Programming

The programming of authorization checks in customer-specific reports is a topic that shouldn't be neglected in HCM projects. In addition to logical databases, numerous other tools also play a significant role.

8.1 Authorizations in Reports Without Logical Databases

A programmer will initially try to use one of the logical databases for implementing a requirement, which were described in Chapter 5. So in this chapter, we'll also detail which authorization checks are implemented by the respective logical database.

There are some situations in which this is not sufficient. These include:

Sometimes logical databases are not sufficient

▶ Necessary checks for authorization objects that are not carried out by the logical database, for example, the cluster authorization object, P_PCLX

▶ Reading of data that belongs to a logical database, which is not the actual logical database of the report; for instance, reading of personnel administration data from the organizational management reports

▶ Reports with critical performance for which the logical database isn't fast enough

▶ Reading of HCM data in function modules that are called, for example, from another ERP component or from web applications (The logical database can only be used for reports.)

The authorization checks must be programmed explicitly for all of these situations. To do this, you're provided with various methods that we'll present in the following sections.

8.1.1 SAP Function Modules with Authorization Check

Generally speaking, the best way to read data is to use existing SAP function modules that usually implement all required authorization checks.

The most critical function modules for reading HCM data are listed in Table 8.1. Even though this list isn't particularly long, it's still sufficient in most cases.

Technical name	Meaning
HR_READ_INFOTYPE	Reading of infotypes in personnel administration and (former) recruitment
HR_READ_SUBTYPE	Reading of infotypes and subtypes in personnel administration and (former) recruitment
RH_READ_INFTY	Reading of any infotypes of the HRP* tables (including data from Organizational Management, Training and Event Management, and all other HCM components outside of personnel administration and applicant management)

Table 8.1 Function Modules for HCM Data

8.1.2 Deactivating the Authorization Check using SAP function modules

The deactivation of authorization checks in reports should be treated with special care. As a basic rule, you either generally prohibit it in your development guidelines or subject it to considerably high check requirements. In individual cases, however, it may be necessary to deactivate the authorization check for reading specific infotypes. This is done for technical reasons, as you'll see in the following example:

Example [Ex]

Users may not see Infotype 0008 (Basic pay), for example. However, the pay scale group/level is supposed to be displayed for the user. And this pay scale group/level is stored in Infotype 0008. In the standard version, you would have to assign read authorization for Infotype 0008 to the users. As a result, the users could view, for example, all salary data using Transaction PA20 (Display HR Master Data).

If you want to display only the pay scale group/level, the report must either work without any authorization check (Authorization Object P_ABAP, simplification degree 2 — in Chapter 5, on the Authorization Object P_ABAP) or the customer-specific report works without any authorization check for reading Infotype 0008.

In addition, performance aspects could result in the deactivation of authorization checks for specific data accesses or in certain reports. In this case, it's very important to implement the deactivation separately according to general and structural checks.

Performance aspects

The deactivation of the authorization check in Organizational Management or in all HCM components that work with the HRP* tables is very simple. Here, virtually all function modules reading infotypes are equipped with import parameters for deactivating the authorization check. An example would be the RH_READ_INFTY function module. It includes two import parameters that are relevant for checking the authorizations. The first parameter controlling the general authorization check is called `authority`. The second parameter, `with_stru_auth`, is used to check the structural authorization. Listing 8.1 shows the reading of the customer-specific Infotype 9605.

Deactivating the check via parameters

```
CALL FUNCTION 'RH_READ_INFTY'
  EXPORTING
    authority        = 'DISP'
    with_stru_auth   = 'X'
    infty            = '9605'
    begda            = p9603-begda
    endda            = p9603-endda
  TABLES
    innnn            = i9605
  OBJECTS            = i_object
```

```
EXCEPTIONS
    all_infty_with_subty = 1
    nothing_found        = 2
    no_objects           = 3
    wrong_condition      = 4
    wrong_parameters     = 5
    OTHERS               = 6.
```

Listing 8.1 Reading an Infotype with Activated Authorization Check in Organizational Management

The required general authorization is the reading (Function Code DISP). In addition, the structural authorization check is activated. To deactivate the general authorization check, you must enter the value " " (blank) under `authority`. To deactivate the structural check, also enter " " (blank) under `with_stru_auth`.

Infotypes PA* and PB*

For personnel administration and the (former) applicant management, the HR_READ_SUBTYPE function module works with an import parameter (`NO_AUTH_CHECK`) to deactivate the authorization check. This can only be controlled generally, however. A differentiation by general and structural authorization isn't possible.

The HR_READ_INFOTYPE function module also reads the infotypes of personnel administration and the (former) applicant management. However, it is not provided with a parameter for controlling the authorization check.

Deactivating the check via modules

In order to work with the HR_READ_INFOTYPE function module and to bypass the authorization check in certain situations, you can use the special HR_READ_INFOTYPE_AUTHC_DISABLE function module. It deactivates the authorization check in personnel administration and the (former) applicant management for exactly one access. This means that the authorization check is active again for the next call of HR_READ_INFOTYPE.

Listing 8.2 shows how you can deactivate the authorization check for reading Infotype 0008:

```
call function 'HR_READ_INFOTYPE_AUTHC_DISABLE'.
CALL FUNCTION 'HR_READ_INFOTYPE'
EXPORTING
```

```
      tclas = 'A'
      pernr = pernr-pernr
      infty = '0008'
      begda = pn-begda
      endda = pn-endda
*     BYPASS_BUFFER= ' '
*     LEGACY_MODE= ' '
*  IMPORTING
*  SUBRC=
   TABLES
      infty_tab= p0008
*  EXCEPTIONS
*     INFTY_NOT_FOUND= 1
*     OTHERS = 2
```

Listing 8.2 Deactivating the Authorization Check for Reading Infotype 0008

In Organizational Management, there are also function modules to activate and deactivate the authorization check.

Function modules for deactivating the authorization check in OM

▶ **RH_AUTHORITY_CHECK_OFF**
The authorization check is generally deactivated (general and structural at the same time).

▶ **RH_AUTHORITY_CHECK_ON**
The authorization check is generally activated.

▶ **RH_AUTHORITY_CHECK_STATUS**
The function module checks whether the authorization check is activated or deactivated.

▶ **RH_DEACTIVATE_STUCTURED_AC**
The function module deactivates the structural authorization.

Warning	[!]

In certain situations it's possible that a TIME_OUT or memory overflow can occur when you process structural authorizations. In this case we recommend checking whether SAP Note 1047995 (Error during processing of structural authorizations) is relevant for you.

8.1.3 Authorization Check Directly in Coding

If none of the previously described options meets your requirements, you as the programmer can use ABAP Command `AUTHORITY-CHECK` to call the respective authorization object. Figure 8.1 shows how you can integrate this command in your coding in the ABAP Editor (Transaction SE80 or SE38) using the Pattern button while simultaneously entering the required authorization object.

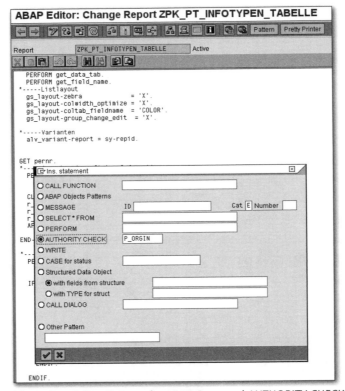

Figure 8.1 Calling Patterns for ABAP Command AUTHORITY-CHECK

Listing 8.3 shows the result that is displayed in the source code. In this case, exactly those fields that belong to the respective authorization object (in this case: P_ORGIN (HR: Master Data)) are listed. You should provide all these fields with a value.

```
AUTHORITY-CHECK OBJECT 'P_ORGIN'
         ID 'INFTY' FIELD '_____'
         ID 'SUBTY' FIELD '_____'
         ID 'AUTHC' FIELD '_____'
         ID 'PERSA' FIELD '_____'
         ID 'PERSG' FIELD '_____'
         ID 'PERSK' FIELD '_____'
         ID 'VDSK1' FIELD '_____'.
```

Listing 8.3 Patterns of ABAP Command AUTHORITY-CHECK

Example [Ex]

You can read the change documents of personnel administration in a customer-specific report. The documents are stored in clusters LA (long-term documents) and SA (short-term documents). To do this, you must check the authorization in object P_PCLX (HR: Cluster). Read authorization (authorization level R) is sufficient here.

Listing 8.4 shows how you can implement the example described previously for checking the read authorization for clusters LA and SA.

```
AUTHORITY-CHECK OBJECT 'P_PCLX'
         ID 'RELID' FIELD 'LA'
         ID 'AUTHC' FIELD 'R'.
IF sy-subrc NE 0.
  MESSAGE e003(y1). "No authorization for cluster LA (long-
term documents).
ENDIF.

AUTHORITY-CHECK OBJECT 'P_PCLX'
         ID 'RELID' FIELD 'SA'
         ID 'AUTHC' FIELD 'R'.

IF sy-subrc NE 0.
  MESSAGE e004(y1). "No authorization for cluster SA (short-
term documents).
ENDIF.
```

Listing 8.4 Example of Checking the Read Authorization for Clusters

[+] **Tip**

The most critical authorization objects for programming are also described back in Chapter 2, section 2.3, Authorization Objects. You can also refer to Appendix B if you require other objects for special purposes. There, you can find a list of all HCM authorization objects, including references to the sections in which they are described.

8.2 How the Logical Databases Handle Missing Authorizations

The logical databases display an object only if the calling user is assigned to the authorization for the infotype used in this report. If the authorization is missing even only for an infotype or subtype, the entire object, such as the personnel number is not displayed. This makes sense, for example, in the payroll driver, because otherwise the payroll results would be different depending on the authorization of the calling user.

Disadvantage of the standard

In practice it's preferable that in other reports the object is displayed, but not the information for which no authorization is available. For example, the system could display the names and telephone numbers in an employee list; the salary, however, could only be viewed with the appropriate authorization.

Programming a deviating procedure

The method just described constitutes the default behavior of all logical databases. If you want to have a different behavior for your own reports, the following procedure will work:

1. Declare the critical infotypes with INFOTYPES nnnn MODE N instead of INFOTYPES nnnn. In doing so, you make sure the infotype is not imported by the logical database and no authorization check is performed.

2. After the GET event has been run in the logical database, you read the declared infotypes directly or using function modules. You can implement the authorization check as required for the concrete case.

For more details refer to SAP Note 142865 (SAPDBPNP authorization check is too strict). Here you can also find a sample coding.

Alternatively, you can also use the PNP_SW_SKIP_PERNR switch in coding during INITIALIZATION. This switch is set to "Y" by default. If you set the switch to "N," the personnel numbers are not skipped, but you are provided with the infotypes for which the user has authorization.

Alternative procedure

8.3 Enterprise-Specific Database with Own Authorization Check

The logical databases of the standard version (see Chapter 5.1, Logical Databases) and their underlying data structures form the basis of all forms of reporting described in this book. However, its shortcomings, particularly with regard to the aggregation and selection options, occur in nearly all reports.

One alternative is the enterprise-specific logical database. A separate logical database can encapsulate a large portion of the enterprise-specific logic, which means it does not have to be reprogrammed for every report. The programming of a separate logical database ensures a virtually unlimited flexibility, also for the authorization concept. That's because the access to reports isn't restricted by the structural organization and the check performed on personnel master data. You can also assign employees to VIP levels, for instance, VIP 1 = executive board, managing director, VIP 2 = manager, and so on, based on different criteria. Depending on the target group, you can also design the selection screen, choice of fields, and the option to change the layout of a report.

Higher flexibility for authorization checks

Now let's move on to describe how a customer-specific logical database was combined with a customer-specific authorization concept for reporting in a specific project.

Logical database for reporting

The users of the reports who work with the customer-specific logical database are assigned to roles. The roles relate to function owners, such as "Controller," "Personnel Attendant," "Manager". These roles are only relevant within personnel reporting, and the roles contain the authorized reports.

For each report, you can specify the following checks via Customizing tables:

Options in the authorization concept

▶ **Access indicator**
Which employees can be accessed? For this purpose, the employees are assigned to an access level according to the position (executive board, head of department, and so on).

▶ **Structural authorization**
Which organizational units can be accessed? This is implemented by defining various levels, such as 1 = all organizational units, 2 = directly assigned organizational units, 3 = only own organizational units, and so on.

▶ **Selection variant**
Which selection criteria are available? Here, you define selection variants with permitted selection fields.

▶ **Filter criterion**
Which employee groups can be accessed? For this purpose, the employees are assigned to a filter criterion based on different indicators (e.g., disability, sales employee).

▶ **Output variant**
Which report content is supposed to be output? Here, you control the indicators per report content in the program.

▶ **Projection mode**
Are reorganizations to be compensated so that you can compare different key days?

▶ **Layout variant**
Do you want to change and store defined layout variants (e.g., by differentiating end user, key user, and power user)?

Assigning the role to the user In a customer-specific PA Infotype, *Personnel reporting role*, the role is assigned to the user based on a specific period. The user can be assigned both multiple roles and an excerpt of a role by limiting the quantity of authorized reports for the individual case within a role. The benefit of this is that changes to this infotype are automatically logged in a revision-proof form.

[+] **Tip**

The SAP PRESS book, *HR Reporting with SAP*, comprehensively presents the options of an enterprise-specific logical database.

8.4 Authorizations for Programmers

You should implement programming code exclusively in a development system to avoid transferring incorrect data in infotypes, tables, or clusters to the production system when testing programs that change the data. Therefore, programmers shouldn't have the authorization to develop workbench objects in an integration system or production system. The right to debug programs may neither be assigned, because this can also modify data. The debugging authorization can be issued also in production systems in combination with a pure read authorization for development objects (Authorization Object, S_DEVELOP – ABAP Workbench), because then changes to data are not permitted during debugging.

To enable programmers to intervene in critical situations, it makes sense to create emergency users with secret passwords in the production system. These secret passwords are only released in case of an emergency that requires immediate action in the production system. To avoid misuse, a second employee from the specialist department may be present during the recovery operation to control the work of the programmer.

To avoid the unwanted reading and changing of data, you must pay special attention to the following points.

▶ Within a system, the changes to programs become effective immediately after generating the report in all clients. So if the developer has the authorization to start a report in a client of the development system and if real data, which was copied for test purposes, is provided in this client, he may access data that he wouldn't be able to view under normal circumstances. It usually makes sense to only use anonymized data in all clients of a development system.

▶ If the developer uses the SELECT command in combination with the CLIENT SPECIFIED addition for reading tables, he can read data from other clients of the same system. Typically, it's not allowed to work with this addition because it can also be used to process infotype tables to which the programmers are not supposed to have access. It's reasonable to check the programs for this addition at regular intervals.

▶ Programs are migrated from the development system to other systems, so, you can take measures to only authorize the SAP Basis or a similar institution to migrate workbench objects. Before the programs are released and migrated to the production system, you should check whether they comply with the internal programming guidelines.

▶ You can implement the check of the programming guideline compliance by means of regular spot checks or regular utilization of appropriate analysis reports. By default, the following options are available:

Transaction S_ALR_87101287 (Report RSABAPSC – Statistical program analysis to find ABAP lang. commands). In this case, you can only evaluate single reports individually.

Program RPINCL10 (String Search in Reports): Enables generic searches, for example, in reports named ZP* using strings of your choice.

Programming guidelines Programming guidelines that are meaningful from the point of view of authorizations:

▶ Prohibiting the CLIENT SPECIFIED addition

▶ Prohibiting SELECTS on tables containing application data (in HCM, particularly PA*, PB*, HRP*) with exceptional rules

▶ Prohibiting the calling of function modules without authorization check and deactivating authorization checks via function modules; again with exceptional rules

8.5 Downloading from Reports

The S_GUI authorization object (Authorization for GUI activities) checks, among other things, the export of data to Microsoft Excel, for example. We would like to deal with two requirements of programming in this context.

Removing the download button The download of HCM data, for example, to Microsoft Excel, frequently simplifies your work; however, it is often considered as critical from the data protection and co-determination points of view. For this reason, the Excel button has become a "red rag," because it's not working in case of missing authorizations (Figure 8.2).

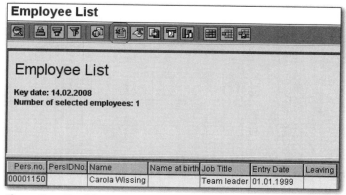

Figure 8.2 Excel Button in Output List

Listing 8.5 shows the options to suppress the display of this button for customer reports. First define the following subroutine:

```
FORM set_pf_status USING rt_extab TYPE slis_t_extab.
  DATA: func LIKE rsmpe-func.
  func = '&vexcel'.
  APPEND func TO rt_extab.
* Set status
  SET pf_status 'standard_fullscr_hr' EXCLUDING rt_extab.
ENDFORM."set_pf_status
```

Subroutine SET_PF_STATUS must then be transferred to function module REUSE_ALV_GRID_DISPLAY:

```
* Display List
CALL FUNCTION 'REUSE_ALV_GRID_DISPLAY'
  EXPORTING
      i_background_id    = 'ALV_BACKGROUND'
      i_buffer_active    = 'X'
      i_callback_program = g_repid
      i_callback_pf_status_set = 'SET_PF_STATUS'
      i_structure_name   = 'SFLIGHT'
      is_layout          = gs_layout
      i_save             = g_save
      is_variant         = gs_variant
      it_events          = gt_events[]
*     I_SCREEN_START_COLUMN   = 0      "Use coordinates for
*     I_SCREEN_START_
LINE      = 0      "display as dialog box
```

```
*       I_SCREEN_END_COLUMN      = 0
*       I_SCREEN_END_LINE        = 0
  IMPORTING
        e_exit_caused_by_caller = g_exit_caused_by_caller
        es_exit_caused_by_user  = gs_exit_caused_by_user
  TABLES
        t_outtab = gt_outtab
  EXCEPTIONS
        program_error = 1
        OTHERS        = 2.
```

Listing 8.5 Suppressing the Display of the Download Button to Microsoft Excel

Using this very simple method enables you to remove the ▦ Microsoft Excel button from the output list in customer-specific reports that are programmed correspondingly.

Download only in exceptional cases

Often, the following situation arises: As a general rule, the download authorization is not assigned. But for specific reports, selected users are supposed to be able to implement a download. To do this, you have two options in your customer-specific reporting:

▶ In the report, you completely set up the table to be output — including the separator for Microsoft Excel. Then you transfer the table to the GUI_DOWNLOAD function module, including the NO_AUTH_CHECK parameter with value "X."

▶ If you implement the download using the convenient tools of the ALV grid and want to omit the authorization check, the programming work is much more complex. (A description would go beyond the scope of this book; however, you can contact the authors to obtain more information.)

8.6 Critical Success Factors

To end this chapter, let's summarize the key things to remember to ensure a careful handling of the authorization check in your customer-specific reporting:

▶ Ensure that the development guidelines contain clear specifications for handling the authorizations topic.

▶ Pay attention to the methods — either automated or supported by procedures — that control the compliance with the development guidelines.

▶ Make provisions for exceptional situations in which deviations from the guideline occur.

▶ Assign the authorization for program developers with care.

▶ Always ensure compliance with the data protection guidelines valid for your enterprise, and, if possible, involve the departments responsible for data protection and auditing, as well as the co-determination aspect.

If the system denies you access to data, this usually involves an authorization problem. In this chapter, we'll describe how you can analyze authorization problems and which tools are available to use.

9   Troubleshooting

Your HCM system has gone live; the authorizations were tested elaborately and have gone live as well. But it doesn't take long for the first users to call: They can't view or maintain specific data, although they should be authorized to do so. What needs to be done in this case?

This chapter provides you with various ways and tools that enable you to search, detect, and remedy errors within the general, structural, and context-dependent authorization check.

9.1   Troubleshooting in General Authorizations

The general authorization check provides two tools that are described in detail in the following sections. After that, we'll provide some tips on how you can track down tenacious errors.

9.1.1   Authorization Error Analysis Using Transaction SU53

Transaction SU53 (Display Authorization Data) should be available in the authorizations of every user, because if a transaction is denied due to a missing authorization, the user can directly call Transaction SU53 and directly describe the error to the authorization administrator during reporting based on the information displayed on screen (Figure 9.1).

Reporting an error using Transaction SU53

The transaction code can be called in all modes. The only prerequisite is that you call it immediately after the denial. Instead of entering the

transaction code directly, you can also call it via SYSTEM • UTILITIES • DIS-
PLAY AUTHORIZATION CHECK.

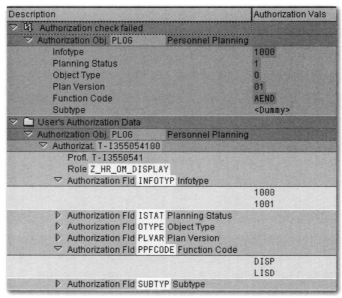

Description	Authorization Vals
▽ 🔲 Authorization check failed	
▽ Authorization Obj. PLOG Personnel Planning	
Infotype	1000
Planning Status	1
Object Type	O
Plan Version	01
Function Code	AEND
Subtype	<Dummy>
▽ 🗁 User's Authorization Data	
▽ Authorization Obj. PLOG Personnel Planning	
▽ Authorizat. T-I355054100	
Profl. T-I3550541	
Role Z_HR_OM_DISPLAY	
▽ Authorization Fld INFOTYP Infotype	
	1000
	1001
▷ Authorization Fld ISTAT Planning Status	
▷ Authorization Fld OTYPE Object Type	
▷ Authorization Fld PLVAR Plan Version	
▽ Authorization Fld PPFCODE Function Code	
	DISP
	LISD
▷ Authorization Fld SUBTYP Subtype	

Figure 9.1 Result of the Authorization Error Analysis: The User May Display (DISP)
Infotype 1001, But Not Change It

More details about the example

Figure 9.1 shows the call of SU53 after the user attempted to call the
changing of relationships within Maintenance Transaction PP01 of Organizational Management.

In the upper part of the screen — AUTHORIZATION CHECK FAILED — the
system displays which authorization is required in the PLOG AUTHORIZA-
TION object (Personnel planning): The changing (function code AEND)
of Infotype 1001 for object type O (organizational unit) with planning
status 1 (active) and plan version 01.

The lower part of the screen — USER'S AUTHORIZATION DATA — provides
a list of the existing user authorizations in the required authorization
object. In this example, only the display authorization (function codes
DISP and LISD) for Infotypes 1000 and 1001 are available.

Deficiencies of SU53

Frequently, the authorization error analysis using Transaction SU53 is
not sufficient to completely retrace the authorization checks because:

▶ some authorization objects are not evaluated properly (e.g., P_PERNR).

▶ often, the entire check flow is vital; however, Transaction SU53 only provides the last check (frequently for P_ABAP, the error lies further in the past).

▶ the problem does not occur for a dialog user, but for an RFC user, for example.

▶ it makes a statement about the failed checks, but provides no information about what is actually checked.

Therefore, the following section presents another method for error analysis that you can use to record checked authorizations.

9.1.2 Authorization Trace

Using the system trace function you can record the complete authorization check for any action and system user. Here, all check authorization objects, including the object fields and the tested values, are recorded.

To create an authorization trace, you should proceed as follows:

Creating a system trace

1. In the SAP EASY ACCESS menu, select TOOLS • ADMINISTRATION • MONITOR • TRACES • SYSTEM TRACE, or start Transaction ST01, and activate the authorization check option.

2. The trace would now record the authorization checks of all users. You can limit the recording to your own users. To do so, select **Edit • Filter • Shared** and enter your user names or the name of the user who has the authorization problem under TRACE FOR USER ONLY .

3. Start the trace by clicking the TRACE ON button (Figure 9.2).

4. Then perform the actions to be traced or have them performed by the appropriate user.

5. After having completed the actions, click the TRACE OFF button and then the ANALYSIS button.

6. If required, change the user name if another user has executed the actions in the system, and start the analysis.

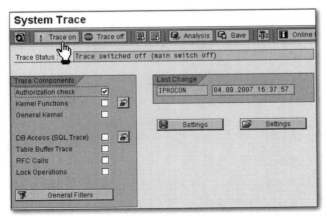

Figure 9.2 Starting the System Trace to Record Authorization Checks

Results of the authorization trace

7. After carrying out the first steps, you obtain a comprehensive file containing the checked objects (Figure 9.3). The return code (RC) after the object indicates whether the check was successful (0) or not (>0). In the TEXT column, you can find the authorization fields and the checked (required) values.

8. Figure 9.3 provides an example with a small excerpt of a trace analysis. It shows two authorization checks (see AUTH under TYPE), both in the PLOG authorization object (under OBJECT). The following authorizations were required:

   ▶ Display (function code DISP) in plan version 01 for object type O (organizational unit) for any infotype, subtype, and planning status

   ▶ Change (function code AEND) in plan version 01 for object type O (organizational unit) for any infotype and subtype in planning status 1

9. The first check was successful (RC = 0), the second check failed (RC = 4).

[+]

Differentiation Through Return Codes

A differentiation of unsuccessful checks through different return codes normally makes no sense, because the return codes are highly program specific. To understand them, you must have extensive background knowledge.

```
Client:      800 User:        IPROCON1    Transaction P010              D5F35ADCE09DF1DE8275001372646C6A
Work Process            2 PID            Date: 04.09.2007              Start:16:33:58:424.806Finish:16:33:58:448.571
First Block of Dialog Step              Last Block in Dialog Step
Block Version:          702 No. of Records:            1 File Version: 1
```

hh:mm:ss:ms	Type	Lasts(us)	Object		Text
16:33:58:425	AUTH	- - -	PLOG	RC=4	PPFCODE=AEND;PLVAR=01;OTYPE=0;INFOTYP=1000;SUBTYP= ;ISTAT=1;

```
Client:      800 User:        IPROCON1    Transaction P010              40F45ADCA0D4F11C8275001372646C6A
Work Process            2 PID            Date: 04.09.2007              Start:16:37:42:983.037Finish:16:37:42:8.469
First Block of Dialog Step              Last Block in Dialog Step
Block Version:          1226 No. of Records:           3 File Version: 1
```

hh:mm:ss:ms	Type	Lasts(us)	Object		Text
16:37:42:983	AUTH	- - -	S_TCODE	RC=0	TCD=P010;
16:37:42:984	AUTH	- - -	PLOG	RC=0	INFOTYP= ;ISTAT= ;OTYPE=0;PLVAR= ;PPFCODE= ;SUBTYP= ;
16:37:42:993	AUTH	- - -	PLOG	RC=0	PPFCODE=DISP;PLVAR=01;OTYPE=0;INFOTYP= ;SUBTYP= ;ISTAT= ;

Figure 9.3 Evaluation of an Authorization Check Record

> **Tip** [+]
>
> The system trace is very useful for analyzing errors, but it can also support you in assigning the authorizations. If you initially implement the actions via a user who has comprehensive authorization, you can see which authorizations you must assign to the user.

Note that the system trace does not always return all authorization data. Sometimes, you perform checks for objects that are not necessarily required. For example, Display Transaction PA20 for HR master data checks authorization object S_GUI (Authorization for GUI Activities) using activity 61 (Export). For this check, the system ignores that this authorization (RC = 4) is missing.

Limitations of the trace

The check method is also very program specific. Some programmers implement very simple authorization checks due to performance reasons and refine them as required at a later point. So when they start the PA transactions, the system checks globally whether any authorization is available in any master data authorization object. The authorizations for infotypes, which are displayed in the transaction, are only checked during a later program step.

Consequently, reading authorization traces requires a sound knowledge about the respective application and can only be done by an HCM expert.

9.1.3 Manual Troubleshooting

If the error analysis using the tools presented so far was not successful, you need to detect the error manually. Here, it is useful for you to know which authorizations a user has for a specific object. For this purpose, use report RHUSERRELATIONS or Transaction SU56 (see Section 7.2, Overview of the Most Vital Authorizations of a User, and Section 7.3, Overview of all Authorization Objects of a User). Using report RHUSERRELATIONS also enables you to check the settings of the authorization main switches.

In addition, you must precisely analyze the reason of the authorization problem:

▶ **The authorization problems only occur for certain infotypes**
Check the infotype settings of the ACCESS AUTHORIZATION indicator in Table T582A (see Section 2.6, Period of Responsibility and Time Logic).

[Ex]

> **Example**
>
> If a user has no access to Infotype 0006 (Addresses), that is, to a person for which the user is no longer responsible, but for which he still has to check historical data, it could be due to the indicator (Figure 9.4) set for Infotype 0006.
>
> Write access for ESS users is assigned via P_PERNR for your own address data. If you mistakenly enter "*," the authorization for this infotype (0006) is assigned negatively (Figure 9.5).

▶ **The problems occur only for one user and one single personnel number**
This is often caused by a wrong setting of the P_PERNR authorization object (see Section 2.3.3, Additional Authorization Objects for Master and Time Data). If you don't enter an „I" under Interpretation of Assigned Personnel Number (authorization for your own personnel number), but an "E" or "*," "E" is always assumed to be the basis (excluding the authorization for your own personnel number).

▶ **Multiple users have an authorization problem for one single personnel number**
You should carefully check the organizational assignment and the relationship with the organizational structure of this personnel number. To do this, use Infotype 0001 (Organizational assignment) or the Transactions of Organizational Management.

Additionally, check the settings of the AUTSW ADAYS authorization main switch in Table T77S0 (see Section 2.6, Period of Responsibility and Time Logic). After an organizational change, this extends the period of responsibility for an administrator by a tolerance period beyond the previous organizational assignment.

▸ **The authorization problems occur in an unknown program**
Provided that you have the debugging authorization, set a breakpoint on AUTHORITY-CHECK and/or MESSAGE, execute the program, and analyze the program behavior.

▸ **The error occurs after you've imported support packages**
For errors of this type, we recommend searching for coding changes, both in the classes, CL_HRPAD00AUTH_CHECK_STD and CL_HRPAD-00AUTH_CHECK_FAST, in Report SAPFP50P, and in function group HRAC. Smaller coding parts can also be found in reports SAPDBPAP, SAPDBPNP, and SAPFP50M. These development objects all contain authorization coding.

▸ **You use customer-specific authorization objects or you've customized the authorization BAdIs**
Set breakpoints or implement careful analyses to ensure that the checks implemented there are correct.

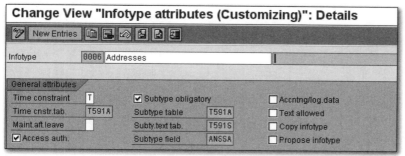

Figure 9.4 Infotype 0006 Switch for Date-Dependent Authorization Check

Figure 9.5 Wrong Entry in the P_PERNR Authorization Object

9.2 Troubleshooting in Structural Authorizations

Detecting errors in structural authorizations is slightly more difficult. Here, you are not provided with any tools like the ones described earlier.

[!]

> **Warning**
>
> The structural authorizations are neither contained in Transaction SU53 nor in the authorization trace. Because this is a pure HCM tool, you can't use the tools of the general authorization.

You can use the ▣ button in Transaction OOSB (Assignment of Structural Profiles to Users) to search errors in the structural authorization (see Section 3.2, Maintaining the Structural Profiles).

Using this button, you call report RHAUTH01 that lists all object types with object ID contained in the structural profile and indicates the total number. If you can't find an object in the list, the structural authorization denies the access.

In the following sections, we'll describe two examples of troubleshooting in the structural authorization check:

[Ex]

> **Example 1**
>
> User CHICAGO can't edit certain event types, for example, he may not maintain any pre-bookings.

Figure 9.6 shows the structurally permitted event types for user CHICAGO. If the event type is not included (or if no maintenance flag is set), the user has no access or at least can't make any changes. The reason is that the event type is not contained in the permitted evaluation path for the respective root object.

Show Authorization Views

Auth.profile	No.	PV	OT	RootObType	ObjectID	RootObject ID	EvalPath	StatV	Depth	M	Period	Begda	Endda	Exclusion	FM
CHICAGO	080	01	D						0	X					
CHICAGO	010			L	50012249	50000467	L-D-E	12	0	X		29.05.1997	31.12.9999		
CHICAGO	010			L	50013228	50000467	L-D-E	12	0	X		01.01.1997	31.12.9999		
CHICAGO	010			L	50013822	50000467	L-D-E	12	0	X		01.01.1997	31.12.9999		
CHICAGO	010			L	50013824	50000467	L-D-E	12	0	X		01.01.1997	31.12.9999		
CHICAGO	010			L	50013835	50000467	L-D-E	12	0	X		01.01.1997	31.12.9999		
CHICAGO	010			L	50015898	50000467	L-D-E	12	0	X		01.01.2001	31.12.9999		
CHICAGO	010			L	50016253	50000467	L-D-E	12	0	X		01.01.2001	31.12.9999		
CHICAGO	010			L	50016254	50000467	L-D-E	12	0	X		01.01.2001	31.12.9999		
CHICAGO	010			L	50016255	50000467	L-D-E	12	0	X		01.01.2001	31.12.9999		
CHICAGO	010			L	50016257	50000467	L-D-E	12	0	X		01.01.2001	31.12.9999		
CHICAGO	010			L	50016258	50000467	L-D-E	12	0	X		01.01.2001	31.12.9999		
CHICAGO	010			L	50021350	50000467	L-D-E	12	0	X		01.01.2000	31.12.9999		
CHICAGO	010			L	50024214	50000467	L-D-E	12	0	X		01.01.2000	31.12.9999		
CHICAGO	010			L	50024423	50000467	L-D-E	12	0	X		13.07.2000	31.12.9999		
CHICAGO	010			L	50024426	50000467	L-D-E	12	0	X		13.07.2000	31.12.9999		
CHICAGO	010			L	50025697	50000467	L-D-E	12	0	X		01.01.2002	31.12.9999		
CHICAGO	010			L	50025997	50000467	L-D-E	12	0	X		01.11.2000	31.12.9999		
CHICAGO	010			L	50026584	50000467	L-D-E	12	0	X		01.01.2001	31.12.9999		
CHICAGO	010			L	50026597	50000467	L-D-E	12	0	X		01.01.2001	31.12.9999		
CHICAGO	010			L	50028560	50000467	L-D-E	12	0	X		01.01.2002	31.12.9999		
CHICAGO	010			L	50029726	50000467	L-D-E	12	0	X		01.01.2003	31.12.9999		
CHICAGO	010			L	50031958	50000467	L-D-E	12	0	X		01.01.2001	31.12.9999		
CHICAGO	010			L	50033273	50000467	L-D-E	12	0	X		01.01.2004	31.12.9999		
CHICAGO	010			L	50035829	50000467	L-D-E	12	0	X		01.01.2005	31.12.9999		
CHICAGO	010			L	50036002	50000467	L-D-E	12	0	X		01.01.2005	31.12.9999		

Figure 9.6 Structurally Permitted Objects (List from RHAUTH01)

Moreover, it can be very helpful to delimit the problem step by step by separating the individual components of a profile. Here, different object types, root objects, and evaluation paths are often combined in an unclear manner.

Reaching the goal step by step

Example 2 [Ex]

A personnel development manager can't maintain the qualifications for specific persons.

The general authorizations don't have errors, so missing structural authorizations may be the cause of the problem. Figure 9.7 shows the structural profile of the personnel development manager. Obviously, there are maintenance and display accesses both for qualifications and for persons depending on the root object.

For error analysis, you can generally assign the access to persons on a trial basis, that is without evaluation path or root object. It would then be clear whether the structural accesses for the qualifications are correct. In the following step, you would have to precisely examine the branch in which the problems occur. In this case, you need to consult the organizational management or the qualification catalog considering the following questions:

▸ Is the ID of the root object correct in the system in which the problem occurs?

▸ Do the relevant objects, in this case, the person and qualification, belong to the root object?

▸ Are there any problems regarding the period of time? Does the PERIOD field of the structural profile contain the value "D" (for key date), and is the qualification only valid as of the beginning of the next month? More information can be found in Section 3.6, Assigning Structural Profiles to Users.

Auth.profile	No.	Plan Vers.	Obj.Type	Object I	Maint.	Eval.path	Status vec
PE	5	01	B		☑		
PE	10	01	LB		☑		
PE	15	01	QK	50023467	☑	QUALCATA	12
PE	16	01	QK	50001000	☐	QUALCATA	12
PE	20	01	O	51000032	☑	PERSON	12
PE	25	01	O	51000321	☐	PERSON	12

Figure 9.7 Structural Profile with Differentiated Authorizations per Root Object

If nothing else helps

If you have the debugging authorization, you can set breakpoints in the function module of the structural authorization, RH_STRU_AUTHORITY_CHECK_PP01, for particularly difficult cases in order to find out where exactly the structural check fails for specific objects.

9.3   Troubleshooting in Context-Dependent Authorizations

There are no special analysis tools for the context-dependent authorization check either. If errors occur for certain users, you should proceed as follows:

1. Check whether all structural profiles that you use in the valid context- **Gradual procedure**
dependent authorization objects are entered in Transaction OOSP
(Change User Authorizations) for these users.

> **Example** **[Ex]**
>
> You use the structural profile, ZB_EIGEN (Own organizational unit), in the
> authorizations for the time data and the ZPA01_GESAMT profile in the au-
> thorizations for the organizational units that the user may edit as the person-
> nel administrator. If you haven't assigned the latter profile to user MAES, as
> shown in Figure 9.8, these authorizations aren't available for him.

2. Check the two components of context-dependent authorizations
independent of each other. Set the AUTHORIZATION PROFILE field in
the context-dependent objects to "*" and check whether the general
authorizations are correct.

3. Then test the used structural profiles one after the other.

Even though you put the components back together after these checks,
you should always reduce the complexity, if possible. Set up the authorizations one after the other, and combine them until you have found the
erroneous authorization.

Change View "User Authorizations": Overview

User name	Auth.profile	Start date	End date	Exclusion	Display Objects
CHICAGO	CHICAGO	01.01.1900	31.12.9999	☐	🚹
COMMCLERK_A	COMMCLERK_A	01.01.1900	31.12.9999	☐	🚹
HASSMANN	ALL	01.01.1900	31.12.9999	☐	🚹
IPROCON1	BEURTEILER	01.01.1800	31.12.9999	☐	🚹
MAES	ZB_EIGEN	07.01.2000	31.12.9999	☐	🚹
MAESTEST	Z_APPEE_JK	07.01.2000	31.12.9999	☐	🚹

Figure 9.8 Missing Structural Profile for Context-Dependent Authorization

9.4   Summary and Critical Success Factors

Troubleshooting is never an easy task. This is especially true for errors in
authorizations. Due to the multitude of tools used, ranging from general

checks to numerous BAdIs and Customizing settings, the number of possible causes is considerable.

Eliminating errors Once an error has occurred, you need to patiently implement analyses and gradual procedures. You can either start with the simple things and increase the level of complexity step by step, or successively reduce the complex error situation. The tips contained in this chapter will support you in developing ideas.

Avoiding errors Of course, it makes more sense to avoid errors from the outset. Especially for authorizations, a clear organization is of utmost importance:

▶ Structure your roles comprehensively and according to tasks.

▶ Use uniform, clear naming conventions both for the roles and the structural profiles.

▶ Handle the Profile Generator with care. The Profile Generator settings should ensure that they support daily maintenance.

▶ Tidy up regularly. Remove obsolete authorizations, combine them, and comment your roles.

All of these factors should ensure that your authorization roles and profiles don't become more complex than necessary. Then — and only then — you can control errors.

In the context of authorizations, tricky problems occur relatively often. This chapter describes selected requirements and their solutions for real-life situations.

10 Selected Problem Areas and Their Solutions

If you have a specific problem regarding your HCM authorizations and haven't been able to solve it although you've read the previous chapters carefully, this chapter is the last chance to find the solution to your problem. With some help from our customers, we compiled a selection of problems from real-life projects and their solutions.

10.1 Authorizations from Organizational Management (Schaeffler KG)

Schaeffler KG is a component manufacturer from the industrial and automotive supplier sector with an approximate total of 63,000 employees in 180 locations across more than 50 countries with annual revenues of approximately 8.3 billion euros. The company uses an untypical approach to manage authorizations in SAP systems.

The administrated SAP landscape is comprised of more than 100 systems and approximately 30,000 active users worldwide. The users and roles in the systems must be administrated, too, but this can't be done centrally.

Problem: 30,000 users and more than 100 systems

The following approach has been selected:

The head office is responsible for providing the roles and users in systems. Managers request the relevant roles via a web transaction. In Organizational Management, the roles are linked to the positions, and the

Central user administration and assignment via OM

287

OM is transferred into a central user administration. There, the accesses for the individual systems are assigned to the users. The roles, including the user assignments, are distributed across the systems. Figure 10.1 shows an extract of the distribution processes.

Not only HCM roles It's essential that Schaeffler KG manages all authorization roles in all components using this procedure, because not only the HCM system is affected.

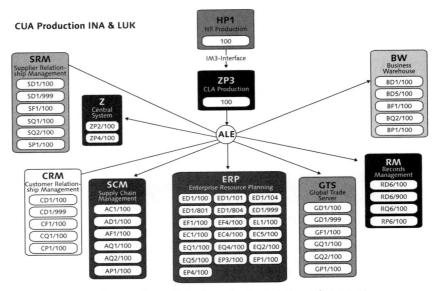

Figure 10.1 Distribution of User Roles from the Central User Administration

Positions to roles The positions are linked to the roles in the Organizational Management section of the HCM system. For this purpose, the relationship between the position and object type AG (role) is used. You have the following options to write this relationship:

▶ In Transaction PFCG (Role Maintenance), you can use the ORGANIZATIONAL MANAGEMENT button in the User tab (see Section 2.2.1, Role Assignment)

▶ By assigning roles via a maintenance interface of Organizational Management (e.g., Transaction PPOM_OLD)

▶ Schaeffler KG additionally assigns roles to positions via a customer-specific program (via standard SAP function components as well). This program issues authorizations for positions on the basis of the organizational assignment of employees in Infotype 0001. However, it's not used for HCM data because this is considered too sensitive.

Based on these procedures, the roles are assigned as follows:

Assigning roles

▶ There are two role classes — first, the functional roles that contain the transactions and technical authorization objects, such as Transaction KS01. Managers can request these roles via the intranet and the person responsible for the role of this department approves them. Example: Can Transaction KS01 be assigned to the position holder?

▶ The second role class — the organizational roles — determines which data you can access (for example, cost centers in company code X). These roles determine the role assignment automatically on the basis of Infotype 0001 (outside the HCM system). The organizational roles are assigned to the position in correspondence with the location of the employee that holds the position.

The SAP users and personnel numbers are linked via Infotype 0105 (Communication), subtype 0001 (System user name) as it is common in the standard version. A customer-specific program checks whether a user master record is created for each personnel number that is linked to a role via a position. If not, the user master record is written automatically using the BAPI_USER_CREATE function module.

Users to persons

Positions, roles, and users are compared every hour by scheduling the PFCG_TIME_DEPENDENCY or RHAUTHUPD_NEW report (see Section 2.6, Period of Responsibility and Time Logic). In this case, the HR ORGANIZATIONAL MANAGEMENT: RECONCILIATION flag must be set. The report identifies the assignment of roles to the users by date.

Automated comparison

The performance of the automatic comparison was critical, and an entire weekend was needed for the initial run. With a great deal of effort, the hourly run had to be optimized by issuing indexes and increasing the system resources before it could be used in real life.

Performance

However, how can the structural authorizations be used in this concept? In the standard version, they cannot be directly linked with the position

Structural authorizations

— not considering Infotype 1017 (PD profile) that is no longer in use, as far as we know.

For Schaeffler, the solution is: Structural profiles are only created by means of function components in order to determine the root object dynamically. The function components directly access Organizational Management and are thus implicitly contained in the solution described previously. This includes the RH_GET_MANAGER_ASSIGNMENT function component that determines the manager of an employee in the standard version (see Chapter 3, Structural Authorization Check).

Consequences After the authorizations have been set up once for each position (either during the implementation of the concept or an SAP rollout), the following things happen:

▶ **Leaving**
The user of the employee loses all authorizations.

▶ **Entry and organizational change for reassigning a position**
The user loses roles of the old position due to the change and is assigned with the roles of the new position (if the predecessor has worked in the SAP system).

▶ **Entry and organizational change for a new position**
The roles have to be assigned to the position when it is described.

Risks You must consider the following aspects when using the described solution:

▶ The maintenance processes must always be carried out in advance.

▶ The employees in the HR department must carry out the maintenance processes correctly (they shouldn't simply exclude old positions and create new ones). Very precise knowledge of SAP ERP HCM is required here.

▶ In HR management, maintenance errors can lead to a loss of roles.

▶ If the responsibilities change, the tasks must be quickly transferred in order to enable the new administrator to maintain the entire data when the old authorizations are removed.

Frequently, employees take tasks of the old position temporarily with them to the new position, but lose their old authorizations. At first glance, this seems to be an obstacle, but it can be used as an advantage. In this way, the system forces you to assign the position to the new employee as soon as possible because only the new employee can assume the tasks related to the position in the system. Alternatively, you can temporarily issue old roles for a transition period. But then again, this involves more administration work.

Figure 10.2 provides an overview of the entire process, from Organizational Management to the distribution of the roles for each user:

1. The HR department creates a person in the HCM system Ð HCM master data to user database.

2. User IDs to the HCM system

3. HCM Organizational Management and HCM HR mini-master record to ZP3

4. User data from the HCM master into ZP3

5. Manager requests roles + workflow + assignment to user

6. Distribution of users across other SAP systems

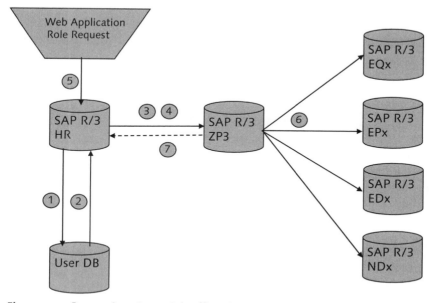

Figure 10.2 Process Overview at Schaeffler KG

In general, Schaeffler KG is very satisfied with the selected procedure. The role assignment process is automated by 95 %. The users can quickly process their respective tasks in the SAP systems. In addition, the accumulation of authorizations by individual users, which could hardly be avoided, and entailed practically uncontrollable impacts, is no longer a problem.

10.2 Starting Reports via Customer Programs (ThyssenKrupp Steel AG)

ThyssenKrupp Steel AG (TKS) in Duisburg, Germany, uses SAP ERP HCM as an integrated system for Personnel Administration, Personnel Development, Time Management, and Payroll. HCM is operated as a shared-service system that enables TKS to settle payroll processes for other companies and which these companies can also use for their own HR processes.

When the authorization concept was designed, it was decided early on that reports should be launched only by means of transactions. In real life, this requires maintaining the respective transactions. However, it's a secure procedure to implement the strictly purpose-related data accesses of the different HR departments, sites, and time administrators, as well as the shared-service center via the corresponding authorizations.

Starting background programs Another requirement was that certain users of the department required the authorization to execute programs in the background. As described in Chapter 2, section 2.4.1, Checks When Calling Reports, standard transactions are not well protected for this.

Therefore, TKS decided to develop and use the following customer-specific solution for the second task:

Programs are assigned to subject areas A customer-specific table was used to assign the programs to be started to specific subject areas. The developer had previously defined these subject areas as the value range of the domain, which the SUBJECT AREA table field describes in a technical way. The customer-specific tables are maintained via a maintenance dialog that has been explicitly authorized by specifying an authorization group.

This procedure can be used to allow for a two-level assignment of authorizations to execute a report (Figure 10.3).

Pflegeview für die Tabelle Z96_GROUP_REPORT		
Sachgebiet	+	Programm
EH: Personaleinsatzplanung	15	ZHPMOPL0
EH: Personaleinsatzplanung	20	ZHPTGPL0
EH: Personaleinsatzplanung	25	ZHPDFDA0
Personalmanagement Personalcenter	0	ZHR_PT_00027A
Personalmanagement Personalcenter	5	ZHR_PA_PM_CREATE_APPRAISALS
Personalmanagement Personalcenter	7	ZHR_PA_PM_CREATE_INFO
Personalmanagement Personalcenter	9	ZHR_PA_PM_CREATE_REMIND
Personalmanagement Personalcenter	11	ZHR_PA_PM_QUALITY_DOWNLOAD
Personalmanagement Personalcenter	13	ZHR_PA_PM_RESULT
Zeitauswertungen	0	ZHR_PT_00027A
Veranstaltungsmanagement	5	ZHR_VM_TEILNAHME_ORGEINH
Veranstaltungsmanagement	10	ZHR_VM_TEILNAHME_ORGEINH2

Figure 10.3 Table with Subject Areas and Programs

The selection screen of the ZHR_SACHGEBIET_PROGRAMM program offers the programs that have been added to the table for selection (Figure 10.4). The programs can be optionally started directly in the foreground or in the background. A variant has to be chosen for the execution in the background if the programs expect that entries be made in a selection screen. For the selection of the programs and variants, an input help defined in the report offers objects that are specified exclusively in the system. Standard function components are used to execute the programs in the background. The function components also confirm the report's execution result. This is necessary because the user that executes the program has no authorization for Transaction SM37 (Simple Job Selection) and can't obtain the execution result in any other way.

Auxiliary program for program execution

To assign authorizations to end users for the execution of reports that have been assigned to specific subject areas, the customer-specific authorization object, ZHR_SACHGB, has been created (Figure 10.5). It refers to the same domain as the table field in the program assignment table. This ensures that authorizations can only be issued for the subject areas defined by the developer in the value range of the domain.

Customer-specific authorization object

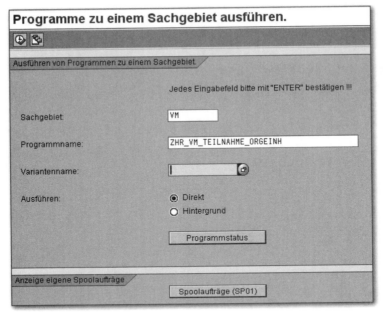

Figure 10.4 Report for Starting Programs

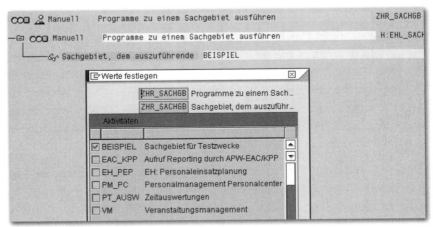

Figure 10.5 Customer-Specific Authorization Object for the Permission of Subject Areas

Consequently, users require the transaction authorization for ZHR_SACH-GEBIET_PROGRAMM as well as the authorization for specific subject areas in the ZHR_SACHGB authorization object to execute programs with the customer-specific report.

The solution described here reduced the administration effort for authorizations considerably; moreover, it enabled department employees to execute programs in the background without having the authorization for executing the program (Transaction SA38).

10.3 Minimizing the Number of Roles and Decentralized Assignment (B. Braun)

B. Braun provides the global health care market with products for anesthetics, intensive care, cardiology, extracorporeal blood purification, and surgery, as well as services for hospitals, practices, and the homecare sector. In 2006, B. Braun achieved total revenues of approximately 3.3 billion Euros with 33,000 employees in 50 countries.

B. Braun has many areas whose administration is decentralized. Basically, this includes all components that work with the PD structures, such as Training and Event Management, Organizational Management, Qualification Catalog, and Job Catalog for Personnel Development.

Decentralized administration

This causes the following two problems:

The decentralized responsibility for processing a specific person subgroup could only be inaccurately mapped with the classic authorization fields of Infotype 0001 (administrator, organizational key, and so on). It could only be precisely defined via structural profiles (persons of an organizational unit).

Structural authorization problems

The initial concept was to create a separate profile for each root node in a structure (qualification catalog, business event catalog, and so on). This led to a relatively large number of profiles in Table T77PR (approx. 200) as well as to a large number of entries in Table T77UA (approx. 1,800), which maps the assignment of users to profiles. It also involved a great deal of administration work and resulted in a certain degree of intransparency.

Complex and intransparent

To solve the problem of the large number of profiles, the standard SAP system provides the option to use a function module in order to deter-

SAP standard

mine the root objects in the structural profiles dynamically. Based on the logged-on user, it determines the relevant node in a structure. Of course, as a prerequisite, a respective relationship of the user must exist in the structure. Because this relationship hasn't been provided (for example, in the qualification catalog) or wasn't suited to determine the root object, B. Braun has created additional customer-specific relationships. The definition of these relationships is based on the function of the person that is responsible for the respective component (Figure 10.6).

Change View "Links": Overview of Selected Set

Dialog Structure	Relat'ship	Relationship bottom up	Relationship top down
▽ 🗁 Links	ZCO	is CO- Agent for	has CO- Agent
🗀 Relationship Charac	ZOM	is OM- Agent for	has OM- Agent
🗀 Additional Data on R	ZPD	is PD- Agent for	has PD- Agent
🗀 Allowed Relationship	ZPE	is PE- Agent for	has PE- Agent
🗀 External Relationship	ZTV	is Travel- Agent for	has Travel- Agent
🗀 Time constraints	ZVM	is EM- Agent for	has EM- Agent
🗀 Relationship abbreviatio			

Figure 10.6 Customer-Specific Relationships for a Structural Authorization

In the allowed relationships, only relationships from a position to the relevant root object types were permitted. As a prerequisite, the employee must have a valid user name in Infotype 0105 (Communication) and his personnel number must be linked to a position. In the example of the event management agent, the position was linked with the object types L (Business event group), QK (Qualification group), and O (Organizational unit) (Figure 10.7).

Change View "Allowed Relationships": Overview

New Entries

Dialog Structure	OT	Object type text	A/B	Rel	Relationship name	RelObjType	Not mair
▽ 🗀 Links	L	Business Event Group	B	ZVM	has EM- Agent	S	☐
🗀 Relationship Charac	O	Organizational unit	B	ZVM	has EM- Agent	S	☐
🗀 Additional Data on R	QK	Qualification group	B	ZVM	has EM- Agent	S	☐
🗁 Allowed Relationship	S	Position	A	ZVM	is EM- Agent for	L	☐
🗀 External Relationship	S	Position	A	ZVM	is EM- Agent for	O	☐
🗀 Time constraints	S	Position	A	ZVM	is EM- Agent for	QK	☐
🗀 Relationship abbreviatio							

Figure 10.7 Allowed Relationships Between Object Types

In addition to the relationships of the respective component responsibility, Table T77PR contains the corresponding structural profiles (Figure 10.8).

Authoriz. profile	Auth.profile name	Info
RESPO_CO	Area CO- Agent	
RESPO_OM	Area OM- Agent	
RESPO_PD	Area PD- Agent	
RESPO_PE	Area PE- Agent	
RESPO_TV	Area Travel- Agent	
RESPO_VM	Area EM- Agent	

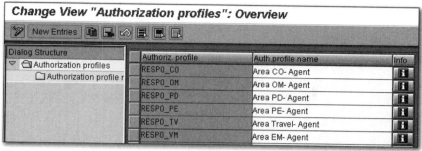

Figure 10.8 Authorization Profiles per Component Responsibility (Table T77PR)

In the structural profiles, the authorized objects are determined via an evaluation path that is specifically created for this purpose (Figure 10.9).

No.	Obj.Type	A/B	Relat'ship	Relationship name	Priority	Rel.obj.type
1	*	B	008	Holder	*	S
2	US	A	208	is identical to	*	P
3	S	A	ZVM	is EM- Agent for	*	L
4	S	A	ZVM	is EM- Agent for	*	QK
5	S	A	ZVM	is EM- Agent for	*	O
6	S	A	ZDV	can see Event - kat.	*	L

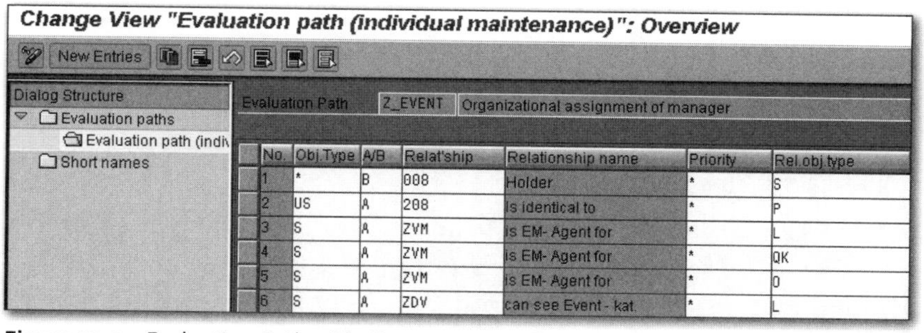

Figure 10.9 Evaluation Path with Customer-Specific Relationships

Furthermore, a customer-specific function component determines the root object (Figure 10.10).

Auth.profile	No.	Pl.	O	Object I	Maint.	Eval.path	Function module
RESPO_VM	1	01	L		☑	L-D-E	Z_HR_XX_CHECK_AUTH_STRUC
RESPO_VM	2	01	QK		☐	QUALCATA	Z_HR_XX_CHECK_AUTH_STRUC
RESPO_VM	3	01	O		☑	O-S-P	Z_HR_XX_CHECK_AUTH_STRUC
RESPO_VM	4	01	Q		☑		
RESPO_VM	5	01	U		☑		
RESPO_VM	6	01	H		☑		
RESPO_VM	7	01	G		☑		
RESPO_VM	8	01	F		☑		
RESPO_VM	9	01	R		☑		

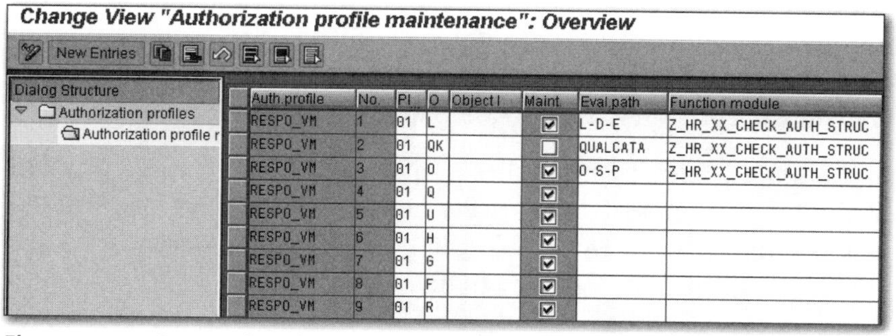

Figure 10.10 Structural Profile with Function Module

Implementing the context authorization

A relationship to an organizational unit is provided for all component-specific structural profiles or evaluation paths. This relationship is used to replace the usual authorizations, based on Infotype 0001 (Organizational Assignment), via the context-dependent authorization object. This solves the complexity problem. If a user is responsible for several components, the context dependency ensures a restriction of the access to persons, depending on the current task area.

Checking SAP*

After the check for the context-dependent authorization object, P_ORGINCON (AUTSW INCON switch in Table T77S0), has been activated, the profile of the SAP* entry in Table T77UA should be checked. It must be ensured that this profile doesn't contain object type P, because if it does, users without a structural profile may access all persons.

Performance optimization

In addition, you should pay particular attention to possible performance problems. The standard enables users with considerably complex structural authorizations to store user data in the SAP memory. You can find a detailed description of this via the following IMG path: PERSONNEL MANAGEMENT • ORGANIZATIONAL MANAGEMENT • BASIC SETTINGS • AUTHORIZATION MANAGEMENT • STRUCTURAL AUTHORIZATION • SAVE USER DATA IN SAP MEMORY.

Regarding transitions, it can be generally said that a structural profile doesn't have to be defined for each user in the context-dependent authorization object. If the SAP* entry doesn't exist, it's copied from Table T77UA to be able to continue to use the usual authorization check in the typical areas (PA, PY, PT, and so on).

Additional problem: too many roles in Travel Management

From Release 4.7 onward, you no longer have to assign the users to the structural profiles in Table T77UA. Instead, you can assign them via the structural authorization object (P_ORGINCON). To do this, you need to implement the BAdI, HRBAS00_GET_PROFL. You can also use this BAdI if the check for the context-dependent authorization object in Table T77S0 is not activated. In this case, Table T77UA becomes obsolete.

B. Braun also uses a decentralized travel management. Previously, the definition was implemented via the COST CENTER field in the P_TRAVL authorization object. This led to a large number of different roles and involved a great deal of administration work.

In Travel Management, the FITV_PERSNO_AUTH_CHK BAdI additionally enables the user to issue person authorizations via structural profiles. Once the BAdI had been implemented, one role and one structural profile were sufficient for all travel agents. A power user carries out the continuous authorization administration in the department by maintaining the customer-specific relationships and assigning the roles. For this purpose, the IT department provided supporting maintenance transactions and reporting options.

Success: only one role and one profile in Travel Management

Power users that must be specified maintain the customer-specific relationships in a decentralized way. For this purpose, specific maintenance transactions were created that all use the RH_OM_MAINTAIN_STRUCTURE function module (Figure 10.11).

Specific maintenance transaction for relationships

In addition, the authorization agents for components were provided with the respective reporting tools (e.g., a list of all EM agents, determination of the responsible EM agent for an employee, and so on). This could be easily implemented via customized reports and transactions.

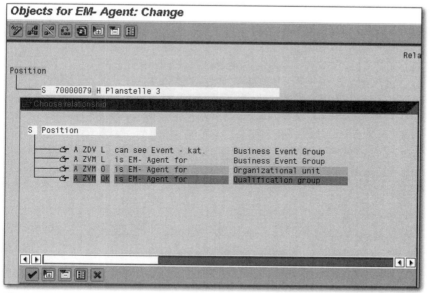

Figure 10.11 Specific Transaction for a Decentralized Relationship Maintenance

10.4 Hiding Specific Fields in Infotypes

In decentralized maintenance, the following question often arises: Can we modify the user interface of the infotypes for specific users, that is, hide fields or change input fields to output fields?

[Ex]

Example

You want to have the ADDITIONAL INDICATOR FOR TIME MANAGEMENT field in Infotype 0007 (Planned Working Time) maintained in a decentralized way. Users that are supposed to maintain the field, however, may not maintain other fields of this infotype. This means that the other fields must become mere display fields for those user groups.

UGR user parameter

Before you start developing a customer-specific program, you should check if the *UGR* user parameter in combination with the infotype control for the screen modification could be a solution.

You can navigate to the infotype screen control in the IMG via PERSONNEL MANAGEMENT • PERSONNEL ADMINISTRATION • CUSTOMIZING USER INTERFACES • CHANGE SCREEN MODIFICATIONS. Figure 10.12 shows the corresponding default entries for the single screen of Infotype 0007.

Change View "Infotype Screen Control": Overview

New Entries

Mod. Pool	Screen	Feature	Variable key	Alt. screen	Next screen
MP000700	2000	P0007		2000	0
MP000700	2000		06_FP	2306	0
MP000700	2000		07	2000	0
MP000700	2000		10	2000	0
MP000700	2000		12	2012	0
MP000700	2000		17	2000	0
MP000700	2000		32	2000	0
MP000700	2000		37	2000	0
MP000700	2000		44	2000	0

Figure 10.12 Variants for Infotype 0007

Before we discuss the UGR user parameter, you need to understand how the different screen variants are created and how you can decide which variant is used when. The P0007 feature shown in the first row of Figure 10.12 indicates the variable key. The variable key in combination with the infotype number is the key for the screen control. Figure 10.13 shows the content of the screen control, for example, for variable key 17. In contrast to the standard version, the ADDITIONAL INDICATOR FOR TIME MANAGEMENT field is hidden and the WORKING WEEK field is defined as a required entry field.

Change View "Infotype Screen Control": Details

New Entries

Module Pool	MP000700	Variable key	17
Standard screen	2000	Feature	
Alternative screen	2000	Feature	
Next screen			

Scrn control

Grp	Field name	Field text	Std	RF	OF	Outp	Hide	Init
001	P0007-SCHKZ	Work Schedule Rule	●	○	○	○	○	○
002	P0007-ZTERF	Employee Time Management Status	●	○	○	○	○	○
003	P0007-EMPCT	Employment percentage	●	○	○	○	○	○
004	P0007-TEILK	Indicator Part-Time Employee	●	○	○	○	○	○
004	P0007-TEILK	Indicator Part-Time Employee						
005	P0007-ARBST	Daily Working Hours	●	○	○	○	○	○
006	P0007-MINTA	Minimum number of work hours per	●	○	○	○	○	○
007	P0007-MAXTA	Maximum number of work hours per	●	○	○	○	○	○
008	P0007-WOSTD	Hours per week	●	○	○	○	○	○
009	P0007-MINWO	Minimum weekly working hours	●	○	○	○	○	○
010	P0007-MAXWO	Maximum number of work hours per	●	○	○	○	○	○
011	P0007-MOSTD	Monthly hours	●	○	○	○	○	○
012	P0007-MINMO	Minimum number of work hours per	●	○	○	○	○	○
013	P0007-MAXMO	Maximum number of work hours per	●	○	○	○	○	○
014	P0007-JRSTD	Annual working hours	●	○	○	○	○	○
015	P0007-MINJA	Minimum annual working hours	●	○	○	○	○	○
016	P0007-MAXJA	Maximum Number of Working Hours	●	○	○	○	○	○
017	P0007-WKWDY	Weekly Workdays	●	○	○	○	○	○
018	P0007-DYSCH	Create Daily Work Schedule Dynam	●	○	○	○	○	○
018	P0007-DYSCH	Create Daily Work Schedule Dynam						
019	P0007-KZTIM	Additional indicator for time ma	○	○	○	○	●	○
020	P0007-WWEEK	Working week	○	●	○	○	○	○

Figure 10.13 Variable Key 17: Hiding and Required Entry Field

What does this have to do with the UGR user parameter? Well, this exact parameter can — in addition to other characteristics — be queried in feature P0007 and all other features for the infotype screen control. As shown in Figure 10.14, the user group indicates which variable key is selected. Consequently, you can maintain a variant of the dynpro that —

UGR user parameter

according to the previous example — changes all fields to display fields, except for the ADDITIONAL INDICATOR FOR TIME MANAGEMENT field.

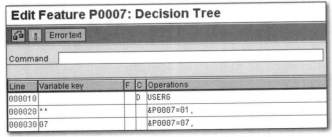

Figure 10.14 Feature P0007 with Query on the User Group

> **Warning**
>
> If you link authorizations to the user group as described previously, you must ensure that the users cannot maintain them by themselves. Transactions SU2 and SU3 (Maintain User Profile) may not be assigned to them. Otherwise, it's possible that the users can assign themselves to a user group that can view data they are not authorized to view.

10.5 Supporting the Workflow with the Double-Verification Principle

The double-verification principle we discussed in Chapter 2 is often essential to improve data quality; however, it may cause delays in processing.

[Ex]

> **Example**
>
> For example, how can you ensure that locked records of Infotype 0008 (Basic Pay) that are written by one administrator are immediately checked and released by a second administrator?

Dynamic actions For this purpose, use the dynamic actions whose Customizing you can find under PERSONNEL MANAGEMENT • PERSONNEL ADMINISTRATION • CUSTOMIZING PROCEDURES • DYNAMIC ACTIONS.

Figure 10.15 shows a template of how an email is sent when changes are made to the PAYROLL ADMINISTRATOR field. The dispatch is defined by the M0001 feature – one of the reference features that serve to send emails from dynamic actions. You can find the respective documentation in the MOESS feature. The reference features show different sample combinations that you can and must customize according to your requirements.

Change View "Dynamic Actions": Overview

ITy	STy.	Field N	F	No	S	Variable function part
0001		SACHA	06	0		*-SEND MAILS AFTER CHANGING P0001-SACHA -----
0001		SACHA	06	1	P	PSPAR-TCLAS='A'
0001		SACHA	06	2	M	M0001|

Figure 10.15 Template for an Email from a Dynamic Action

If you want to send an email when changes have been made to an info- **Sending emails**
type in the "locked" status, you should use the table for the dynamic actions and consider the following aspects:

▶ The infotype is "locked" in the table for dynamic actions when the lock indicator, SPRPS field name (for example, P0008-SPRPS), is set to "X."

▶ The receiver is, for example, one of the administrators from Infotype 0001. In this case, the feature uses the transferred values, RECV1/2/3 (see documentation on MOESS). Figure 10.16 illustrates the assignment of the SAP user names to the administrators of Infotype 0001 (IMG: PERSONNEL MANAGEMENT • PERSONNEL ADMINISTRATION • ORGA-NIZATIONAL DATA • ORGANIZATIONAL ASSIGNMENT • DEFINE ADMINIS-TRATOR). The receiver's email address is determined by means of his or her entry in Infotype 0105 (Communication). The subtype — usu-ally 0010 (Email) — is determined via the „SUBTY" return value of the feature.

▶ The email can be sent as „executable" by transferring the fields TCODE, and so on (see documentation on MOESS). Then, a link to the locked record of Infotype 0008 is indicated in the email. That means the receiver can directly navigate from the email (in SAP Business Workplace) to the infotype record, check it, and release it.

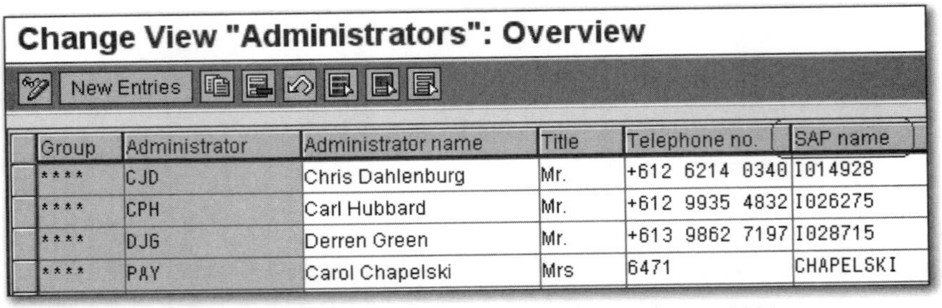
Change View "Administrators": Overview

New Entries

Group	Administrator	Administrator name	Title	Telephone no.	SAP name
****	CJD	Chris Dahlenburg	Mr.	+612 6214 0340	I014928
****	CPH	Carl Hubbard	Mr.	+612 9935 4832	I026275
****	DJG	Derren Green	Mr.	+613 9862 7197	I028715
****	PAY	Carol Chapelski	Mrs	6471	CHAPELSKI

Figure 10.16 Assigning SAP Users to Administrators from Infotype 0001

The use of dynamic actions for infotype changes described in this section always simplifies the work processes in master data maintenance if changes are not completed until a second administrator releases them.

10.6 Authorization-Relevant Switches in Queries

You can use *switches* to influence the processing logic of an InfoSet. The PROC_PERNR_PARTIAL_AUT switch is a general switch, that is, it always influences all infotypes of the InfoSet. If this switch is activated in the InfoSet, persons for which only a partial authorization is available are also processed.

In general, the query excludes all personnel numbers if the evaluation includes an infotype for which the user is only authorized to view some of the subtypes. That means the user can also not view the authorized subtypes for these persons.

Only for PNP

This only concerns InfoSets that have been created on the basis of the logical databases, PNP or PNPCE.

A user with full authorization obtains the result shown in Figure 10.17. In this example, there are two records of Infotype 0021 for Franz Beckenbauer and no records maintained for Stefanie Graf.

Pers.No.	Name of employee or applicant	Type of Family Record	First name
00090009	Franz Beckenbauer	Spouse	Bärbel
00090009	Franz Beckenbauer	Child	Maja
00090010	Stefanie Graf		

Figure 10.17 Results with Full Authorization for Infotype 0021

If the user has only the authorization for subtype 1 (Spouse) in Infotype 0021 (Family Member/Dependents), the result is displayed in Figure 10.18. The user cannot view the spouse of Franz Beckenbauer, although he has an authorization for subtype 1. This represents the standard behavior of the query.

Pers.No.	Name of employee or applicant	Type of Family Record	First name
00090010	Stefanie Graf		

Figure 10.18 Results in Case of Partial Authorization and Without Switch

Only after the PROC_PERNR_PARTIAL_AUT switch has been integrated in the underlying InfoSet can the user view the "spouse" subtype (Figure 10.19).

Pers.No.	Name of employee or applicant	Type of Family Record	First name
00090009	Franz Beckenbauer	Spouse	Bärbel
00090010	Stefanie Graf		

Figure 10.19 Results in Case of Partial Authorization with Switch

Tip	**[+]**
You can find a detailed description of all switches in the IMG documentation under **Personnel Management • Human Resources Information System • HR Settings for SAP Query • Create InfoSets for HR.**	

Switches are integrated using additional coding in the InfoSet. In InfoSet maintenance, click on the Extras button and then select the CODE tab on the right of the screen and DATA in the CODE SECTION field (Figure 10.20). The [Common] within square brackets refers to all infotypes.

Integrating switches

```
*$HR$ [Common]
*$HR$ PROC_PERNR_PARTIAL_AUT = 'X'
```

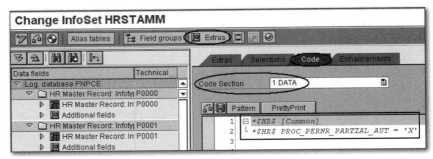

Figure 10.20 Integrating a Switch into an InfoSet

[+]

Tip

The switches are available as of SAP R/3 Enterprise. For earlier releases, refer to SAP Note 305118 (Elimination of Various Query Problems in HR).

Note that queries must be re-generated after you've added or changed a switch. It's not sufficient to execute them again. In Transaction SQ01, select the query that is supposed to be generated, and then select QUERY • MORE FUNCTIONS • GENERATE PROGRAM.

10.7 Transaction Variants

Modifying user interfaces of transactions

Transaction variants enable you to change user interfaces comparable to the screen modification for infotypes (Table T588M). That means you can hide fields, define fields as required entry fields, specify field contents, or only view contents. You can also deactivate buttons and menu functions. By creating a transaction variant you can generate a modified version of an executable transaction. You can define this modified transaction as a standard transaction. In this case, every user can view the changed version when he calls the standard transaction code (e.g., PA30 – Maintain HR Master Data). You can also assign a new transaction code to this variant transaction, for example, ZPA30, and add it only to the user menu of specific users via role maintenance (Transaction PFCG, see Chapter 2, General Authorization Check).

We have experienced the use of transaction variants for the following customer requirements:

▶ **Travel management**
In contrast to travel expenses, the user interface of the travel request of Transaction TRIP (Travel Manager) cannot be adjusted in Customizing. However, in almost all cases it is necessary that one or more fields that aren't needed (often task type or advances) can be hidden. Here, the only option is to use a variant transaction that is usually defined as a standard transaction.

▶ **Master data maintenance**
Some users are not supposed to have the authorization to select additional infotypes in Transaction PA30 (Maintain Personnel Master Data) and are only supposed to be authorized to select the infotypes that are provided in the tabs. (You can exclude the processing of infotypes that are not allowed via an authorization object.)

▶ **Only display schemas, rules, and features**
You want some users to be authorized to view only Transactions PE01 (Personnel Calculation Schemas), PE02 (Personnel Calculation Rules), PE03 (HR: Features). Because authorization objects P_PE01 and P_PE02, which are provided for this purpose, don't work yet, you can create a variant transaction where all buttons and menu functions enabling changes are hidden (Figure 10.21).

Figure 10.21 Result of the Variant Transaction — Displaying Features is the Only Option

The following sections describe the procedure for implementing this requirement.

Creating a transaction variant

To create a transaction variant with hidden change buttons in Transaction PE03, you must proceed as follows:

1. Select Transaction SHD0 to create cross-client transaction variants (Figure 10.22). (for client-dependent transaction variants choose Transaction SHD0_MANDT.)

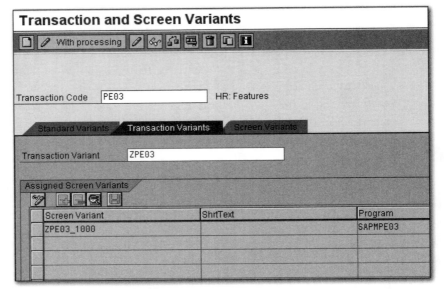

Figure 10.22 SHD0 – Initial Screen

2. In the TRANSACTION CODE field, enter the standard transaction code PE03, and select a new name in the customer name space (starting with Y or Z) of the TRANSACTION VARIANT field, for example, ZPE03.

3. Click on the CREATE button. This calls the application transaction.

[+]   **Tip**

From Release 4.6A onward, a transaction variant consists of several screen variants.

4. Press ⎡Enter⎤. A dialog window opens and displays the first dynpro (main screen) with the individual fields and tabs (Figure 10.23). The following settings are possible:

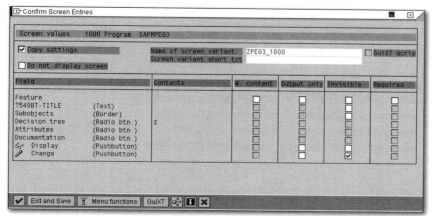

Figure 10.23 Creating a Screen Variant

- ▶ If COPY SETTINGS is not checked, you delete the entire screen from the variant or the assignment of the screen variant to the transaction variant.

- ▶ If DO NOT DISPLAY SCREEN is activated, you hide the entire screen (in this case, values must be usually transferred).

- ▶ If WITH CONTENT is checked, the respective field contains the value you entered in the application transaction. The value is indicated in the CONTENTS column.

- ▶ If Output Only is checked, no entries can be made in the field.

- ▶ If INVISIBLE is checked, the field will be hidden.

- ▶ If REQUIRED is checked, the field becomes a required entry field.

- ▶ Only for tables, if ADOPT COLUMN SEQUENCE/COLUMN WIDTH is checked, the changed column sequence and/or column width is copied to the dynpro.

5. Enter a name for the screen variant if no name has been proposed (e.g., <name of transaction variant>_(<client>)_<dynpro number>) and a short text.

6. If required, select the Menu Functions button to hide functions, such as Back, Cancel, or icons in the application toolbar. Place the cursor on a function, and click on the second button from the left (Figure 10.24). Ensure that you also deactivate the functions for the hidden buttons in the menu.

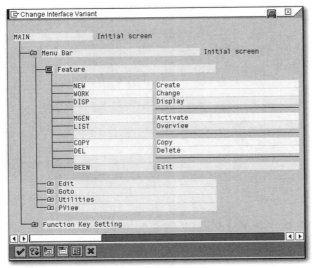

Figure 10.24 Deactivating Function Codes

7. Select NEXT (Enter) in the dialog window. Any existing additional dynpros (subscreens) of the application transaction are called. After the last subscreen has been called, the system returns to the transaction. Press Enter once again to return to the last dialog window and save the changes.

8. In the dialog window, click on EXIT and SAVE to exit the application transaction. The system displays a list of all screens of the application transaction for which new screen variants are created (you can also navigate to the list using the CHANGE button in the initial screen of Transaction SHD0). If required, make additional changes here, enter a short text for the transaction variant, and then save the settings. (Note: These are workbench objects.)

Specific transaction code To assign an executable transaction to the variant transaction, proceed as follows:

1. In the menu of the initial screen, select GOTO • CREATE VARIANT TRANSACTION.

2. In the TRANSACTION CODE field, enter the desired name from the customer namespace, and select the TRANSACTION WITH VARIANT (Variant transaction) option (Figure 10.25).

3. Press [Enter], and select Inherit GUI Attributes in the next screen. Save the settings.

4. You can now add this transaction code to the PFCG role maintenance of the user menu. The Profile Generator proposes the same authorization objects as for the standard transaction. Only the S_TCODE object contains the code of the variant transaction.

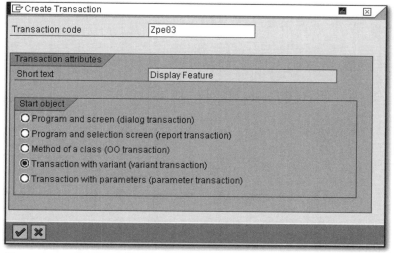

Figure 10.25 Creating a Variant Transaction (Executable Transaction Code)

You have two options to change a transaction variant:

Change the values using the CHANGE WITH PROCESSING button. Then, the transaction is called, and you can change parameters that require information on the runtime of the application transaction, copy contents, or define default values.

If you change the values using the CHANGE (WITHOUT PROCESSING) button, you can only modify the output characteristics of the field values.

Changing a transaction variant

10.8 Summary

Authorizations in SAP ERP HCM is a very complex topic. At the beginning, this chapter used several customer scenarios to describe how this topic is addressed and managed in real life, and how SAP tools can implement comprehensive requirements for the authorization system. Later on, the chapter explained how you can use additional tools of the HCM system to solve authorization problems.

We hope that these examples, as well as the entire book, provided helpful information about:

- how you can use the standard tools of the HCM authorizations intelligently.
- where and how extensions can best assist you.
- how you can use different tools of the HCM system in innovative ways to solve your authorization problems efficiently.

Appendices

A Transactions for Authorization Management

Table A.1 lists the transactions for the authorization management.

Transaction Code	Meaning
OOSB	Assigning Structural Profiles to Users
OOSP	Maintenance of Structural Profiles
PFCG	Maintenance of Standard Roles (includes composite roles and reference roles as well as assigning them to the user)
SU21	Maintenance of Authorization Objects (Development)
SU24	Maintenance of the Profile Generator
SU53	Analysis of the Authorization Check by the User
SU56	Authorizations Entered in the Buffer of the Logged-On User (it is possible to change the user)
ST01	Authorization Trace (what is being checked?)

Table A.1 Transactions for Authorization Management

B Authorization Objects of the SAP HCM System

Table B.1 lists all authorization objects of the HCM system, including references to the respective sections in the book.

Technical Name	Description	Discussed in Section
P_ABAP	HR: Reporting	5.16.3
P_APPL	HR: Applicants	5.13
P_ASRCONT	Authorization for Process Content	5.7
P_B2A	HR-B2A: B2A Manager	5.1.1
P_CATSXT	HR: Time Sheet for Service Providers Type/Level Check	5.4
P_DEL_PERNR	Deletion of Personnel Numbers in Live Systems	2.4.7
P_ENCTYPE	HR: PBC – Financing	5.3
P_ENGINE	HR: PBC – Authorization for Automatic Commitment Creation	5.3
P_EXMGRP	HR: PBC – Exceptions for Financing Rules	5.3
P_FINADM	HR: PBC – Changes in the Financing Past	5.3
P_HAP_DOC	Appraisal Systems: Appraisal	5.11
P_HRF_INFO	HR: Authorization Check Infodata Maintenance for HR Forms	5.1.2
P_HRF_META	HR: Authorization Check Metadata Maintenance for HR Forms	5.1.2
P_LSO_FOUP	Authorization Object for Participation Follow-Up	5.20
P_LSO_TU	Authorization for LSO Content Management	5.20

Table B.1 Authorization Objects of the HCM System, Including References to the Respective Sections in the Book

Technical Name	Description	Discussed in Section
P_NNNNN	Customer-specific object	2.8.1
P_NNNNNCON	Customer-specific object (context)	4.2
P_ORGIN	HR: Master Data	2.3.2
P_ORGINCON	HR: Master Data with Context	4.2
P_ORGXX	HR: Master Data – Extended Check	2.3.3
P_ORGXXCON	HR: Master Data – Extended Check with Context	4.2
P_PBSPWE	for the Process Workbench Engine (PWE) authorization	5.1.1
P_PCLX	HR: Cluster	2.3.4
P_PCR	HR: Payroll Control Record	5.1.1
P_PEPSVAR	Shift Planning: User-Independent Sort Variants	5.14
P_PERNR	HR: Master Data – Personnel Number Check	2.3.3
P_PYEVDOC	HR: Posting Document	5.1.1
P_PYEVRUN	HR: Posting Run	5.1.1
P_RCF_ACT	Activities in E-Recruiting	5.5.2
P_RCF_APPL	Applications in E-Recruiting	5.5.2
P_RCF_POOL	Direct Access to Talent Pool	5.5.2
P_RCF_STAT	Object Status in E-Recruiting	5.5.2
P_RCF_VIEW	Data Overview in E-Recruiting	5.5.2
P_RCF_WL	Access to Worklists	5.5.2
P_TCODE	HR: Transaction codes	2.3.1
P_TRAVL	Travel Expenses	5.19
PLOG	Personnel Planning	2.3.5
S_MWB_FCOD	Allowed Function Codes for Manager's Desktop	5.9

Table B.1 Authorization Objects of the HCM System, Including References to the Respective Sections in the Book (Cont.)

C   Authorization Switches

Figure C.1 shows the authorization main switches that are maintained using Transaction OOAC.

Change View "HR: Authorization main switch": Overview

Documentation

System Switch (from Table T77S0)

Group	Sem. abbr.	Value abbr.	Description
AUTSW	ADAYS	15	HR: Tolerance Time for Authorization Check
AUTSW	APPRO	0	HR: Test Procedures
AUTSW	DFCON	1	HR: Default Position (Context)
AUTSW	INCON	0	HR: Master Data (Context)
AUTSW	NNCON	0	HR:Customer-Specific Authorization Check (Context)
AUTSW	NNNNN	0	HR: Customer-Specific Authorization Check
AUTSW	ORGIN	1	HR: Master Data
AUTSW	ORGPD	1	HR: Structural Authorization Check
AUTSW	ORGXX	0	HR: Master Data - Extended Check
AUTSW	PERNR	1	HR: Master Data - Personnel Number Check
AUTSW	XXCON	0	HR: Master Data - Enhanced Check (Context)

Figure C.1   Maintaining the Authorization Main Switches in OOAC

These are complemented by the following additional switches that can only be maintained directly in Table T77S0:

▶ **HAP00 AUTHO**
Activates the Authorization Profile field in the P_HAP_DOC authorization object of performance management

▶ **HRFPM NOPAU**
Deactivates the authorization check for determining the required full-time equivalents in the transactions of personnel budget plan management

▶ **PEINS AUTH**
Deactivates the complete authorization check when you enter the target plan of shift planning (Transaction PP61)

▶ **PLOGI ADAYS**
Tolerance period of the structural authorization check

▶ **PPVAC STRAU**
Activates the structural authorization in the „previous" applicant data administration

Table C.3 indicates the sections of the book that describe the switches in greater detail.

Authorization Switch	Meaning	Discussed in Section
AUTSW ADAYS	Tolerance period	2.6, 3.7
AUTSW APPRO	Test procedures	2.7.2
AUTSW DFCON	Default position (context)	3.8
AUTSW INCON	Master data (context)	4.2
AUTSW NNCON	Customer-specific object (context)	4.2
AUTSW NNNNN	Customer-specific object	2.8.1
AUTSW ORGIN	Master data	2.3.2
AUTSW ORGPD	Master data, structural	3.5, 3.8
AUTSW ORGXX	Master data, extended	2.3.3
AUTSW PERNR	Master data, personnel number	2.3.3
AUTSW XXCON	Master data, extended (context)	4.2
HAP00 AUTHO	Performance management	5.12
HRFPM NOPAU	Personnel budget plan management	5.4
PEINS AUTH	Shift planning	5.15
PLOGI ADAYS	Tolerance period of structural check	3.7
PPVAC STRAU	Applicants (old), structural	5.14

Table C.1 Authorization Switches of the HCM System, Including References to the Respective Sections in the Book

D   Business Add-Ins

Table D.1 contains all Business Add-Ins of the HCM system, including references to the respective sections.

Technical Name	Meaning	Discussed in Section
HRASR00AUTH_CHECK	HR Administrative Services	5.8
HRBAS00_STRUAUTH	Structural Authorization Check	3.10
HRCMP00TCS0006	Total Compensation Statement Pension Fund CH	5.2
HRHAP00_AUTHORITY	Performance Management	5.12
HRPAD00AUTH_CHECK	General Authorization Check	2.8.3
HRPAD00CHECK_TIME	Time Logic in the General Authorization Check	1.6.1
HRPDV00APPRAISAL0005	Appraisals (old)	5.3
HR_PY_AUTH_PU01	Deleting Payroll Results	5.1.5

Table D.1   Business Add-Ins of the HCM System, Including References to the Respective Sections in the Book

E Glossary

General authorization check In contrast to the HCM-specific authorization checks (test procedures, structural authorization, and context-dependent authorization), the general authorization check is an integral part of the SAP NetWeaver basis. Such authorization checks can be found in all components of SAP ERP.

User Logon name that permits the access to the SAP system in combination with a password. Among other things, a user is assigned with authorization roles.

Authorization An authorization is an authorization object that was filled with content by the customer.

Authorization (main) switch There are multiple switches that you can use to influence the authorization checks. Authorization switches are settings that were implemented via the central Control Table T77S0. Authorization main switches, in turn, are authorization switches that can be maintained using Transaction OOAC (HR: Authorization Main Switch).

Authorization object An authorization object is a program module that protects specific data. It contains up to ten fields that allow you to define which data contents are to be protected. A list of the authorization objects discussed in this book can be found in Appendix B,

Authorization Objects of the SAP HCM System.

Authorization profile The combination of different authorizations results in an authorization profile, which in turn belongs to a role. The authorization profile itself is a purely technical value.

Authorization trace The authorization trace is used for troubleshooting and the analysis of the required authorizations. It is part of the system trace and is started using Transaction ST01 (System Trace). See also Chapter 9, Troubleshooting.

Business Add-In (BAdI) BAdIs enable you to implement requirements for the authorization check that exceed the SAP standard without having to modify it. They also enable you to change the standard code at places predefined by SAP and implement customer-specific checks. A list of the BAdIs discussed in this book can be found in Appendix D, Business Add-Ins.

Context-dependent or context-sensitive authorization check Chapter 4, Context-Dependent Authorization Check, comprehensively discusses this tool which combines the general and the structural authorization check. The context-dependent check enables the user to implement different functions for various organizational responsibilities.

Inheritance of roles   See reference role.

Organizational level   The **organizational level** is a specific structure of the reference role. The content of the organizational levels is not inherited when roles are derived (see also reference role). It is the only distinguishing criterion in the derived roles. In the standard version of SAP ERP HCM the plan version is the only organizational level. However, you also have the option to define other fields for the organizational level (see Chapter 2, General Authorization Check).

Performance optimization   Authorization checks are often very complex and therefore they don't always distinguish themselves through high performance. This particularly applies to the structural authorization check. In chapter 3, Structural Authorization Check, we dedicated one section to the optimization of performance.

Profile Generator   When creating a role in Transaction PFCG (Role Maintenance) you first enter transactions in the menu. If you change to the maintenance of the authorizations from there, the Profile Generator proposes authorizations in the different authorization objects based on the entered transactions. The customizing of the Profile Generator is described in great detail in Chapter 2, General Authorization Check.

Test procedure   The test procedures are HCM-specific tools that you can use to at least partially implement a period-related access protection for master data. You can find more information on this topic in Chapter 2, General Authorization Check.

Reference user   The reference user concept generally serves to simplify the authorization maintenance. First, you define a user as the reference user. Then, you assign a different user to the reference user. This user inherits all attributes of the reference user. Reference users are used in e-recruiting for external candidates (see Chapter 5).

Reference role   For the inheritance of role properties, the reference role is the role in which the menu entries and the authorizations are maintained, and which can inherit these properties to the derived roles. In the derived roles, only the organizational levels are maintained. The concept of reference roles is used to simplify the role administration (see Chapter 2, General Authorization Check).

Role   Roles are assigned to users and are responsible for the general authorization check. Role usually stands for a single role. Multiple single roles can be combined to form a composite role.

Composite role   Instead of assigning multiple users with the same functions to the same role individually, you can also combine them in a composite role. Then, you only have to assign a composite role. A composite role can have any number of single roles. Composite roles themselves do not contain any authorizations. For more information refer to Chapter 2, Structural Authorization Check.

Master data authorization   All authorization checks that control the access to infotypes of personnel administration and time management.

Structural authorization check The structural authorization check is only available in the HCM system. It uses the structures of Organizational Management and similar hierarchies to differentiate the authorization check with regard to the areas of responsibility. We dedicated an entire chapter to this subject (Chapter 3, Structural Authorization Check).

System authorizations In addition to the pure HCM authorizations, numerous other system authorizations also play a significant role in the authorization concept of the HCM system. These are authorizations for basic functions in different areas, for example, for processing batch input sessions or interface authorizations for web accesses. Section 2.4, Required System Authorizations, will detail this subject.

F   Recommended Reading

In this appendix, we have listed some publications that provide further details on the topics discussed or cover advanced topics in the SAP ERP environment.

F.1   Books

Further reading on the topic of authorizations:

- Brochhausen, Ewald; Kielisch, Jürgen; Schnerring, Jürgen; Staeck, Jens: *mySAP HR – Technical Principles and Programming*, Chapter 4. 2nd Edition Bonn: SAP PRESS, 2005.

- Linkies, Mario; Off, Frank: *SAP Security and Authorizations:* in particular, Sections 9.3.2 and 9.3.3. Bonn: SAP PRESS, 2006.

- Masters, Jeremy; Kotsakis, Christos: *SAP ERP HCM Performance Management,* Chapter 13. Bonn: SAP PRESS, 2008.

Basic knowledge about SAP ERP HCM:

- Edinger, Jörg; Krämer, Christian; Lübke, Christian; Ringling, Sven: *Mastering HR Management with SAP*. Bonn: SAP PRESS, 2008.

- Figaj, Hans-Jürgen; Haßmann, Richard; Junold, Anja: *HR Reporting with SAP*. Bonn: SAP PRESS, 2007.

- Ringling, Sven; Lübke, Christian; Krämer, Christian: *HR Personnel Planning and Development using SAP*. Bonn: SAP PRESS, 2004.

F.2   Websites

- *help.sap.com (Note: Don't use the prefix "www")*
  Help portal of SAP AG; contains help files for all SAP products in different releases (free of charge, navigation in English, documentation available in multiple languages).

▶ *www.admanus.de/english-newsletter*
Newsletter for SAP ERP HCM and HR processes (free of charge)

▶ *www.asug.com*
Homepage of the American SAP user group. Forums on all SAP topics, materials for download, event calendar (most parts only accessible for ASUG members. Requires membership fee).

▶ *www.iprocon.de/books*
Recommendation of proven books on personnel management, project management, and SAP (free of charge)

▶ *www.hrexpertonline.com*
Online database of the HREXPERT newsletter, expert articles on SAP ERP HCM (requires fee to be paid)

▶ *www.sap.com/community*
Forums on all SAP topics (HCM forum highly frequented), materials for download, online events, newsletter (most sections only for members, free-of-charge registration)

▶ *www.sap.com/usa/index.epx*
Website of the United States country side of SAP AG. A wide choice of documentations, whitepapers, live demos, newsletters, links, support pages, and so on. (Some parts are publicly available, some only available for customers; partly to be paid. Some parts of the documentation only available in English.)

▶ *www.sap.info*
Online version of the SAP INFO magazine. Articles about all topics of the SAP AG offer and newsletter (free of charge).

G   The Authors

Martin Esch is one of the two Managing Directors of Projektkultur GmbH (*www.projektkultur.biz*), a consulting firm that's part of the AdManus Consulting Network (www.admanus.de) and specializes in SAP ERP HCM and project management. He has been specializing in IT-based HR management in the SAP environment since 1993 and has managed numerous projects as a consultant. One of his main focuses in consulting is the authorization system in SAP ERP HCM.

Anja Junold has been working as an SAP ERP HCM Consultant at iProCon GmbH (*www.iprocon.de*) since 2002. During this time, she has gathered experience in both national and international HR departments. Anja is a co-author of the books *HR Reporting with SAP* and *SAP-Personalwirtschaft für Anwender*, both published by SAP PRESS. iProCon GmbH offers services related to SAP ERP HCM. The HR service tree reference model is an iProCon product, which can be ordered at the following URL: *www.iprocon.de/referencemodel*.

Index

Interested in reading more?

Please visit our Web site for all
new book releases from SAP PRESS.

www.sap-press.com